The World after the End of the World

SUNY series in Contemporary Continental Philosophy
─────────
Dennis J. Schmidt, editor

The World after the End of the World

A Spectro-Poetics

Kas Saghafi

Ross Bleckner, *Galaxy Painting*, 60 by 45 in. (152 by 114 cm.), oil/canvas, 1993
Copyright: Ross Bleckner
Courtesy: Mary Boone Gallery, New York
Collection: Linda Pace Foundation, San Antonio

Published by State University of New York Press, Albany

© 2020 State University of New York

All rights reserved

No part of this book may be used or reproduced in any manner whatsoever without written permission. No part of this book may be stored in a retrieval system or transmitted in any form or by any means including electronic, electrostatic, magnetic tape, mechanical, photocopying, recording, or otherwise without the prior permission in writing of the publisher.

For information, contact State University of New York Press, Albany, NY
www.sunypress.edu

Library of Congress Cataloging-in-Publication Data

Names: Saghafi, Kas, author.
Title: The world after the end of the world : a spectro-poetics / Kas Saghafi.
Description: Albany : State University of New York Press, 2020. | Series: SUNY series in contemporary continental philosophy | Includes bibliographical references and index.
Identifiers: LCCN 2019049042 (print) | LCCN 2019049043 (ebook) | ISBN 9781438478210 (hardcover : alk. paper) | ISBN 9781438478227 (ebook)
Subjects: LCSH: Derrida, Jacques. | Nancy, Jean-Luc. | Salvation. | Loss (Psychology) | Death. | Other (Philosophy)
Classification: LCC B2430.D484 S245 2020 (print) | LCC B2430.D484 (ebook) | DDC 194—dc23
LC record available at https://lccn.loc.gov/2019049042
LC ebook record available at https://lccn.loc.gov/2019049043

10 9 8 7 6 5 4 3 2 1

*For the love of my life, Pleshette—
who was my world*

Contents

Acknowledgments	ix
Abbreviations	xi
Prologue: *Salut*—A Spectro-Poetics	xxiii

The End of the World

1. The World after the End of the World	3

Intact

2. Safe, Intact: Derrida, Nancy, and the "Deconstruction of Christianity"	19
The Unscathed	22
Tact and Touch	25
Do Not Wish to Touch Me	27
Intact	30
There's Deconstruction, and then, There's Deconstruction	33

Death

3. Derrida Is the Death of Death	39
Death	39
The Proper Is Stronger than Life and Death	42
Aporias	45
Marranos	48
Side	49

Resurrection

4. Nancy's Resurrection — 55
   - Resurrection — 56
   - Eternal Life — 64
   - Nancy's Eternal Life — 70

Survivance

5. The Desire for Survival? — 77
   - Desire — 80
   - Finitude — 83
   - Immortality — 85
   - Dead—Immortal — 87
   - The Impossibility of Dying — 90
   - The Desire for Survival? — 92

6. For a Time: The Time of Survival — 95

7. Dying Alive: The Phantasmatics of Living-Death — 111
   - The Phantasm — 113
   - The Phantasm of Dying Alive — 116
   - Thinking Death — 118
   - The Intemporality of the Unconscious — 119
   - The Phantasm and the Event — 123
   - Survivance — 124
   - The Weave — 127
   - Ground — 128
   - Perhaps an Other Time, Place, and Logic: Affect, the Phantasm, and the "As If" — 130

Notes — 135

Bibliography — 167

Index — 173

Acknowledgments

This book would not have been written without the moral support of the two J's, my and Pleshette's ever faithful friends, Justine Malle and Joanne Molina.

I wish to extend my profound and warm gratitude to Ester and Dariush Saghafi, Dara and Yoli Saghafi, Alex da Ponte, Karen Mulford, Sally Aron, Jerry Aron, Fern Kelly, and John Rowley.

During the early stages of the manuscript, Dawne McCance and an anonymous reader provided very careful and expert advice, for which I'm grateful. The revised draft profited enormously from Ginette Michaud's very generous and detailed reading and astute comments. I wish to thank my editor Andrew Kenyon, Ryan Morris, Dana Foote and Dennis J. Schmidt, the series editor, for their extremely helpful advice.

I am deeply indebted to Michael Naas—our director, our teacher, our friend—and Pascale-Anne Brault. I am grateful for the friendship and collegiality of Geoffrey Bennington, Peggy Kamuf, Elizabeth Rottenberg, David Wills, Ellen Burt, Kir Kuiken, and Katie Chenoweth, my esteemed fellow travelers and members of the *équipe* at the Derrida Seminars Translation Project (DSTP). In addition to Nicholas Royle, Sarah Wood, and Timothy Clark of the *Oxford Literary Review*, they have been my true intellectual interlocutors.

I am especially grateful for the friendship of Elissa Marder, Kelly Oliver, Jill and Alan Schrift, Sarah Marshall, Chris Vickers, Crina Gschwandtner, David "Topper" Scott, Marygrace Hemme, Nicolas Pernot, Audrey Petit, Dylan Trigg, Ginger Guin, and Adam Rosenthal.

I am grateful to the following friends and colleagues: Amy Allen, Alia Al-Haji, Nicole Anderson, Charles Bambach, Andrew Benjamin, Tina Chanter, Andrew Cutrofello, Paul Davies, Jacques De Ville, Penny

Deutscher, Verena Erlenbusch-Anderson, Rodolphe Gasché, Simon Glendenning, Leigh Johnson, Claire Katz, Shannon Lundeen, Mary Beth Mader, Martin McQuillan, Elaine Miller, Peter Milne, Steven Miller, Andrew Mitchell, Simon Morgan Wortham, Andrew Parker, Eftichis Pirovolakis, Jeffrey Powell, Alison Ross, Isabelle Ullern, Francesco Vitale, Ewa Ziarek, and Kris Ziarek.

I am especially indebted to Anne Laptin, Peg Christopher, Sarah Lebovitz, Melvin Goldin, and Bethany Spiller who provided care in the time of need.

I would be remiss not to thank all the librarians and library staff who have over the years facilitated my research: Wayne Key, Frankie Perry, Paula Phillips, Susan Wood, Blake Galbreath, Zach Sandberg, and Gail Barton.

I would like to thank Heidi Samuelson for the preparation of the index.

Early versions of several chapters have been previously published. An early version of chapter 1, "The World after the End of the World," was published in *Oxford Literary Review* 39, no. 2 (December 2017): 265–276.

An early version of Chapter 2 "Safe, Intact: Derrida, Nancy, and the 'Deconstruction of Christianity,'" appeared in *A Companion to Derrida*, edited by Leonard Lawlor and Zeynep Direk (Walden, MA: Wiley-Blackwell, 2014): 447–463.

Certain passages in Chapters 2 and 4 have been borrowed from "Thomas the Marvelous: Resurrection and Living-Death in Blanchot and Nancy," *Mosaic* 45.3 (September 2012): 1–16.

An early version of chapter 5, "The Desire for Survival?," was published in *Desire in Ashes: Deconstruction, Psychoanalysis, Philosophy*, edited by Simon Morgan Wortham and Chiara Alfano (New York: Bloomsbury, 2015), 139–160.

An early version of chapter 6, "For a Time," was published in *Journal of French and Francophone Philosophy* 23, no. 2 (2015): 122–130.

An early version of chapter 7, "Dying Alive," was published in *Mosaic* 48, no. 3 (September 2015): 15–26.

All chapters have been rewritten and revised.

Abbreviations

Works by Jacques Derrida

All references are given to the French edition, followed by the English edition. Where the translation is not indicated, translations are my own.

A   *Apories*. Paris: Galilée, 1996. *Aporias*. Translated by Thomas Dutoit. Stanford: Stanford University Press, 1993. The English version is a translation of an article, "Apories: Mourir-s'attendre aux limites de la vérité," published in *Le passage des frontières: autour du travail de Jacques Derrida*. Paris: Galilée, 1993.

Ad   *Adieu à Emmanuel Lévinas*. Paris: Galilée, 1997. Translated by Pascale-Anne Brault and Michael Naas as *Adieu: To Emmanuel Levinas*. Stanford: Stanford University Press, 1999.

AF   *Mal d'Archive. Une impression freudienne*. Paris: Galilée, 1995; rpt. 2008. *Archive Fever*. Translated by Eric Prenowitz. Chicago: University of Chicago Press, 1996.

An   *L'animal que donc je suis*. Edited by Marie-Louise Mallet. Paris: Galilée, 2006. *The Animal That Therefore I Am*. Edited by Marie-Louise Mallet, translated by David Wills. New York: Fordham University Press, 2008.

Av   "Avances." In Serge Margel, *Le Tombeau du dieu artisan: Sur Platon*. Paris: Minuit, 1995, 11–43. *Advances*. Translated by Philippe Lynes. Minneapolis: University of Minnesota Press, 2017.

Cir   "Circonfession." In *Jacques Derrida* [with Geoffrey Bennington]. Paris: Seuil, 1991, reed. 2008. Translated by Geoffrey Bennington as "Circumfession," in *Jacques Derrida*. Chicago: University of Chicago Press, 1993.

CFU   *Chaque fois unique, la fin du monde*. Paris: Galilée, 2003. The original English version *The Work of Mourning*. Translated by Pascale-Anne Brault and Michael Naas. Chicago: Chicago University Press, 2001.

CN   "Comment nommer." In *Le poète que je cherche à être*. Edited by Yves Charnet. Paris: La Table Ronde/Belin, 1996, 182–206. Translated by Wilson Baldridge. "How to Name." In Michel Deguy, *Recumbents: Poems*. Middletown, CT: Wesleyan University Press, 2005, 191–221.

"Cnp"   "Comment ne pas trembler." *Annali della Fondazione Europea del Disegno (Fondation Adami)*, vol. 2. Milan: B. Mondadori, 2006.

Con   *Le «concept» du 11 septembre. Dialogues a New York (octobre-decembre 2001) avec Giovanna Borradori*. Paris: Galilée, 2004. Translated by Giovanna Borradori as *Philosophy in a Time of Terror: Dialogues with Jürgen Habermas and Jacques Derrida*. Chicago: University of Chicago Press, 2003.

Cos   *Cosmopolite de tous les pays, encore un effort!* Paris: Galilée, 1997. Translated by Mark Dooley as "On Cosmopolitanism," in *On Cosmopolitanism and Forgiveness*. New York: Routledge, 2016.

D   *Demeure—Maurice Blanchot*. Paris: Galilée, 1998. *Demeure: Fiction and Testimony*. Translated by Elizabeth Rottenberg. Stanford: Stanford University Press, 2000. Published with Maurice Blanchot's *The Instant of My Death*.

DA   "Deconstruction in America: An Interview with Jacques Derrida." *Critical Exchange* 17 (Winter 1985): 1–33.

Dia   "Dialogue entre Jacques Derrida, Philippe Lacoue-Labarthe et Jean-Luc Nancy." *Rue Descartes* 52 (2004): 86–99.

Diss   *La Dissémination*. Paris: Seuil, 1972. *Dissemination*. Translated by Barbara Johnson. Chicago: University of Chicago Press, 1981.

Dr   *Le droit à la philosophie du point de vue cosmopolitique*. Paris: Galilée, 1997.

E	*Echographies—de la télévision (Entretiens filmés avec Bernard Stiegler)*. Paris: Galilée, 1996. *Echographies of Television: Filmed Interviews*. Translated by Jennifer Bajorek. Malden, MA: Blackwell, 2002.
EO	*L'oreille de l'autre: otobiographies, transferts, traductions. Textes et débats avec Jacques Derrida*. Edited by Claude Lévesque and Christie V. McDonald. Montréal: VLB Editions, 1982. *The Ear of the Other: Otobiography, Transference, Translation: Texts and Discussions with Jacques Derrida*. Translated by Peggy Kamuf and Avital Ronell. Lincoln: University of Nebraska Press, 1988. The French edition subsequently appeared as *Otobiographies: l'enseignement de Nietzsche et la politique du nom propre*. Paris: Galilée, 1984. The 1984 edition does not include transcripts of Roundtable discussions included in the English edition.
Ep	"De l'écrit à la parole: table ronde animée par Jacques Munier." *Théatre/Public* 79 (January–February 1988): 40.
FK	"Foi et savoir: Les deux sources de la 'religion' aux limites de la simple raison." In *La Religion*. Edited by Jacques Derrida and Gianni Vattimo. Paris: Seuil, 1996. Translated by Samuel Weber as "Faith and Knowledge: The Two Sources of 'Religion' within the Limits of Mere Reason," in *Religion*, edited by Jacques Derrida and Gianni Vattimo. Stanford: Stanford University Press, 1998. In cases where it may be helpful, paragraph numbers are provided as # following the page number.
"Fors"	"Fors: Les mots anglées de Nicolas Abraham et Maria Torok." In *Le verbier de l'Homme aux loups*. Paris: Flammarion, 1976. Translated by Richard Rand as "Fors: The Anglish Words of Nicolas Abraham and Maria Torok," in *The Wolf Man's Magic Word: A Cryptonymy*. Minneapolis: University of Minnesota Press, 1986.
FWT	*De quoi demain . . . Dialogue* [with Elisabeth Roudinesco]. Paris: Fayard/Galilée, 2001. *For What Tomorrow . . . : A Dialogue*. Translated by Jeff Fort. Stanford: Stanford University Press, 2004.
Glas	*Glas*. Paris: Galilée, 1974. *Glas*. Translated by John P. Leavey Jr. and Richard Rand. Lincoln: University of Nebraska Press, 1986.

GT   *Donner le temps: 1. La fausse monnaie*. Paris: Galilée, 1991. *Given Time: 1. Counterfeit Money*. Translated by Peggy Kamuf. Chicago: University of Chicago Press, 1992.

H. C.   "*H. C. pour la vie, c'est a dire* . . ." In *Hélène Cixous croisées d'une œuvre*. Edited by Mireille Calle-Gruber. Paris: Galilée, 2000. *H. C. pour la vie, c'est a dire* . . . Paris: Galilée, 2002; *H. C. for Life, That Is to Say* . . . Translated by Laurent Milesi and Stefan Herbrechter. Stanford: Stanford University Press, 2006.

"ICM"   "Il courait mort : salut, salut." In *Papier machine*. Paris: Galilée, 2001. Translated as "'Dead Man Running': Salut, Salut," in *Negotiations: Interventions and Interviews 1971–2001*, edited and translated by Elizabeth Rottenberg. Stanford: Stanford University Press, 2002.

IND   *Idiomes, nationalités, déconstructions: Rencontre de Rabat avec Jacques Derrida*. Special issue, *Cahiers Intersignes* 13 (Autumn 1998). Casablanca: Editions Toubkal, 1998.

LT   *Le toucher, Jean-Luc Nancy*. Paris: Galilée, 2000.

LTLF   *Apprendre à vivre enfin: Entretien avec Jean Birnbaum*. Paris: Galilée/*Le Monde*, 2005. *Learning to Live Finally: The Last Interview*. Translated by Pascale-Anne Brault and Michael Naas. Hoboken, NJ: Melville House, 2007.

Jsg   "Je suis en guerre contre moi-même." *Le Monde*, October 12, 2004, vi–viii.

M   *Marges—de la philosophie*. Paris: Minuit, 1972. *Margins of Philosophy*. Translated by Alan Bass. Chicago: University of Chicago Press, 1982.

Mem   *Mémoires d'aveugle: L'autoportrait et autres ruines*. Paris: Editions de la Réunion des musées nationaux, 1990. Translated by Pascal-Anne Brault and Michael Naas as *Memoirs of the Blind: The Self-Portrait and Other Ruins*. Chicago: University of Chicago Press, 1993.

Mo   *Le Monolinguisme de l'autre ou la prothèse d'origine*. Paris: Galilée, 1996. *Monolingualism of the Other; or, The Prosthesis of Origin*. Translated by Patrick Mensah. Stanford: Stanford University Press, 1998.

MPD *Mémoires—pour Paul de Man*. Paris: Galilée, 1988. *Memoires: For Paul de Man*. Translated by Cecile Lindsay, Jonathan Culler, Eduardo Cadava, and Peggy Kamuf. New York: Columbia University Press, 1986; 2nd rev. ed. 1989.

OG *De la grammatologie*. Paris: Minuit, 1967. *Of Grammatology*. Translated by Gayatri Chakravorty Spivak. Baltimore: Johns Hopkins University Press, 1974; 2nd corr. ed. 1998.

ON *Sauf le nom*. Paris: Galilée, 1993. "Sauf le nom," translated by John P. Leavey Jr., in *On the Name*, edited by Thomas Dutoit. Stanford: Stanford University Press, 1995.

OrG *Introduction à "L'Origine de la géométrie" de Husserl*. Paris: Presses Universitaires de France, 1962; 2nd ed. 1974. *Edmund Husserl's "Origin of Geometry": An Introduction*. Translated by John P. Leavey Jr. Lincoln: University of Nebraska Press, 1978; 2nd ed. 1989.

P *Passions*. Paris: Galilée, 1993. "Passions," translated by David Wood, in *On the Name*, edited by Thomas Dutoit. Stanford: Stanford University Press, 1995.

Par *Parages*. Paris: Galilée, 1986. *Parages*. Edited by John P. Leavey. Translated by Tom Conley, James Hulbert, John P. Leavey, and Avital Ronell. Nouvelle édition revue et augmentée. Paris: Galilée, 2003. *Parages*. Stanford: Stanford University Press, 2011.

PC *La carte postale: de Socrate à Freud et au-delà*. Paris: Aubier-Flammarion, 1980. *The Post Card: From Socrates to Freud and Beyond*. Translated by Alan Bass. Chicago: University of Chicago Press, 1987.

Pcq "Penser ce qui vient." In *Derrida pour le temps à venir*, edited by René Major. Paris: Stock, 2007.

PFr *Politiques de l'amitié*. Paris: Galilée, 1994. *Politics of Friendship*. Translated by George Collins. New York: Verso, 1997.

PG *Le problème de la genèse dans la philosophie de Husserl*. Paris: Presses Universitaires de France, 1990. *The Problem of Genesis in Husserl's Philosophy*. Translated by Marian Hobson. Chicago: University of Chicago Press, 2003.

PM *Papier machine. Le ruban de machine à écrire et autres réponses.* Paris: Galilée, 2001. *Without Alibi.* Edited and translated by Peggy Kamuf. Stanford: Stanford University Press, 2002. *Paper Machine.* Translated by Rachel Bowlby. Stanford: Stanford University Press, 2005.

Po "Poétique et politique du témoignage." In *Derrida,* edited by Marie-Louise Mallet and Ginette Michaud. Paris: Editions de l'Herne, 2004.

Poi *Points de suspension. Entretiens.* Selected and presented by Elisabeth Weber. Paris: Galilée, 1992. *Points . . . : Interviews, 1974–1994.* Translated by Peggy Kamuf et al. Stanford: Stanford University Press, 1995.

Pos *Positions.* Paris: Minuit, 1972. *Positions.* Translated by Alan Bass. Chicago: University of Chicago Press, 1981.

Psy *Psyché. Invention de l'autre, t. 1 (nouvelle édition augmentée).* Paris: Galilée, [1987] 1998.

Psy2 *Psyché. Invention de l'autre, t. II (nouvelle édition augmentée).* Paris: Galilée, [1987] 2003.

"R" *Béliers. Le dialogue ininterrompu: entre deux infinis, le poème.* Paris: Galilée, 2003. "Rams," in *Sovereignties in Question: The Poetics of Paul Celan,* edited and translated by Thomas Dutoit and Outi Pasanen. New York: Fordham University Press, 2005.

R *Voyous. Deux essais sur la raison.* Paris: Galilée, 2003. *Rogues: Two Essays on Reason.* Translated by Pascale-Anne Brault and Michael Naas. Stanford: Stanford University Press, 2005.

Sh *Schibboleth—Pour Paul Celan.* Paris: Galilée, 1986; rpt. 2003. "Shibboleth: For Paul Celan," translated by Joshua Wilner, in *Word Traces: Readings of Paul Celan,* ed. Aris Fioretos. Baltimore: Johns Hopkins University Press, 1994.

SM *Spectres de Marx. L'Etat de la dette, le travail du deuil et la nouvelle Internationale.* Paris: Galilée, 1993. *Specters of Marx: The State of the Debt, the Work of Mourning, and the New International.* Translated by Peggy Kamuf. New York: Routledge, 1993.

Sp	*Eperons. Les styles de Nietzsche*. Paris: Flammarion, 1976; rpt. 1978. *Spurs: Nietzsche's Styles*. Translated by Barbara Harlow. Chicago: University of Chicago Press, 1979.
SPLJ	*Surtout, pas des journalistes!* Paris: Galilée, 2016. Originally published in English translation as "Above All, No Journalists!," in *Religion and Media*, edited by Hent de Vries and Samuel Weber. New York: Fordham University Press, 2001.
"TA"	"Le temps des adieux : Heidegger (lu par) Hegel (lu par) Malabou." *Revue philosophique de la France et de L'Etranger* 188, no. 1 (January–March 1998): 3–47. Translated by Joseph D. Cohen as "A Time for Farewells: Heidegger (read by) Hegel (read by) Malabou," in his preface to Catherine Malabou, *The Future of Hegel: Plasticity, Temporality and Dialectic*, translated by Lisabeth During. London: Routledge, 2005.
"Th"	"The Three Ages of Jacques Derrida," interview with Kristine McKenna. *LA Weekly*, November 8–14, 2002.
TP	*La vérité en peinture*. Paris: Aubier-Flammarion, 1978. *The Truth in Painting*. Translated by Geoffrey Bennington and Ian McLeod. Chicago: University of Chicago Press, 1987.
TS	*Il Gusto del Segreto*. Edited by Giacomo Donis and David Webb. Rome-Bari: Gius. Laterza & Figli Spa, 1997. [With Maurizio Ferraris,] *A Taste for the Secret*. Translated by Giacomo Donis. Malden, MA: Polity Press, 2001.
VP	*La voix et le phénomène*. Paris: Presses Universitaires de France, 1967. *Voice and Phenomenon*. Translated by Leonard Lawlor. Evanston, IL: Northwestern University Press, 2011.
WA	*Without Alibi*. Edited, translated, and with an introduction by Peggy Kamuf. Stanford: Stanford University Press, 2002.
WD	*L'Ecriture et la différance*. Paris: Seuil, 1967. *Writing and Difference*. Translated by Alan Bass. Chicago: University of Chicago Press, 1978.
WM	*The Work of Mourning*. Edited by Pascale-Anne Brault and Michael Naas. Chicago: University of Chicago Press, 2001.

Seminars

BSI *Séminaire La bête et le souverain, Volume I (2001–2002)*. Paris: Galilée, 2008. *The Beast and the Sovereign*, volume 1. Edited by Michel Lisse, Marie-Louise Mallet, and Ginette Michaud. Translated by Geoffrey Bennington. Chicago: University of Chicago Press, 2009.

BSII *Séminaire La bête et le souverain, Volume II (2002–2003)*. Paris: Galilée, 2010. *The Beast and the Sovereign*, volume 2. Edited by Michel Lisse, Marie-Louise Mallet, and Ginette Michaud. Translated by Geoffrey Bennington. Chicago: University of Chicago Press, 2011.

DP1 *La peine de mort, Volume I (1999–2000)*. Paris: Galilée, 2012. *The Death Penalty, Volume I*. Edited by Geoffrey Bennington, Marc Crépon, and Thomas Dutoit. Translated by Peggy Kamuf. Chicago: University of Chicago Press, 2014.

DP2 *La peine de mort, Volume II (2000–2001)*. Paris: Galilée, 2012. *The Death Penalty, Volume II*. Edited by Geoffrey Bennington and Marc Crépon. Translated by Elizabeth Rottenberg. Chicago: University of Chicago Press, 2017.

Works by Jean-Luc Nancy

Ad *L'adoration (Déconstruction du christianisme, 2)*. Paris: Galilée, 2010. *Adoration: The Deconstruction of Christianity II*. Translated by John McKeane. New York: Fordham University Press, 2013.

C *Corpus*. Paris: Métailié, 1992.

"CD" "Consolation, désolation." *Magazine littéraire*, April 2004, 58–60.

"DC" "La déconstruction du christianisme." *Les Etudes philosophiques* 4 (1998): 503–19. Translated by Simon Sparks as "The Deconstruction of Christianity," in *Religion and Media*, edited by Hent de Vries and Samuel Weber. Stanford: Stanford University Press, 2001. Subsequently appeared in *La Déclosion*.

Déc	*La Déclosion (Deconstruction du christianisme, 1)*. Paris: Galilée, 2005. *Dis-Enclosure: The Deconstruction of Christianity*. Translated by Bettina Bergo, Gabriel Malenfant, and Michael B. Smith. New York: Fordham University Press.
"FC"	"Fin du colloque." In *Maurice Blanchot: Récits critiques*. Tours: Editions Farrago/Léo Scheer, 2003.
I	*L'intrus*. Paris: Galilée, 2000. Translated by Susan Hanson as "L'intrus." *CR: The New Centennial Review* 2, no. 3 (Fall 2002): 1–14.
JPR	"Lettre à Jean-Pierre Rehm." *Journal FIDMarseille-04.07.05*, Festival International du Documentaire, Marseille (2005): 2.
Mu	*Les muses*. Paris: Galilée, 1994. *The Muses*. Translated by Peggy Kamuf. Stanford: Stanford University Press, 1996.
NMT	*Noli me tangere. Essai sur la levée du corps*. Paris: Bayard, 2003. *Noli me tangere: On the Raising of the Body*. Translated by Sarah Clift. New York: Fordham University Press, 2008.
Pa	*Partir—Le départ*. Montrouge: Bayard, 2011.
Rv	"Reste, viens." *Le monde*, October 12, 2004, x.
Sa	"Salut à toi, salut aux aveugles que nous devenons." *Libération*, October 11, 2004, my translation.
Tr	"Tenue, retenue." In *Lucile Bertrand: Sculptures*. Paris: L'Arbre à Lettres, 1995. Translated by Simon Sparks as "Held, Held Back," in *Multiple Arts*, edited by Simon Sparks. Stanford: Stanford University Press, 2006.

Other Works

Works by Sigmund Freud

GW	*Gesammelte Werke*. 18 vols. Edited by Anna Freud et al. Frankfurt am Main: S. Fischer Verlag, 1960–.
SA	*Studienausgabe*. 10 vols. Edited by Alexander Mitscherlich, Angela Richards, and James Strachey. Frankfurt am Main: Fischer Verlag, 1969–1975.

SE *Standard Edition of the Complete Psychological Works of Sigmund Freud.* 24 vols. Translated and edited by James Strachey et al. London: The Hogarth Press, 1953–1974.

Works by Martin Heidegger

NII *Nietzsche. Zweiter Band.* Pfullingen: Verlag Günther Neske, 1961. *Nietzsche*, vol. 4. Edited by David Farrell Krell, translated by Joan Stambaugh, David Farrell Krell, and Frank Capuzzi. San Francisco: HarperCollins, 1991.

SZ *Sein und Zeit.* Tübingen: Max Niemeyer Verlag, 1953. *Being and Time.* Translated by John Macquarrie and Edward Robinson. New York: Harper & Row, 1962.

VA "Das Ding." In *Vorträge und Aufsätze* (1954), 171. Translated by Albert Hofstadter as "The Thing," in *Poetry, Language, Thought.* New York: Harper & Row, 1971.

Weg "Vom Wesen des Grundes." In *Wegmarken.* Frankfurt am Main: Vittorio Klostermann, 1967. Translated by William McNeill as "On the Essence of Ground," in *Pathmarks*, edited by William McNeill. Cambridge: Cambridge University Press, 1998.

ZSD *Zur Sache des Denkens.* Tübingen: Max Niemeyer, 1976. Translated by Joan Stambaugh as "The End of Philosophy and the Task of Thinking," in *Basic Writings*, revised and expanded edition, edited by David Farrell Krell. New York: HarperCollins, 1993.

All citations to GA refer to Martin Heidegger, *Gesamtausgabe.* Frankfurt am Main: Vittorio Klostermann, 1976– .

GA 10 *Der Satz vom Grund.* Frankfurt: Klostermann 1976. *The Principle of Reason.* Translated by Reginald Lilly. Bloomington: Indiana University Press, 1991.

GA 20 *Prolegomena zur Geschichte. History of the Concept of Time: Prolegomena.* Translated by Theodor Kisiel. Bloomington: Indiana University Press, 1985.

GA 26 *Metaphysische Anfangsgründe der Logik im Ausgang von Logik.* Frankfurt: Klostermann, 1978. *The Metaphysical Foundations of Logic.* Translated by Michael Heim. Bloomington: Indiana University Press, 1984.

GA 65 *Beiträge zur Philosophie (Vom Ereignis)*. Frankfurt: Klostermann, 1989. *Contributions to Philosophy (Of the Event)*. Translated by Richard Rojcewicz and Daniella Vallega-Neu. Bloomington: Indiana University Press, 2012.

GA 66 *Besinnung (1938/39)*. Frankfurt: Klostermann, 1997. *Mindfulness*. Translated by Parvis Emad and Thomas Kalary. New York: Continuum, 2006.

WORKS BY MAURICE BLANCHOT

Ec *L'écriture du désastre*. Paris: Gallimard, 1980. *The Writing of the Disaster*. Translated by Ann Smock. Lincoln: University of Nebraska Press, 1986.

EL *L'espace littéraire*. Paris: Gallimard, 1955. *The Space of Literature*. Translated by Ann Smock. Lincoln: University of Nebraska Press, 1982.

PF *La part du feu*. Paris: Gallimard, 1949. *The Work of Fire*. Translated by Charlotte Mandell. Stanford: Stanford University Press, 1995.

For abbreviations of ancient authors and works, see *Liddell-Scott-Jones Greek-English Lexicon* (9th edition).

Prologue

Salut—A Spectro-Poetics

One of us, one of the two, "*will have* had [*aura été*] to remain alone" ("R" 22/140). One of us, doomed to carry the world, the world of the other (*le monde de l'autre*), will have had to endure the loss of the world (22/140). "The world after the end of the world [*le monde après la fin du monde*]" (22–23/140). This lone, solitary clause without verb describes not only the condition of the survivor who has to carry the other and the world of the other, but also expresses what death—every death—does to the world. The clause says, declares, a new definition of the world. The other's death brings to a close the world in the same way that the other opens the world. Death marks each time the end of the one and only world, the end of the unique world. And the survivor remains alone, "assigned to carry both the other and *her* world, the other and *the* world that have disappeared" (23/140). He will have to bear "the end of the world" brought on by the other's death.

A heartrending, ravaging event in "my" world led me, forced me, in my grief to think about and evaluate several motifs from Derrida's later writings that he had been developing over a number of publications and that I had been struggling to come to grips with. Over time, it became my conviction that these motifs could not be treated separately or in isolation and required being thought together, with each other. *The World after the End of the World* is an attempt to think the intricate relation between these tightly knit motifs—world, death, mourning, survival, the end of the world, the phantasm, and the French term *salut*—each of which would justifiably merit a book-length study.

From 2003 onward the syntagma "the end of the world," not to be mistaken with the more familiar eschatological, apocalyptic notion, became linked in Derrida's thought to a thinking of the other's death. This expression or syntagma arose arguably in part in the context of, and as a reaction to, the publication in English of *The Work of Mourning* (2001) and its subsequent appearance in French as *Chaque fois unique, la fin du monde* (2003), a collection of pieces penned after the passing away of close friends and colleagues. The polemical preface ("Avant-propos") to *Chaque fois unique, la fin du monde*, and related publications of around the same time, displayed a rethinking or a complete reassessment of the notion of "world" in Derrida's thinking. It is as if Derrida were asking, "What if there has never been such a thing as '*the* world?'" And further, "What becomes of the common notion 'world' if one were to proclaim that the world ended?" It is one of my contentions that "the end of the world" puts an end to (a thinking of) the world as we know it.

In the early '90s, Derrida's work displays a resistance to a certain rhetoric of *globalization* in contemporary political discourse and the media. Confronting the dominance of this politics of globalization, founded on a legal, economic, techno-scientific, linguistic-cultural "homo-hegemony," and observing that the concept of the world gestures toward a history and an Abrahamic filiation, Derrida challenges and deconstructs the common, long-standing definition of "the world."[1] His mournful bearing witness to the death of close friends and colleagues coupled with his own avowed obsession with death, is sustained by a non-apocalyptic thinking of "the end of the world."[2] His late texts pursue the link between the end of the world and the death of the other first mentioned in *Aporias*.[3]

In "Faith and Knowledge," his major work on the question of "religion," and numerous subsequent publications, Derrida linked religion to what, in *Monolingualism of the Other* (1996), he referred to as "that strange French word *le salut*" (Mo 56/30, trans. mod.).[4]

Salut, a rich, multivalent, polysemic, yet "equivocal word," is pivotal for Derrida's work on topics such as religion, immunity, health and well-being, security, safety, redemption and salvation. The promise of what is commonly known as "religion"—even though after "Faith and Knowledge" we can no longer innocently operate with a naïve notion of this term—is salvation (*salut*).[5] When used as a performative, *salut* is part of daily conversation in French uttered as a greeting to say hello or good-bye or as a send-off. When used as a noun or as a substantive, *salut* means salvation and designates being whole, safe, unscathed, immune, intact, or being restored to this state by being indemnified, saved, redeemed, and made whole. To indemnify is to restore, to restitute in order to render intact. What does this indemnification involve? The desire for indemnity and "immunological salvation" is a wish to protect what is believed to be intact or unharmed ("ICM" 183n/269fn9). A process of immunization and indemnification against what is considered unclean, unhealthy, or unholy, *salut* is also a desire to restore some thing to a supposedly original or uncompromised state. Thus, it is not only to keep safe and sound, protected and unscathed, but also to heal, to make whole, to restitute, and to restore. In *Le toucher, Jean-Luc Nancy* Derrida refers to being safe, searching for immunity, redemption, or salvation as "Christian values" (LT 249). One need only turn to St. Paul's Letter to Timothy in the New Testament: "God our Savior, who desires that all men be saved" (NRSV 1 Timothy 2: 4).

Though Derrida uses terms having to do with saving (*sauver*) in his early writings (for example, in *The Truth in Painting* [1978]), it is not until the 1990s, starting from "Faith and Knowledge," that he delves into and explores the various senses of *salut* (TP 263/229). The semantic series of terms borrowed from Émile Benveniste (*heilig*, holy, *sacré*, *sain et sauf*, *indemne*, *intact*, *immune*) are a common feature of many of his texts. References to the two aspects of *salut* date back at least to "Avances" (1995), and are further developed in texts since 1996, such as "Faith and Knowledge" (1996), *Adieu to Emmanuel Levinas* (1997), *Demeure—Maurice Blanchot* (1998), and *Rogues* (2003). In "Avances," his extended appreciation of Serge Margel's book on Plato's *Timaeus*, *Le tombeau du dieu artisan*, Derrida makes a passing reference to *salut*, listing terms whose repetition becomes a familiar feature of his writings on *salut*: "être sain et sauf, saint et sauf (hieros, hagios, hosios, sacer, sanctus, heilig, holy, *sacré, saint, indemne, immun*)" (Av 38/47). A year later, in "Faith and Knowledge" (1996), he comments on "a discourse on salvation [*salut*], that is on the holy, the sacred, the safe and sound, the unscathed, the immune [*le sain, le saint, le sacré, le sauf, l'indemne, l'immun*] (*sacer, sanctus, heilig*, holy and their alleged equivalents in so many languages)." Is *salut*, queries Derrida, "necessarily redemption, before or after evil, fault or sin?" (FK 10/2). In *Demeure—Maurice Blanchot*, a text in which Derrida explores the rich vocabulary of *salut*, he describes how the narrator of Blanchot's *The Instant of My Death* saves himself without fleeing, "saves himself without saving himself [*sauvé sans se sauver*]," assures his salvation without having run away (D 100/76). Elsewhere, in a text dedicated to Sarah Kofman, Derrida detects in her work an "absence of salvation [*l'absence de salut*]" (CFU 136/173) that did not promise either resurrection or redemption (150/181).⁶ A continued probing of the two irreducibly proximate senses or uses of *salut*, "two contrary, sometimes contradictory *saluts*," *at the same time* inseparable and inextricable, which operate *within* one another, haunt each other, yet remain apart, takes place in earnest in the mid-'90s ("TA" 35/xxxvi, second emphasis mine).⁷

The notion of *salut* also appears in Jean-Luc Nancy's writings with greater frequency in the 1990s. We also see in Nancy a resistance to *salut* as salvation. In *The Muses* (1994), describing a painting of Caravaggio entitled *The Death of the Virgin*, where several people have gathered around the reclining body of a woman, Nancy affirms: "There is neither resurrection nor assumption [. . .] there is neither abyss, nor ecstasy, nor salvation [*salut*]" (Mu 113/65). A bit further on he repeats this claim: "It is not salvation [*salut*], it is not redemption" (114/66). A few years later, on the back of the jacket of the French edition of *La pensée derobée* (2001), considering a notion that he explores in the book, Nancy responds to the question that he himself poses, "How to think, how to start again to think nudity?" "No 'salvation' [*Pas de 'salut'*], no 'end' [*pas de 'fin'*]," he writes, "but on the contrary, at each moment, a singular opening of the sense of being without end [*sens d'être sans fin*]." In *L'intrus*, a meditation on his heart transplant, Nancy wonders about the "proper" life that needs to be "saved [*sauver*]" (I 27/7).

In his later writings, Nancy's references are increasingly to *salut* as salvation, for example, in *Dis-Enclosure* and *Noli me tangere*. Nonetheless, *salut* as a greeting also does appear in his texts, for example, in a chapter of *The Muses*, "The Vestige of Art," where employing the word *pas*, he observes that, for him, invoking the notion of *pas* is "to salute Blanchot and Derrida" (Mu 156n/98fn19). A bit further on in the same essay on the "remains" of art, Nancy sends out a greeting to a distinguished theorist of art, remarking that "this time the salute goes to Thierry de Duve" (158/99fn22). One of the aims of the present book is to compare the employment of the vocabulary of *salut* by Derrida and Nancy so as to distinguish Derrida's work from, the sometimes subtle, differences with the work of Jean-Luc Nancy and while doing so, to demarcate their different senses of deconstruction.⁸

Turning on its head the question that Derrida poses in "Faith and Knowledge" regarding the link between religion and *salut*, the present book poses the following question: Can a discourse on *salut* be dissociated from a discourse on religion? In a critical essay on naming, calling, and mourning in Michel Deguy's poetry entitled "How to Name?" Derrida refers to the "singular bivocity" of the two *salut*s.[9] Describing the metonymy of the two meanings of *salut* as saving and greeting, he calls them a "metonymical doublet" (CN 185/194). "The two *salut*s," he writes, "greet each other [*se saluent*] from near or from afar, one *as* well *as* the other [*l'un* comme *l'autre*], one operating and co-operating within the other that remains nevertheless apart" (185/194, trans. mod.).

Even though he delineates the dual structure of *salut* and the "duplicity" of the two meanings (CN 185/195), and even though the two senses of *salut* contaminate and haunt one another, where, in a language hearkening back to *Dissemination*, there is a *passage* between the opposing senses or values of the same word, Derrida insists on the absolute heterogeneity and the "irreconcilable difference" between the two *salut*s, wishing to keep them separate (203/218). As Derrida writes in *Rogues*, "If, as I have attempted and am still tempted to do elsewhere, one were to separate [*dissocie*] as irreconcilable the notion of *salut* as greeting or salutation to the other [*salut à l'autre*] from every *salut* as salvation (in the sense of the safe, the immune, health, and security), if one were to consider the greeting or salutation of the other, of what comes, as irreducible and heterogeneous to any seeking of *salut* as salvation, you can guess into what abysses we would be drawn" (R 160/114). It is one of this book's goals to explore these abysses mentioned by Derrida. It is crucial to stress that *salut* in Derrida's writings operates undecidably, the structural undecidability of *salut* allowing the tension between *salut*'s two meanings, as greeting and salvation, to remain *suspended*.[10] The use of the article would allow the reader to know how *salut* is meant to function (as a noun or as a performative) yet its usage without the article compels the reader to constantly keep the double meaning in mind.

Derrida's taking up of the notion of "the end of the world," this book argues, dictates an engagement with the thought of *salut*, for, if the death of the other—a parting—signifies the end of the world, this departure then necessitates, stressing the performative, a *salut*-ation. At every end, at every leave-taking, there must be a good-bye, but also a "see you," "see you later," or "I will see you again." I aim to show that this other performative sense of *salut*, the greeting, the *adieu*, disturbs, gently troubles, the wish or desire for safety and salvation that is the first sense of *salut*. How does this seemingly unremarkable gesture, one may ask, endanger or disturb the sense of *salut* as salvation, the desire for being saved, which as Derrida has diagnosed, is at the root of "religion"?

Just as Derrida wishes to dissociate the two senses of *salut*, this book will place its emphasis, on the less-discussed aspect of *salut*—*salut* as the coming or visitation of the other, an originary greeting, or an originary turn toward or address to the other—acknowledging that it will not be a matter of choice.[11] The wager would be to see if this salutation, foreign to the *salut* of salvation, can prove itself resistant to the economy of salvation. The originary performative greeting of the other would take place on the threshold, "on the forever uncertain border" between *salut* and *salut*.[12] Only on this threshold can the *salut* of salutation be dissociated from the *salut* of "redemptive economy" (Kamuf 105–106). Not redemption (restoration) or indemnity (protection), not remaining intact and unscathed, not being made whole and restored, but *salut*, if there is any, will have to be *un salut sans salut*, or as Derrida writes at the end of *Le toucher*: "Just *salut*, greeting without salvation; just a *salut* to come [*un salut sans salvation, un salut juste à venir*]" (LT 348).[13] A new reading of *salut* as greeting, I suggest, would require "a certain poetics [*une certaine poétique*]" (R 23/5), a "poetics of *salut* [*poétique du salut*]" (CN 185/196)—what in "How to Name" Derrida calls "a spectro-poetics" (CN 201/216)—that can "inflect differently [*détourner*]" a dominant interpretation, modifying and transforming the common meaning of phrases (R 23/5).

∽

Mourning no longer waits. Discussing his encounter with Hans-Georg Gadamer, in the lecture delivered at Heidelberg University entitled *Rams: Uninterrupted Dialogue—Between Two Infinities* (2003), Derrida writes that from the very first encounter between the two, interruption anticipates death. One the two *will have* had to carry alone, in himself, the dialogue and the memory of the first interruption. The other, Pleshette DeArmitt, who is named as she is called, "she: [. . .] is the one whose name one must keep. One must recall her name and what she is called. To salute is not only to name, it is to call the other [*appeler l'autre*]" (CN 184/194, trans. mod.). She is the one "whose name it is necessary to keep through mourning [*il faut que le nom soit gardé dans le deuil*]" (203/217). In "How to Name?" Derrida writes, "To greet, to salute is to name the other precisely where the other is called, named [*s'appelle*], that is, called from an other place [*depuis un autre lieu*] which will have had to be her end [*qui aura du être sa fin*]" (203/217, trans. mod.). At "the end," from *this place*, the "other place" where she may be, this other place from where she is called, where all horizon is lacking, "where the two meanings of *salut* part [*se séparent*] and say goodbye or farewell [*adieu*] to one another," there is no being saved, no safety, in a survivance that is neither life nor death (203/217, trans. mod.).¹⁴

This is where "the 'singular bivocity' of the word *salut* must, as it were, part with itself [*se séparer*] forever, and that one *salut* must never be like the other" (CN 203/217–218). Derrida names this "dissociation," this "absolute heterogeneity, irreconcilable difference [*différend*]" between the two *salut*s "Necessity"—fond of capitalizing it "as if it were someone else's proper name, like *Khôra*" (203/218). Yet the possibility of "the non-*salut* of salvation or health" must always "haunt le *salut* as calling [*le salut en appel*]" (203/218). For, in order to "be able to call, where saluting is more than naming," it is essential and necessary that *le salut* of salvation, health, redemption, and resurrection never be assured, "that it always *could* be refused, threatened, forbidden, lost, gone" (203/218).

"One can only call to the other [*appeler l'autre*], and greet [. . .] as living [*vivant*], that is to say, as dying [*mourant*], in her *mourance* and mine, in a survivance that is neither life nor death," where there is no longer any "assured salvation, no salvation on the horizon" (CN 203/218, trans. mod.). This salutation "calls out to the other without hope"—not hopelessly, but "without any assurance of salvation" (204/218). Derrida calls this *salut*-ation to the other "irreducible reference, absolute difference which at once shapes and makes reference possible, and respect for the absolute referent which the other is, whatever happens [*quoi qu'il arrive*]" (204/218). There "must no longer [*il ne doit plus*] be" a horizon for this, as the lack of a horizon is "the condition for something, *something other* [quelque chose d'autre] to happen, some to-come [*quelque à-venir*] [. . .] absolute surprise, trauma without horizon, without the structure of a horizon" (204/218, trans. mod.). If what is coming appears against the contours of a horizon, it will no longer be an unanticipated surprise. As awaiting of what is already expected, it will be predicted, programmed, and precomprehended. The *salut* without salvation, *salut*-ation to the other, "the *ferance* of absolute difference, that is to say, different, unforeseeable, and heterogeneous reference, the event, the irruptive coming [*venue*], the *arrivance* of the other or death," in contrast, "all presuppose a radical and consistent calling into question" of all that pertains to a horizon (204/218–219). What is called for is "an other discourse on *salut*, an other *salut*,"[15] a spectro-poetic discourse that would not only "think justice and the gift otherwise" (CN 213/292) but would also acknowledge, address, reach out to, respond to, greet, welcome, and salute—the other.

While Derrida links the syntagma "the end of the world" with the other's death and mourning, he also continues a questioning of the notion of death in his last seminars. Derrida, whose preoccupation with the notion of death and whose abiding meditation on the inextricability and contamination of life with death led to their incessant interrogation, in his last seminars, in particular in *The Beast and the Sovereign, 2*, extended his examination of what earlier he had labeled "life death [*la vie la mort*]" to the notion of "living death [*la mort vivant*]." In his seminar on Heidegger and Defoe, which displays his dissatisfaction with the Heideggerian approach to the question of death, Derrida has recourse to an entirely new notion of the phantasm in order to think the phantasm of "dying alive." Since there can be no objective or scientific determination of the state of death, since as Derrida believes, life and death as such are not separable and since it is not possible to have direct access to death *as such*, living death can only be approached as a phantasm (this, of course, leads to a rethinking of phantasm: to be thought not simply using the Platonic philosophical register of truth/untruth, reality/fantasy, but in relation to the event as the coming or the happening of the event).[16] The death of the other and the end of the world, besides urging a thinking of living death as a phantasm, also inevitably set in motion a thinking of *survivance*. Yet Derrida's survivance, as this book will demonstrate, is not simply a matter of surviving in general, a continued persistence after an end—the end of the world—or even *my* own survival, but of an irreducible, originary trace anterior to the distinction between life and death, making both of them possible.

What remains? An address to the singular other, a supplicating address to the other *as other*, to *you*; a prayer, devoted to *you*. A salutation not to save but to greet, to salute from afar, "an utterly close experience of the distant [*toute proche expérience du lointain*]," a *salut*, an *envoi* worlds apart from the usual send-offs, a call, a poem-prayer challenging its constative use (CN 187/ 272).[17] In a living-dying-surviving,[18] what remains but to carry you?[19]

Not simply good-bye, a bidding farewell. Salut! is an address to and by the other, "be well," "fare well," wherever you may be, "until we meet again." A wave of the hand in acknowledgment, in recognition, as when children speaking in French play hide-and-seek and say, "Coucou. Hey there! I see you."

The End of the World

1

The World after the End of the World

> To be able to bear to bring to bear [*supporter de porter*] on death this mourning gaze [*regard endeuillé*] that is enduring and durable, to bear the weight of this bearing [*portée*], of the gaze brought to bear and the mourning borne [*porté*], the courage to bear death [*porter la mort*], one needs, I would say, something like a fidelity to death, to what dies and to who dies, as such, as dead: fidelity to death, fiance, confidence, faith, fidelity-to-death to the death [*fidelité à mort à la mort*], to whom and to what happens to be dead [*se trouve mort*]. This fidelity and loyalty not only require time: there would be no time without them.
>
> —Jacques Derrida, *Séminaire La bête et le souverain, Volume II (2002–2003)*

> La mort, c'est un monde qui disparaît. Et si chaque mort est la fin d'un monde, il y a une infinité de mondes.
>
> —Jacques Derrida, *Idiomes, Nationalités, Déconstructions*

"The world" is gone.[1]

There is no world when *you*'re gone. The moment that I'm obligated, as soon as I am obligated *to you*—and it is your death that obligates me, makes *me* obligated, responsible *for* you and *to* you—no world can be there. There is no ground—or a third—between us. No world can support us or serve as mediation for us. I am all alone.

"The world has gone, already, the world has left us, the world is no more, the world is far off, the world is lost, the world is lost from sight, the world is out of sight . . . the world has departed, the world has died" ("R" 46/149). On the occasion of the other's death, each time, it is the end of the world. Farewell to the world, for upon the other's death the world has departed.

In the last few years of his life, Derrida on a number of occasions wrote about and commented on Paul Celan's poem "Grosse, Glühende Wölbung" from *Atemwende*, which ends with the line "*Die Welt ist fort, ich muss dich tragen.*"[2] "This poem," Derrida writes in *Rams*, "says the world, the origin and the history of the world, the archeology and eschatology of the concept, the very *conception* of the world: how the world was *conceived*, how it is born and straightaway is no longer, how it goes away [*s'éloigne*] and leaves us, how its end is announced" ("R" 77/162). Derrida's writings on Celan's poem bear on a host of important motifs, motifs such as world (including the phenomenological concept of the world), death, the death of the other, survival, melancholy, mourning, solitude, and survivance. What can be learned from these writings can be summarized all too brutally and quickly as follows: There is no such thing as the One universal world that is shared by all; the world is not that within which all beings live or what they inhabit, the intersubjective accomplishment of a transcendental ego or *the* horizon against which everything is supposed to occur; death marks every time the absolute end of the world; the death of the other entails the disappearance of *the* world, marking, every time, each time singularly, the absolute end of the one and only world, *the end of the world*. To state this boldly: for Derrida, whatever we are to understand by "world" is determined out of, determined from, determined by "death"—the death of the other. Derrida's writings force us to think the notion of "world" starting from, out of, or on behalf of, the other. In other words, we are forced to rethink the very thought of the world on the basis of, setting out from "*ich muss dich tragen.*"[3]

Moreover, in his various remarks on Celan's poem, Derrida reformulates, what may advisedly be called, the "mortal" condition as "carrying the other in me." In his meditations on the verb *tragen*, particularly in Celan and in Heidegger, and on *porter*, to carry, to bear, to wear, Derrida places a great emphasis on the experience of carrying the other in oneself. At both ends of life's spectrum, at birth and at death, I carry or bear the other in myself. For the mother, in the experience of *carrying* a child before birth, *Die Welt is fort*, the world disappears—it is far away. For the one who mourns and endures the melancholy of a loss, what is left is to carry or bear the other. That is the survivor's condition: to live with the melancholy of the end of the world.

In speaking about the end of the world, I am following a path, which may by now be considered well trodden, a trail already expertly blazed by the remarkable analyses of Michael Naas, Rodolphe Gasché, Ginette Michaud, Geoffrey Bennington, J. Hillis Miller, and Peggy Kamuf, who each in his or her own way has helped us better understand Derrida's very curious formulation "the end of the world."[4]

From the first encounter between us there is melancholy, the melancholy that one day death will separate us. We know, we are aware, that one of us will have to go before the other, leaving the other alone. But mourning does not wait for death, its implacable temporality of the future anterior dictates that one of us will have been "dedicated [*voué*]" ("R" 22) to carry the other, to carry "the world after the end of the world" ("R" 23/140).

For, as Derrida writes in *Rams*, death is not, as we customarily think, the end of *a* world, "the end of someone or something *in the world*," the end of one world among others, but the absolute end of the one and only world. Each time, each time singularly, death is nothing other than the end *of the* world (23/140). Death marks, each and every time, the end of the one and only world, the very world that "each one [*chacun*] opens as the origin of the world" (23/140).

The world is gone. It is no more. The world died; it ended. But what *was* the world? Has there ever been such a thing as *the* world? Which world?

∼

Rather than give a historical genealogy of a concept, it may be more helpful to provide some markers in what we might call the history of the world.[5] The notion of "world" was developed gradually in ancient Greece.[6] Homer (10th c. BCE) juxtaposed sky, earth, sea, and so on, when he wished to speak of all things. He also used the phrase "the heaven and the earth," while Hesiod used the plural neutral adjective *panta*, "all [things]," in the *Theogony* (730–700 BCE).[7] The adjective *ta panta*, all things, also makes an appearance in Heraclitus (ca. 500 BCE),[8] whereas Empedocles (ca. 485–425 BCE) makes use of the singular adjective *to pan*, "the All."⁹ Elsewhere, around 600 BCE, the prophet Jeremiah states that the God of Israel has made "*the* whole": "He is the one who formed all things."¹⁰ The innovation introduced by the Greeks was to give the world a name of its own, *kosmos*. Its meaning, beginning with its use in the *Iliad*, is "order" in the expression *kata kosmon*, "in good order" or "ornament." The term designates order and beauty, particularly the beauty resulting from order, the beauty that is implied today by an activity that obtains its name from the word—"cosmetics." Similarly, the Latin *mundus*, world, is the same word as *mundus*, the French *toilette* or "woman's ornamentation." At least, this is according to Pliny the Elder, who asserts: "What the Greeks call *kosmos*, we call *mundus* due to its perfect and faultless elegance."¹¹ The word *elegantia* used by Pliny is a direct reference to the cosmetic usage of the term *mundus*. The two meanings of the word coexisted together and persisted.

The first application of *kosmos* to the "world" is attributed to Pythagoras by later authors: "Pythagoras was the first to call 'kosmos' the encompassing of all things (*hē tōn holōn periokhē*), because of the order (*taxis*) that reigns in it" (Aetius, *Placita*, 2.1.1, p. 327, DK 14 A21). We may be dealing with Platonic conceptions retroactively projected onto Pythagoras, but the term is also encountered in various pre-Socratic authors (among them, Anaxagoras DK 59 B8, Diogenes of Apollonia DK 64 B2 or 4 Laks). *Kosmos* is found several times in Heraclitus's fragments. In Fragment 30 the idea of "an ordered totality sufficient in itself" that does not require the involvement of an exterior stimulus is affirmed (Brague 20). This fragment is credited with having created the meaning of the word *kosmos*. By the time of Plato's writings, the word *kosmos* was understood in "the exclusive sense of a cosmic order" (Brague 21). Xenophon writes that "the action of the gods is carried out to ensure the 'order of all things' (*hē tōn holōn taxis*), a synonym for 'the totality of the world' (*ho holos kosmos*)" (*Mem* 4.3.13 and *Cyr* 8.7.22) (22).

Brague considers Plato's work as "representing a decisive point of departure" (22). It was with Plato that the word *kosmos* was installed definitively and without ambiguity in its meaning as "world."¹² By providing the first description of reality as forming an ordered whole, both good and beautiful, Brague maintains, Plato's *Timaeus* "causes the concept of *kosmos* to function" (22).¹³ The dialogue's final words fortify the description of the world: "this Heaven (*heis ouranos hode*) single in its kind and one" (92c7–d3). That which is initially designated "the heavens *and* the earth" is merged, so to speak, with the sky and the world becomes identified with the heavens or the sky. Aristotle distinguishes three meanings of the word "sky" (*ouranos*) (a) the substance of the last sphere of the universe or the natural body that is found in that sphere; (b) the body that is continuous with the last sphere of the universe, (c) the body enveloped by the last sphere" (*Cael* 1.9.278b11–21). The sky, no longer imagined as a flat plane above the earth, but now considered to be rounded and enveloping the earth on all sides, would also be all that the sky contains (the container and the contents, as it were, become one). An interpretation of the world taking its pattern from the sky begins to emerge (23).

According to Brague, "The 'world' has never designated a simple description of reality: it has always translated a value judgment, the fruit of a sort of act of faith" (23). Indeed, "Greek scientists were aware that they not only had a knowledge of the *kosmos*, but that their use of the term had essentially constructed the *kosmos* as such, as a *kosmos*" (23). For the Greeks "the world and its human subjects were primarily connected through the existence of laws that governed them all, and [. . .] those laws were of a moral nature. This idea was not specifically Greek. It can be found, for example, in Persia," as evinced in the Zoroastrian conception of the universe as a struggle between good and evil (29).

In his many writings on the notion of the world, Heidegger claimed that the concept of world was masked by that of nature and it was necessary to distinguish the phenomenological concept of the world from that of nature (*phyè, physis*), which was often conflated with it.[14] The phenomenon of the world, Heidegger argued, had heretofore never been acknowledged in philosophy (GA 20 231, 250). Greek ontology is, before all, oriented by the cosmos—the paradigm to grasp all that is. The world does not designate anything worldly or cosmic; rather, it designates that "in" which the Dasein that we are lives (27). Thus, the world is a characteristic and feature of Dasein and not of things, still less that of their organized gathering.

Brague argues that the concept that Heidegger relies on is not at all Greek. Rather, it is Germanic, as indicated by the etymology of the terms translated by "world" in these languages: *Welt, world,* and the Dutch *wereld*, which bring together the first element that means "man" (the Latin *vir*) and a second meaning "age" (the English *old*). Does the syntagma "I am, we are in the world," he asks, exist in Hellenism? Brague believes that the notion of "being-in-the-world" coined by Heidegger does not have a Greek equivalent. That we are *in* something called a world did not make sense for the Greeks. The notion that birth is "coming to the world" and dying is "to leave the world" was hardly meditated by them. It was not until Christianity that being in the world received a meaning, in particular with St. Paul and St. John, signifying the state of man separated from God (Weg 40/112).

Brague's decisive question is: "Has Greek thought ever thought the relation of man to the world otherwise than that of the part to the whole (e.g., *Laws* X, 903b–d)?" (37). "The Greeks think the totality of *what is present* but leave aside the totality of *presence* itself" (44). "Being in the world does not mean that we are in the midst of the things, which form the totality of what there is" (44). We are in the world "totally and permanently [*façon totale*]" (44). In his book Brague argues that Greek thought says everything about the world apart from the fact that *we are here*, we have always already been in the world (47). "It thinks the site that we occupy," remarks Brague, "but not our situation (being-situated)," which is ours (48). It thinks the being *of the* world and not being *in* the world. It thinks the belonging of man to the world, but not *my* presence in the world. It is fascinated by the contents of the world and forgets that the being-in-the-world that is mine goes hand in hand with it. Thus, for Greek cosmology there is no difference between "I am" in the world and that there are stars, gods, animals in the world.

In "On the Essence of Ground" (written in 1928), Heidegger investigates transcendence as the fundamental constitution of Dasein (Weg 108). He provides an interpretation of the phenomenon of world that will serve to illuminate transcendence. Heidegger names "*world* that *toward which* Dasein as such transcends, thus determining transcendence as *being-in-the-world*" (109). In *The Metaphysical Foundations of Logic* (1928) Heidegger also describes his aim as looking at "what is signified by 'world' as a feature of transcendence as such" (GA 26, 218/170). He goes on to define transcendence as "being-in-the-world" (218/170). In "On the Essence of Ground" he writes that the concept of world is taken not in a pre-philosophical sense but in a transcendental one. World, for Heidegger, does not signify "the totality of those beings that are present at hand" (Weg 110). He states that "*kósmos* does not refer to all beings taken together" but rather to "a state of affairs [*Zustand*], i.e., *how* beings, indeed beings *as a whole* are" (111). The world thus belongs precisely to Dasein, even though it embraces in its whole all beings (112). *Kósmos* comes to be used as a term for a particular kind of human existence, the kind of stance he takes *toward* the cosmos.

With the advent of Christianity, the world came to be viewed as the terrestrial "globe," designating the world of human beings or living beings. In the Gospel of St. John *kósmos* refers to the fundamental form of human Dasein removed from God. According to Heidegger, this coining of the meaning of *kósmos* that begins in the New Testament also appears in Augustine and Aquinas. For Augustine *mundus* refers to the whole of created beings, but also "those who delight in the world, the impious, the carnal" (Weg 113). World, Heidegger summarizes, means "beings as a whole" and the way Dasein maintains itself in relation to beings. Aquinas, too, on occasion uses *mundus* as synonymous with *universum*, the whole world of creatures, but also *saeculum*, the worldly way of thinking.

From the intricate thinking of world and the infinity of possible ways of creating the world in Leibniz, to Kant's examination of the concept of the world in the *First Critique*, from Schopenhauer's *The World as Will and Representation* to the phenomenology of Husserl, Fink, Heidegger, Merleau-Ponty, and Sartre, from the thought of "existence without a world [*existence sans monde*]" in Levinas to Blanchot's "solitude in the world," the notion of world has played a significant role and has exercised tremendous influence in Western philosophical thought.

∽

What, then, is the world? The "world is what is always already there."[15] It is understood as the "ground," the background, or "the total horizon of our experience" (121). We call the world "the spatiotemporal totality of being" (121). It forms "the frame of reference of any possible truth, certainty, validity, judgment, opinion, knowledge, value, and so forth" (121). It is the common horizon of experience; the "soil" that we are rooted in.

The world, Derrida writes, "has at least as a minimal sense the designation of *that within which* [ce dans quoi]" all living beings are born, live, inhabit, and die (BSII 365/264). It is said that all living beings inhabit a common world—the *same* world—the world that they cohabit as inhabitants, for whom it serves as the common horizon. The world is also considered to be "an arrangement, an order, an order of ends, a juridical, moral, political order, an international order" (359/260). Yet, for Derrida, this is a *presumed, anticipated* unity, a supposed unity or identity that "one can always question" (366/265). As he writes in the second volume of *The Beast and the Sovereign*: "No one will ever be able to demonstrate, what is called *demonstrate* in all rigor, that two human beings, you and I for example, inhabit the same world, that the world is one and the same thing for both of us" (366/265). He goes on to state that "*there is not the world* [il n'y a pas le monde], that nothing is less certain than the world itself, that there is perhaps no longer a world and no doubt there never was one as totality of anything at all [*totalité de quoi que ce soit*]" (366/266). He reiterates this a little further by saying that "perhaps there is no world. Not yet and perhaps not since ever [*depuis toujours*] and perhaps not ever" (367/266). For, what has been called the world is nothing but an "arbitrary, conventional and artificial, historical, non-natural contract," an "agreement inherited over millennia between living beings" (368/267). According to Derrida, there is such an "uncrossable difference" between us that it has been necessary for the sake of survival to make *as if*, to go along with a ruse (368/267) to give the same meaning to similar vocables or signs, to pretend "*as if* we were inhabiting the same world" (369/268).[16]

Having briefly established Derrida's views on "world," one path to take would be to pursue the philosophical notion of "the world" in order to show how Derrida's differs from its phenomenological predecessors (for whom the world forms *the* horizon). But perhaps a more interesting approach would be to explore the deconstruction of the world through a discussion of *the end* of the world. In retrospect, we can say that this is exactly what was taking place in Derrida's last seminar *The Beast and the Sovereign, 2* (2002–2003), devoted in part to Heidegger's 1929/1930 lecture course *The Fundamental Concepts of Metaphysics*, that is, the meticulous but utter reformulation, revaluation, in other words, deconstruction of each of the terms of its subtitle: world, finitude, solitude. There, through a silent reading of the last line of Celan's poem, each of the three terms of Heidegger's lecture course is thoroughly worked over and reinterpreted by Derrida.

The world is gone. The world is no more and the survivor remains alone. The survivor remains "before [*en deçà*] and beyond the world" of the other—before the world itself ("R" 23/140). On this side, below, and "before" the world, because with the other's death there is no world, the world is gone and "beyond" because (the survivor is) far removed from the world that is gone. The survivor is, as it were, "in the world outside the world [*dans le monde hors du monde*]" (23/140). Alone, deprived of the world, "he feels solely responsible, assigned to carry the other and *her* world" (23/140). He is responsible "without world (*weltlos*), without the ground of any world [*sans le sol d'aucun monde*], thus in a world without world" (23/140, trans. mod).

In *Rams*, a talk delivered on February 5, 2003, and published in the same year, while honoring Hans-Georg Gadamer and declaring his admiration for him, Derrida turns to a discussion of Celan's poem, in particular its last line: *Die Welt ist fort, ich muss dich tragen*. Not because, like Gadamer, who believes that the last line "bears the stress of the poem," Derrida is following a "hermeneutic principle," but because this line, separated, solitary, all alone, allows him to speculate on the import of Celan's words ("R" 30/142).

On a first reading, there seems to be a radical heterogeneity between the two clauses of the last line of the poem. What demonstrable link can there be between them? Michael Naas (233) and Ginette Michaud have both emphasized the chiasmatic structure of the last line, Celan's double proposition that contains a constative (it's the end of the world) and a performative (a commitment, a promise, an oath, a duty, an "inflexible injunction": I must carry you). But if it is the end of the world, why must I still carry you? "When the world is no more (*n'est plus*), when it has gone far away [*au loin parti*] (*fort*), then I must carry *you*, you all alone [*toi tout seul*], you alone in me or on me alone [*tout seul en moi ou sur moi seul*]" (68/158). If one were to invert the order, the sequence of the two parts of the last line of Celan's poem, in other words, "if one were to invert the consequence of *if, then* [*si, alors*]: if (where) [*si (là où)*] there is a necessity or duty toward you, if (where) *I* must [*doit*], myself, carry you, bear you [*te porter*], yourself [*toi*], well, then," Derrida notes, "the world tends to disappear [*tend à disparaître*]" (68/158). What is called the world tends to disappear when I become responsible, when I am responsible. It is the other's death that immediately obligates me. "As soon as I am obliged, from the instant when I am obliged *to you*, when I owe, when I owe it *to you*, owe it *to myself* to carry *you*, as soon as I speak to you and am responsible to you, or before [*devant*] you, there can no longer, essentially, be any world [*aucun monde, pour l'essentiel, ne peut plus être là*]. No world can support us, serve as mediation, as ground, as earth, as foundation or as alibi." For, there is "no longer anything but the abyssal altitude of a sky" (68/158).

Where there's no longer any world, I am alone. "I am alone with you [. . .] we are alone"—and this is a declaration as well as an engagement (69/158). Where there's no world and I'm alone, "I am alone in the world as soon as I owe myself to you [*je me dois à toi*], as soon as you depend on me, as soon as I bear, and must assume" without the mediation of a go-between, without ground, "the responsibility for which I must answer in front of you for you" (68–69/158). According to Derrida, all the protagonists and the reader of Celan's poem "hear themselves called [*s'entendent appeler*] [. . .] as soon as the poem is entrusted to our care and as soon as we must carry it." To bear this poem is "to give it to the other to bear [*donner à porter*]" (69/158–159).

In the tenth session of *The Beast and the Sovereign* Derrida asks, "What does *porter*, [to carry, to bear, *tragen*] mean"? (BSII 357/258). (Later in the seminar, he also pays attention to the lexicon of *tragen* in Heidegger [*Übertragung, Auftrag*, and *Austrag*] in *Identity and Difference* and the relationship between *tragen* and *Walten*.) Derrida devotes an analysis to the term *tragen* in Celan's poem in the fifth section of *Rams*, where he develops a remarkable description of an experience—the experience of carrying the other in the self—in which *I must* prevails over *I am*. Before *I am*, I carry. Before being, I carry.[17]

In spoken German, *tragen* refers to the experience of *carrying* a child prior to its birth ("R" 72/159). Derrida glosses this further as he puts a twist on Levinas's notion of "the other in me": "Between the mother and the child, the one in the other and the one for the other, in this singular couple of solitary beings, in the shared solitude between one and two bodies, the world disappears" (72/159). The world is far away for the mother who carries the child (72/159). As well as speaking the language of birth, *tragen* can also be addressed to the dead, to the survivor or to his or her specter in the same experience of carrying the other in the self. I keep the other in me in mourning, something that I was already doing while the other was still living. According to Derrida, "I welcome in me, I take into myself this end of the world, I must carry the other and the other's world, the world in me: introjection, interiorization of memory (*Erinnerung*), idealization" (74/160). "But if *I must* (and this is ethics itself) carry the other in myself in order to be faithful to that other, to respect its singular alterity, a certain melancholia must still protest against normal mourning" (74/160, trans. mod.). Melancholia is *necessary* so that I do not keep the other within myself, *as myself.*

The world is gone; it is in retreat. In *Rams* Derrida addresses the Husserlian-inspired thought of the annihilation of the world (*Weltvernichtung*), referring to this "retreat [*retrait*]" of the world to "the point of the possibility of its annihilation" as "the most insane experience of a transcendental phenomenology" (74/160). In §49 of *Ideas I* Husserl explains that "access to the absolute egological consciousness" necessitates the suspension of the existence of the transcendent world in a radical *epokhē*" (75/161). The hypothesis of the annihilation of the world does not only threaten the sphere of pure egological experience but also opens access to this sphere. According to Derrida, Celan's poem "pushes to its limit the experience of the possible annihilation of the world," that is, "its sense for 'me,' for a pure *ego*" (75/161). But in this solitude of the pure *ego*, the alter ego that is "constituted in the ego is no longer accessible in an originary intuition." The *alter ego* can be constituted "only by *analogy*, by *appresentation*, indirectly, inside of me, who then carries it there where there is no longer a transcendent world" (76/161). "I must then carry it, carry *you*, there where the world gives way [*se dérobe*]" (76/161). This is my responsibility; but I can only carry you without appropriating you to myself. This carrying can no longer mean to include or comprehend the other in oneself; but rather, "to bear oneself toward [*se porter vers*] the infinite inappropriability of the other, [. . .] in me outside of me" (76/161). I can only be "starting from this strange, dislocated bearing [*portée disloquée*] of the infinitely other in me" (76/161). Highlighting the plurivocity of the *dich* in the last line of Celan's poem, Derrida writes, "I must carry the other, and carry you, the other must carry me [. . .] even there where the world is no longer between us or beneath" us (76/161). My solitude is such that "I am alone with the other [. . .] without world," "wherever the 'I must' [. . .] forever prevails over the 'I am'" (76/161).

A few months after giving the talk on Gadamer, in the preface to *Chaque fois unique, la fin du monde* (published in October 2003) Derrida claims: "the death of the other, not only *but especially if one loves the other* [*surtout si on l'aime*]" does not simply declare the "absence," the "disappearance [*disparition*], the end of *this or that* life," in other words "the possibility for a world (always unique) to appear to a *given* living being" (CFU 9, first emphasis mine).[18] Rather, "death declares *each time the end of the world entirely* [en totalité], the end of every possible world, and *each time the end of the world as a unique, and thus singular, and thus infinite, totality*" (9).

The death of the other is "as if the *repetition* of the end of an infinite whole [*d'un tout infini*] were still possible: the end of the world *itself*, the only world there is, every time. Singularly, irreversibly" (9). It is as if this end of the world were possible "for the other and in a strange way also for the provisional survivor who endures its impossible experience" (9). It is as if every time the repetition of the death of another—the end of the world *itself*, the only world there is—were possible. What is referred to as an "impossible experience" is this aporetic experience of the repetition of the end of the world (each time the end and then its repetition).

As Rodolphe Gasché observes, "To repeat the unique disappearance of the one and only world after the death of an other also means that in every singular case in which a death occurs, and one world (which is also the world itself) disappears, there is no more return of the world itself."[19] And this is how Derrida defines "the world," showing that its meaning is entirely derived from death: "That is what 'the world' would mean. This meaning is conferred on it only by what is called 'death'" (CFU 9). The other does not come back. There is no more return of the world. The death of a singular other confronts the survivor with "the always open possibility, indeed the necessity of a possible non-return," the necessity that non-return be possible. This necessity of the possibility of *non-return*, this end of the world, signals the end of all resurrection (CFU 11).[20]

Commenting on Nancy's notion of resurrection, what Derrida finds troubling is that *anastasis* "postulates both the existence of some God and that the end of *a* world will not be . . . the end of *the* world" (CFU 11). As Derrida explains, "'God' means: death can put an end to *a* world, it would not be *the* end of the world. A world, one world can always survive another. There is more than one world. More than one possible world [or: more than one world possible—*un monde possible*]. That is what we would wish to believe, as little as we believe or believe to believe in 'God.'" However, "death, death itself, if there is such a thing," acts as a countermeasure against this thought of God, because it leaves no room [*aucune place*], not the least chance [*pas la moindre chance*], for the replacement or for the survival of the sole and unique world, of the "sole and unique" that makes of each living being (animal, human, or divine), a sole and unique living being (CFU 11).

That the other does not come back spells the end of all resurrection.

After Derrida's writings on the end of the world we can no longer accept the definition of the world as the totality of what there is. The world cannot be thought of as an all-encompassing, universal totality to be grasped synoptically or viewed from a satellite as a globe.²¹ Rather, the world is that which is uniquely opened up by the other, the totality of what is for a unique "being" that being's world, and what comes to an end upon the other's death.

The discussion of "the end of the world" can be linked to one of the terms or tropes appearing regularly in Derrida's later seminars—the abyss.²² The effect of the reading of the end of the world presented earlier, beyond its significance on death, the other, mourning, melancholy, world, solitude, resurrection, and so on, could be explored on Derrida's almost contemporaneous reading of the notion of *Grund* (ground, principle, axiom, etc.) in Heidegger, a reading that Derrida takes up over a number of his seminars, for example, the *Death Penalty* seminar and *The Beast and the Sovereign, 1*.²³ Why would such a reading be important?²⁴ Being for Heidegger is ground, a point that he underscores on a number of occasions. As he writes in "The End of Philosophy and the Task of Thinking": "Since the beginning of philosophy and with that beginning, the Being of beings [*das Sein des Seienden*] has showed itself as the ground (*arché, aition*, principle), has been considered as ground. The ground is that from which beings as such are what they are in their becoming, perishing, and persisting" (ZSD 62/374). Being is the ultimate ground. *Grund* may be *arché*, beginning or first principle but it is certainly not the cause. Thus, for Heidegger, Being as *Grund* is not being as *ratio* but a ground without ground. The ground is an *Ab-grund*, an abyss; however, with this *Ab-grund*, Derrida suggests, Heidegger is still positing some form of ground—an originary ground (*Urgrund*) that is also a non-ground (*Ungrund*) underlying everything. The abyss, then, still seems to belong to some primordial *Urgrund*.²⁵

In contrast, for Derrida, a consideration of ground is not an ontological matter. Each and every other constitutes a ground, rests on a ground. Consequently, with the death of every other, a world goes away; the ground (*le fond*) gives way and is lost. The death of every other signals an absence of bottom, ground, or foundation. With the other's death, there is no ground—an abyss gapes open. The other's death leaves the survivor with the abyss of without world. Since there is no such thing as *the* abyss, as Derrida tells us in session 12 of *The Beast and the Sovereign, 1*, there is *more than one* [*plus d'un*] ground.²⁶ With the passing away of every other, a ground founders. There is no *Ur*-abyss, no abyssal substratum, but abysses everywhere.

Your loss has swept away the ground beneath your feet. Your ground. With no ground below you, I stare into the void.

Alone. I am alone—with you. I am alone, only for you. I am alone "only for you, that is, yours [seul pour toi et à toi]: without world [sans monde]" ("R" 76/161).

With you gone, the ground has given way. In the wake of your death I remain turned toward you. It is you "in me," speaking to me, leaving "in me" your spectral traces. I appear before your gaze; I am an "image" for you. I bear in me the gaze that you bear on me. I will bear, "in this strange dislocated bearing" of you ("R" 76/161), what you have "left living in me" (CFU 123/94), thus keeping you—without keeping—in my heart, alive, in me outside of me. "At that end of the world that every death is" (BSII 244/170), where there is no longer any world between us, where there is an abyss between the two islands, there where "I am alone with you" ("R" 69/158) without the ground of any world, in a world without world, I must carry you, bear you.

Intact

2

Safe, Intact

Derrida, Nancy, and the "Deconstruction of Christianity"

> safe, sound, intact, virgin, unhurt, *heilig*, holy
>
> —Jacques Derrida, *The Death Penalty, Volume I*

> intact adj.—Lat. *intactus* (1498), ME *intacte* fr. L *intactus*, fr. *in* + *tactus*, pp. of *tangere* to touch
>
> intact adj.—1. "A quoi l'on n'a pas touché" (1835), "Qui n'a pas subi d'altération, de dommage" = entier 2. Vierge 3. sauf
>
> —*Le Petit Robert: Dictionnaire de la langue française*

> intact adj.1. untouched especially by anything that harms or diminishes: entire; uninjured
>
> —*Webster's Ninth Collegiate Dictionary*

It is a safe bet to say that whenever there is a discussion of "the unscathed" in Derrida's work, the terms "safe" and "intact" almost always accompany one another, while in the work of Jean-Luc Nancy these two terms are held apart. An exploration of the occurrence of these two words in the later writings of Derrida and Nancy, I would like to suggest, allows us to catch a glimpse of some of the differences between the later work of these two thinkers as well as to distinguish the most salient features of their interpretations of deconstruction.

Since his heart transplant, Jean-Luc Nancy seems to have had a new lease on life. Nancy has been an extremely prolific thinker and writer, recently bringing out a healthy number of texts on a variety of subjects—democracy, justice, love, sleep, identity, the city, art—at an enviable pace.[1] Arguably, his major texts have mostly been authored after this transplant and the ensuing illness caused by an antirejection drug. In a number of these works, Nancy has been vigorously engaged in the project of the "deconstruction of Christianity," which to date spans two books, *Dis-Enclosure* and *Adoration*, and other related publications. As well as being a thinker of extraordinary caliber in his own right, Jean-Luc Nancy, as an interlocutor and friend of Jacques Derrida for decades, has also been at the vanguard of deconstruction, such that after Derrida's death he has been treated as an inheritor of or a kind of spokesperson for deconstruction. While Derrida and Nancy's relationship is extremely complex and interwoven and would require several volumes to carefully explicate, it is worthwhile to make an attempt, however modest, to differentiate their projects and their approaches to deconstruction. It is true that a cluster of shared themes, terms, motifs, and methodologies link the two thinkers, and for any attentive reader of their work, their disagreements regarding certain themes (like community, fraternity, democracy, generosity, faith, and belief) will not be new. Their abiding friendship also speaks to the fact that neither views friendship as the necessity to be in agreement about everything.[2] What marks out the singularity of each thinker, I would like to argue, is the way each understands the meaning of deconstruction.

Over the decades that they knew each other, Derrida and Nancy collaborated on a variety of projects. After Derrida's first visit to Strasbourg in 1970, Nancy and his colleague Philippe Lacoue-Labarthe participated in Derrida's seminars at the École Normale Supérieure in the early 1970s. All three were involved in GREPH (Groupe de Recherches sur l'Enseignement Philosophique), which lobbied for the earlier instruction of philosophy in the French educational system (resulting in the publication of the collective volume *Qui a peur de la philosophie?* [Who is afraid of philosophy?] in 1977, and in editing the book series La philosophie en effet with Sarah Kofman, initially for the publisher Flammarion in 1975 and then for Galilée starting in 1985. In 1980 Nancy, with Lacoue-Labarthe, also organized the first Cerisy conference devoted to Derrida's work, Les fins de l'homme, and at the invitation of Derrida both formed the Centre de Recherches Philosophiques sur le

Politique at the École Normale, lasting from 1980 to 1984, producing two volumes investigating the relationship between deconstruction and the political. In the later years, Derrida and Nancy often appeared together at countless conferences. Their long friendship, however, did not prevent Derrida from expressing his philosophical disagreements with Nancy, given voice to in his *Politics of Friendship* (regarding the question of community and fraternity), *Le toucher* (concerning the prominence and privilege bestowed upon the sense of touch since philosophy's inception), and *Rogues* (in particular, on the subject of freedom). This chapter aims to concentrate on how the later writings of Derrida and Nancy intersect concerning the general subject of religion (and related topics). What is of particular interest is the significant role that the interpretation of the term *salut*—which in French has two meanings, "greeting, salutation" as well as "salvation"—plays in this interaction.[3]

In broad outlines, as it will be seen, the goal of "religion," if it can be said to have one, is to keep the living—the adherents of religion—safe, unscathed, and intact. The "unscathed [*indemne*]"—the untouched, the uncontaminated, *heilig*, safe and sound—is that which has not suffered damage. It can refer to either a virgin state that once existed, in which no damage was suffered, or to a state to which things must be restored as unharmed. "Religion" thus functions to indemnify: to prevent and secure against hurt or damage, to heal, to restore as unscathed, as well as to compensate for incurred loss. Yet that which desires to be intact (unscathed, untouched) cannot sustain its goal. It cannot remain whole nor have perfect integrity because unwittingly it is in-tact, in touch. Its auto-immunity means that what desires to be safe cannot ensure its safety.[4]

Conversely, in Nancy's view, it is only the deceased that is intact. What is safe is that which remains whole, unscathed, and intact. And it is only the dead one that is safe, intact, out of reach.[5] The deceased is untouchable in its death. What death can "do" is to touch—a touch *without contact*—or to greet the intact. *Salut*, according to Nancy, is not a wish to save but an address, an invitation that wishes safety for its addressee. A salutation declares: Be safe, be whole, intact in death. It touches the intact, the untouchable, but without any *contact*. While reserve and restraint are appropriate only for the dead one in Nancy's view, in Derrida's assessment, as we will see, it is the living who have the right to respect and restraint, since it is the task of "religion" to save the living as intact.

The Unscathed

Derrida lays out the core of his views on religion in a series of dense, elliptic paragraphs in "Faith and Knowledge, which are by now familiar and often cited.[6] In "Faith and Knowledge" Derrida writes that a discourse on "religion" cannot be dissociated from a discourse on salvation [*salut*], that is, "to save, be saved, save oneself" (FK 9/2, #2). Early in the text, he asks whether "the unscathed [*indemne*]" is not "the very matter—the thing itself [*la chose même*]—of religion?" (FK 34/23, #27). By the unscathed, Derrida explains in a note, he is referring to "that which has not suffered damage or prejudice, *damnum*" (34n/69–70n16). Thus, the word "unscathed" speaks of "the unimpaired": "the pure, non-contaminated, untouched, the sacred or the holy before every profanation, all injury, all offence, all lesion" (34/69–70).

He also notes that the French word *indemne* has often been used to translate *heilig* ("sacred, safe and sound [*sain et sauf*], intact") in Heidegger (FK 34n12/70n16). In the note mentioned earlier he further elucidates that *damnum* gives the French language the word *dam*, which among other things is tied to the sacrifice offered to the gods as ritual compensation. Thus, a discussion of the unscathed will also involve *indemnification*, "the process of compensation and the restitution, sometimes sacrificial, that *re*constitutes purity intact, renders integrity safe and sound, restores cleanliness and property unimpaired" (34n/69–70n).

In the note, Derrida informs us that throughout "Faith and Knowledge" he will regularly associate the words "unscathed," "indemnity," "indemnification" with the words "immune," "immunity," "immunization," and above all "auto-immune" (FK 34n12/69–70n16, #27). It should be noted that the inclusion of the notion of auto-immunity here, and its association with the unscathed, indicates that the unscathed or the intact is by no means that which remains or can remain whole with perfect integrity, but that which, in the drive to remain whole and unscathed, in order to protect itself, harms itself. In another important note on auto-immunity, Derrida observes that while immunity designates freedom or exemption from charges and obligations, as well as the inviolability of the asylum sought in the Christian church, auto-immunity refers to a living organism protecting itself against its self-protection by destroying its own immune system (59n23/72n27, #37). If the goal of "religion" is defined as the desire to remain unscathed, its association with the auto-immune suggests that this desire for absolute immunity is a structurally untenable phantasm: whatever seeks to be auto-immune cannot be kept intact, for it is vulnerable to self-harm and to sacrificial self-destruction.

Later in the same text Derrida speculates that the religious is in fact bound up with the convergence of two experiences. The two strata or two sources of "religion" are the experience of *belief* [croyance] and the experience of the unscathed, of *sacredness* [sacralité] or of *holiness* [sainteté] (FK 46/33, #32). In French *sainteté* means "saintliness" or "holiness," as well as "sanctity." This allows Derrida to refer later to the "sacrosanct" (derived from Lat. *sacrosanctus*, from *sacer* "sacred" and *sanctus* "holy," "worthy of veneration"; also bearing the ironic modern meaning of "untouchable, taboo"). Benveniste glosses the two terms that compose the compound word. What distinguishes *sacer* from *sanctus* is the difference between "implicit" and "explicit" sacredness. What is *sacer* has its own proper value by itself whereas *sanctus* is "a state resulting from a prohibition for which men are responsible, from an injunction supported by law" (Benveniste 191/455). Thus, *sacrosanctus* is "what is *sanctus* by a *sacrum*: what is defended by a veritable sacrament." In the second part of the essay entitled ". . . and pomegranates," Derrida states that all the values associated with "sacro-sanctity (*heilig*, *holy*, safe and sound, unscathed, intact, immune, free, vital, fecund, fertile, strong, and above all [. . .] 'swollen') (FK 63/48), or what he calls "the semantic genealogy of the unscathed" (64/48), have to be thought together with the "machine-like [*machinique*]" (63/48, #38).

Speaking of this "drive to be unscathed [*la pulsion de l'indemne*]," on the part of that which is allergic to contamination, *save by itself, auto-immunely* [sauf par soi-même, auto-immunément]" (FK 38/25, #28), Derrida further explains:

> We are here in a space where all self-protection of the unscathed, of the safe and sound [*sain(t) et sauf*], of the sacred (*heilig*, holy) must protect itself against its own protection, its own police, its own power of rejection, in short, against its own, which is to say against its own immunity. It is this terrifying but fatal logic of *the auto-immunity of the unscathed* that will always associate Science and Religion. (FK 58/44, #37)

Drawing on Benveniste's "rich chapter" on the Sacred and the Holy [*Le sacré*] in *Le vocabulaire des institutions indo-européennes*, Derrida notes that the holy and sacred character is also defined through a notion of exuberant and fecund force (FK 65fn25/74fn30).[7] Even though Benveniste does not note this fact in his discussion, Derrida adds that there is a necessity for

> (. . . every religion or all sacralization also to be healing [*guérison*]—*heilen, healing* [in English]—health, *salut*, or promise of a cure—*cura, Sorge*—horizon of redemption, of the restoration of unscathed, of *indemnification*). The same must also be said for the English "holy," neighbor of "*whole*" ("entire, intact," therefore "safe, saved, unscathed in its integrity, immune") [. . .]. Whoever possesses le "*salut*," that is, whose physical integrity is intact, is also capable of conferring *le* "*salut*." "To be intact" is the luck that one wishes, predicts or expects. It is natural to have seen in such perfect "integrity" a divine grace, a sacred meaning. By its very nature, divinity possesses the gift of integrity, of *salut*, of luck, and can impart it to human beings. (FK 65n/74–75n25, #39, citing Benveniste 185–187/451–452)

Thus, the "absolute imperative" or the "law of salvation [*loi du salut*]" is "saving the living as intact, the unscathed, the safe [*le sauf*] (*heilig*), which has the right to absolute respect, restraint [*retenue*], modesty (FK 65–66/49, #40).[8] This sets up the necessity of an enormous task: reconstituting the chain of analogous motifs in what Derrida calls "the sacro-sanctifying attitude or intentionality, in relation to that which is, should remain or should be allowed to be what it is (*heilig*, living, strong and fertile, erect and fecund: safe, whole, unscathed, immune, sacred, holy [*saint*] and so on). Salvation and Health [*Salut et santé*]" (66/49).[9]

This intentional attitude, Derrida continues, bears several names belonging to the same family: respect, modesty, restraint, inhibition, *Achtung* (Kant), *Scheu, Verhaltenheit, Gelassenheit* (Heidegger)," all of which mark a restraint or holding-back [*halte*] in general, constituting "a sort of universal structure of religiosity" (FK 67/49, # 40). These terms open the possibility of the religious, a possibility that itself remains divided. On the one hand, it involves "respectful or inhibited abstention before what remains sacred mystery, and what ought to remain intact or inaccessible, like the mystical immunity of a secret." On the other hand, this holding back "opens an access without mediation or representation" to what remains unscathed, but "not without an intuitive violence" (67/49).

All (of the preceding) "stop short of that which must or should remain safe and sound, intact, unscathed, before what must be allowed to be what it ought to be, sometimes even at the cost of sacrificing itself and in prayer: the other" (67/50, #40).

Tact and Touch

In *Le toucher, Jean-Luc Nancy* Derrida's monumental book on touch, touching, the *sense* of touch in the history of philosophy, and Nancy's body of work, the entirety of which is referred to as an "immense philosophic treatise of touch" (LT 125/107), Derrida turns to what links "religion," in this case Christianity, to touching. At the beginning, Derrida comments on a 1978 essay by Nancy entitled "Psyche," written on a phrase from Freud ("Psyche ist ausgedehnt: weiss nichts davon").[10] There Derrida writes of an impassive, untouchable, and intact Psyche ("Psyche the untouchable, Psyche the intact"). Even though Psyche (or in other words, soul or thought) is "extended," this is an extension that is untouchable. This Psyche is "a Psyche that does not touch anything" (LT 28). It has an intangible body, which is also intangible to itself.

Derrida remarks on the Aristotelian legacy that any thought on touching has to concern itself with both the tangible and the intangible. In chapter 4 entitled "The Untouchable, or the Vow of Abstinence," he discusses what he calls "the law of tact." He suggests that the law is the untouchable prior to all the ritual prohibitions imposed on touching by religion or culture. The law enjoins us to respect, which commands us to keep a distance—to not touch. At the origin of law, thus, there is tact and the law (of tact) commands to touch *without* touching. After all, what is tact but "knowing [how] to touch *without* touching, without touching *too much*" (LT 82). There is the law of tact. As Derrida writes, approaching "the *figure* of touching," touching touches what it does not touch. It "brings into contact (without contact) contact *and* noncontact" (90).

There must be some "touchable-untouchable" (LT 93n). We must think, Derrida states, "the logic of an untouchable that remains right at, right on [*reste à même*], if we can say, the touchable" (93n). The touchable-untouchable is not someone and should not be confused with what in certain cultures is called an "untouchable."[11] The untouchable could not be named and identified, Derrida writes, except insofar as "there is some touchable-untouchable in general, before every religion, cult or prohibition" (93n). In fact, "every vow of abstinence experiments with the touchable *as* untouchable" (93n).

Derrida sets up his analysis of Christianity's relation to touch in "Tender," the following chapter. The Gospels, he writes, present the Christic body as a "*touching* body as much as *touched*, as a touching-touched flesh. Between life and death" (LT 117). As Derrida suggests, "One can take the Gospels as a *general haptics*. Salvation [*le salut*] saves by touching, and the savior, that is, the one who touches, is also the touched: saved, safe, unscathed. Touched by grace" (117). Derrida goes on to provide examples of salvation by touching from the Gospels: "Jesus the Savior is 'touching,' he is the One who touches, and most often with his hand, and most often in order to purify, heal, or resuscitate. To save [*sauver*], in a word. He heals or purifies the leper by touching him" (Matt. 8:3) (117). He "heals Peter's mother-in-law by touching her hand with his hand" (Matt. 8:15) (118); "heals the blind by touching their eyes" (Matt. 9: 29–30) (118); "cures the deaf and the mute" (Mark 7: 32–36); "heals and saves from fear" (Matt. 17: 7–8); "he even cures death itself by touching a coffin" (Luke 7: 13–15) (118). Often (vulnerable and innocent) children are touched by Jesus (Luke 18: 15–17) (119). Jesus touches, having been touched to the heart—where he is "first moved and touched" (118).

However, Jesus is not only touching

> the one who Touches, but he is also the Touched [. . .] he is "*to be touched*, he can and must be touched. This is the condition for salvation. To be safe and sound, to attain immunity, *touch*, to touch him [le toucher, *le toucher*], Him. Or better, to touch, without touching that which would come into contact with his body, that is, like a fetish, or the origin of fetishism, his garment, his cloak and thus what saves is not touching, but the faith that this touching signifies and attests to. (LT 119)

Derrida notes that it appears that the "literal allusions to touching are more rare, almost absent in the Gospel according to John" (LT 120). This may be because "Jesus becomes for a moment untouchable" and "the 'Touch me not' (*noli me tangere, me mou haptou*) addressed to Mary Magdalene at the moment when, still in tears near the grave, she has just recognized him" is reported by John (120/102). Moreover, Derrida adds, the motif and the lexicon of touching in the Epistles (in

Corinthians, Colossians, Timothy, Hebrews) are commonly associated with "a prohibition: do not touch, so that it remains untouchable" (120fn2).

What comes to pass when one has to touch the untouchable? This theme gets broached in Nancy's text *The Experience of Freedom* published in 1988. There Nancy employs "the figure of touch" in relation to the limit: by being led to the limit, philosophy has touched the limit (LT 121). On the one hand, Derrida explains, no one has ever touched such an abstract thing as a limit, but on the other hand, one only touches a limit: to touch is to touch a limit. This limit, which philosophy will have thus touched (upon), finds itself to be at the same time touchable and untouchable. Thus, there can only be "a *figure* of touch"; for one "only touches by way of a figure," as the touchable is what is impossible to touch. "History of the untouchable, therefore, of immunity, of the unscathed, of the safe [*du sauf*]. Save, safe—touching [*Sauf*—le toucher]" (122/104). However, Derrida expresses a reservation regarding this *figure* of touch: what is the logical or rhetorical legitimacy, the phenomenological status of that which one cannot "without trepidation" call "the *figure* of 'touch'" (124/106)?

Has the entire tradition of Western philosophy not been a "haptology" or what Derrida calls a "haptocentric metaphysics"? Even though touching, for Nancy, is a resistance to all forms of idealism and subjectivism, does it still not function as "the motif of a kind of absolute realism?" (LT 60). Does not this thinking of the body with its connotations of immanence, immediacy, and intuitionism imply an almost seamless relation between that which touches and what is touched? In *Le toucher* Derrida seeks to show the theological foundations of a thinking of the body, its propriety and its integrity; a thinking that privileges the notion of touch as a kind of contact. This thinking, with roots in Christian thought and in the Christian conception of incarnation, where spirit is made flesh in the body of Christ, demonstrates the belonging-together of Western philosophy and Christian theology, of phenomenological thought and a doctrine of incarnation. Derrida labels Nancy's appeal to, and recuperation of, touch a "*quasi*-hyper-transcendental-ontologization of tact" (328).

Do Not Wish to Touch Me

Prompted by Derrida's *Le toucher*, Nancy's *Noli me tangere* may be read as a response (to what Nancy calls Derrida's "rabbinical skepticism" [NMT 25–26n4]), a riposte, an impassioned corrective regarding the question of touch, or an innovative reworking of the notion of resurrection. Devoted to an analysis of exemplary representations of the life of Jesus by artists such as Rembrandt, Dürer, Titian, Pontormo, Cano Alonso, Bronzino, and Correggio, *Noli me tangere* takes the form of meditations on specific episodes or scenes from the Bible. In this short book, Nancy takes up Christ's relation to touching while presenting a new reading of the resurrection of Jesus. It is also Nancy's most extensive meditation on the notion or concept of resurrection in general.[12]

In Christian and post-Christian iconography, moments of the account or narrative of Jesus—an account that is presented as a succession of scenes—have been taken up as motifs by painters and sculptors. If the life of Jesus, Nancy explains, is "a representation of the truth that he claims himself to be," then this life is identical to "the truth that appears in being represented" (NMT 8/4). Thus, underscoring the identity of the truth and its figures (11/5), the *logos* cannot be taken as "distinct from the figure or the image" (9/4).

Nancy writes that the phrase *Noli me tangere* has made touching "a major stake in taboo as the constitutive structure of sacrality" (NMT 26/13).[13] "The *untouchable*," whose most striking example is the Hindu figure of the pariah, Nancy remarks, is "everywhere present wherever there is the sacred, that is, [wherever there is] withdrawal, distinction, and the incommensurable" (26/13–14).[14] However, in Christianity, Nancy contends, nothing and no one is untouchable, particularly because "the very body of God is given to be eaten and drunk" (27/14). One could even say that "Christianity will have been the invention of the religion of touch, of the sensible, of presence that is immediate to the body and to the heart" (27/14). This would thus render the famous scene of *Noli me tangere*, mentioned by Derrida and the subject of Nancy's book, an exception (27/14).

Nancy's proposal is to think together the two sayings, *Noli me tangere* and *Hoc est corpus meum*, "in an oxymoronic or paradoxical mode" (28/14). What is paradoxical and exceptional about the *Noli* scene, he claims, is that "Christ expressly rules out the touching of his resurrected body" (28/14, trans. mod.). While the resurrected body is "tangible," here "it does not present itself as such" (28/14). This is the only time that Christ does not want to be touched, Nancy makes clear, only because he "does not want to be held back, for he is leaving, departing" (29/15).

Nancy presents the nonreligious meaning of "resurrection" as "the departing into which presence actually withdraws [. . .]. Just as it comes, so it goes: that is to say, it *is* not" (NMT 29/15).¹⁵ Resurrection is thus "the uprising, the sudden appearance of the unavailable, of the other and of the disappearing *in the body itself and as the body*" (29/15, trans. mod.). This is because "He dies indefinitely," he is the one who does not "cease to depart" (31/16). The one who says "Do not touch me" is the one whose "presence is that of a disappearance indefinitely renewed or prolonged" (31/16). It is as if, Nancy writes, he is saying, "*I am already going away; I am only in this departure; I am the parting of this departure*" (all italics in the original) (31/16). This, Nancy calls "a stance before death" (33/18), "a standing upright before and in death" (34/18). What is affirmed is "the stance (thus also the reserve, restraint) of an untouchable, of an inaccessible" (33/18). If touching (him) indicates "the immediacy of a presence," then Christ is "the untouchable who holds himself beyond reach" and is not touched by Mary Magdalene (39/21, trans. mod.).

According to Nancy's analysis of the pictorial representation of the resurrection, painters generally depict an episode that is not given to be seen. In the "textual scenes" where the resurrected one appears, however, Jesus invites the disciples to touch him to assure them that he is there in flesh and blood (NMT 42/22). What this demonstrates for Nancy is that "faith [*la foi*]," in contrast to belief [*croyance*], "consists of seeing and hearing *without tampering*" (42/22). In Nancy's assessment, the *Noli* is to be read as "Don't touch me, for I'm touching you, and this touch is such that it holds you at a distance" (60/36). Later in the chapter entitled "The Hands," Nancy qualifies this by adding that *Noli me tangere* does not simply say "Do not touch me" but "do not wish to touch me" (61/37).

In Nancy's estimation, resurrection is not a return to life or a process of regeneration (NMT 32/17). As he writes in *Noli me tangere*, "The resurrection [of Christ] is not a resuscitation [*réanimation*]: it is the infinite continuation of death that displaces and dismantles all the values of presence and absence, of animate and inanimate, of body and soul" (73–74/44, trans. mod.). "This raising [*levée*] of the body is not a 'relève' in the sense given to this word by Derrida to translate the Hegelian *Aufhebung*" (33/18), not a dialecticization or a mediation of death. There is no passage into another life (34/18). In addition, *anastasis* does not come from the self; it comes to the self from the other (35/19). For Nancy, the statement "I am resurrected" does not signify the accomplishment of an I but rather a passivity. This is why he claims that "I am dead" and "I am resurrected" say the same thing (35/19). Resurrection, Nancy writes, "designates the singularity of existence": "everyone resurrects, one by one and body for body" (76/46).

That Nancy is bent on presenting resurrection as a "more discreet," mundane, "familiar," rather than "spectacular," affair (NMT 41/22), with a "less flamboyant," "natural" character rather than a "supernatural" one, can be discerned from his descriptions, as well as from the negative valence he gives to terms such as "a spectral body" (he tells us that the resurrected body is not a spectral body but a tangible one [28]); "supernatural magic" (44); "fantastic film" (the episode of Lazarus is not a fantastic film, we are informed [34]); "magical trick" (29); "apparition" (75); and "miracle" (the episode of Thomas is not at all miraculous [41n5, 86]).[16]

A summary of Nancy's views on resurrection, and other related concepts such as "eternal life," highlights the differences between Derrida and Nancy. Rather than a return to life, resurrection, for Nancy, signifies a reconfiguration of death and dying. He underscores the importance of a notion of death in his analysis when he remarks in *Noli me tangere* that "without death there would only be contact, contiguity, and contagion, a cancerous propagation of life that would as a consequence no longer be life or *existence*" (NMT 74/45). In addition, belief is linked to the spectacular, whereas faith consists of seeing and hearing where there is nothing exceptional for the eyes and ears (42). Faith knows to see and hear without touching. Further, as he argues in *Noli me tangere*, the living (or the adherents of religion) have no desire to be intact. Since Christianity can correctly be described as the religion of touch, it is only the departing body of the resurrected Christ that is untouchable. Therefore, the prescription *Noli me tangere* is to be understood as an exception or an anomaly.

Intact

Nancy returns to Derrida's previous comments on a couple of occasions before and after Derrida's passing away. He takes up Derrida's objections to his portrayal of resurrection in two pieces of writing. It is worth pointing out that the word "intact" occurs on a number of occasions. In the yet to be translated three-page "preface" to *Chaque fois unique, la fin du monde* (published in October 2003), Derrida directly addresses Nancy's uptake of resurrection.[17] Resisting any reworking of resurrection in whatever shape or form, no matter how radical, he contrasts it with what he calls "the end of the world." Writing in the French edition of *The Work of Mourning*, a collection of pieces written after the death of friends and colleagues, Derrida observes that each death and each farewell is unique (hence resists being compared to another and, perhaps, to being gathered together in a collection). Each farewell, he tells the reader, is the farewell of a salutation that is resigned to greet the possibility and necessity that it be not returned and to greet the end of the world as the end of every resurrection—thus putting an end to all resurrection. For, however different it may be from "classical resurrection," *anastasis* will continue to console, a consolation that contains some grain of cruelty. *Anastasis*, for Derrida, "postulates the existence of some God and assures that the end of *a* world will not be the end of *the* world. Each death spells the end of the world. The world has gone away; there can be no world—and this end leaves no room for resurrection (CFU 11).

The dead one is safe, intact, and what is intact is out of reach, not to be touched.[18] This is what Nancy declares in "Consolation, désolation," an essay written for a special issue of *Magazine littéraire* devoted to Jacques Derrida published in April 2004.[19] In this brief piece Nancy relates what is intact to what is dead. In contrast to Derrida's view, for Nancy, it is not the adherents of religion who wish to be safe, but safety is reserved for the dead one, who is greeted. As Nancy explains: "the noun '*salut*' denotes address, invitation or injunction with a view to being safe" ("CD" 58). Discussing the double valences of the word *salut*, Nancy attempts to distinguish that which is "safe [*sauf*]" from "the saved [*le sauvé*]." Safe (*salvus*), he explains, is what remains whole, unscathed, intact. While "the saved" refers to what has "escaped from the injury or the blemish that it had suffered from," safe is "that (or that one, he or she) [*cela (ou celui, celle)*] which remains intact, out of reach." In other words, it is that which has never been touched" (58/99). "Consolation, désolation" develops the relation of *salut* to the one who is dead, asserting that it is the dead one who is safe, intact. What is intact is out of reach, not to be touched. Safety, then, is reserved for "the dead one [*le mort*]," who can only be greeted.

> In this way the dead carry off with them, as we say, the unique and sole world each of them was. They thus carry off the entire world, for never is the world a world if not unique, alone, and entirely intact. *Solus, salvus:* there is salvation only of the sole [*il n'y a de salut que du seul*]. ("CD" 59/99)[20]

Nancy clarifies that "to console," signaled in the title of his essay and referred to by Derrida in his "preface" to *Chaque fois unique, la fin du monde*, is never to comfort, to soothe the pain, or to restore the life of the dead. "*Solor*, to comfort, is foreign to *solus*" but "fortif[ies] desolation," makes "its harshness inflexible and untouchable" ("CD" 58/99). The deceased, whose death is untouchable, thus "disappears in the absolute isolation" of his or her death (59/100). "The salutation desolates [the name] as it desolates itself" (59/100). And before this isolation, "I am alone, each time absolutely alone" (59/100).

Nancy writes that what death can "offer us [*nous offre*]"—But how does death "offer"? What kind of offering could this be?—is to "touch the intact." However, distinguishing between contact and touch, Nancy asserts that "no contact with death is possible (whether sensible, intelligible, or imaginary)" ("CD" 58/100). For "the salutation [*le salut*] touches the untouchable," but it does so only in the form of an address "that confirms for him his death (58–59/100, trans. mod.). This salutation "salutes the other in the untouchable intactness of his or her insignificant propriety or ownness" (58–59/100).

Taking issue with Derrida's suspicion or refusal of any salvation while referring to the sixteen deceased figures eulogized in *Chaque fois unique, la fin du monde*, Nancy writes that "Derrida's *salut* [. . .] still saves no matter what" ("CD" 59/100, trans. mod.). "It does not save anything from the abyss," but it "salutes the abyss saved" (59/100). "To save [*sauver*]," Nancy claims, "is not 'to heal'" (Déc 42/27). Moreover, saving is not a "process, and it is not aimed toward an ultimate 'health' (*salvus* and *sanus* are not the same word). It is a unique and instantaneous act by which the one who is already in the abyss is held back or recovered" (42/27). (The interjection of the role of the abyss here should be noted.) Saving, then, "does not annul the abyss" but "takes place in it" (42/27). In "Consolation, désolation" Nancy declares that *salut* "does not save anything from the abyss," but it "salutes the abyss saved [*salue l'abîme sauf*]" ("CD" 59). Thus, if any salvation is to be found, it is this "being in or unto the abyss [*l'être-dans ou à-l'abîme*] [. . .] within which there is 'salvation [*salut*]'" (Déc 42/27). There is only salutation, Nancy writes, "for there is nothing to save" ("CD" 59/101). "In his or her dying, each one is saluted by himself, inasmuch as this 'himself' is desolated, intact, and does not and will not come back to us or to himself" (59/101, trans. mod.).

In his first item of writing on Derrida penned in October 2004 immediately following his passing away, a brief homage called "Salut à toi, salut aux aveugles que nous devenons," Nancy responds to the notion of *salut* developed in various places by Derrida.[21] Sending Derrida a salutation, Nancy wishes him safety: "salve, be safe! [*salve, sois sauf*]!" Extending this notion to safety *in* death and *as* death, Nancy wishes for Derrida to "be safe not from death but in it, or else if you allow, if it is allowed, be safe as death [*sois sauf comme la mort*]. Immortal like it [death]."[22]

Safety, then, is what is wished for—and reserved for—the dead, not the living.

There's Deconstruction, and then, There's Deconstruction[23]

In a piece entitled "Deconstruction of Christianity," first delivered as a lecture in 1995, published as an article before appearing as a chapter in *Dis-Enclosure*, Nancy claims that "Christianity is the very thing—*the thing itself* [la chose même]—that has to be thought."[24] This statement is of course an alteration of, and a kind of response to, Derrida's insistence in "Faith and Knowledge," previously quoted, regarding the unscathed as being "the very matter, the thing itself" to be thought about religion. Since the appearance of the original article, Nancy has made good on the promise of continuing to pursue a project of the deconstruction of Christianity. It would be impossible to make definitive judgments regarding Nancy's project, which is ongoing and constantly being amended and supplemented by new writings. I will restrict my discussion of this ever-expanding enterprise to the features that specifically distinguish Nancy's sense of deconstruction from that of Derrida.

Writing of "the deconstruction of Christianity" in *Le toucher, Jean-Luc Nancy*, Derrida claims that at the moment when there is a *doxa* spreading powerfully on the subject of "*globalization*," at the moment when Christian discourse informs in a confused but sure way all the import of this *doxa*, a *doxa* that carries with it the "world [*monde*]," with its vague equivalents "globe, universe, earth, or *cosmos* (in its Pauline usage), Nancy's remarks may be intersecting with a strand of the Heideggerian project: to dechristianize the thinking of the world, [of] the 'globalization of the world' [*mondialisation du monde*], of the world insofar as it worldifies or worldizes (*weltet*) itself" (LT 68/54). Nancy's stated project of the deconstruction of Christianity, Derrida writes, "will be the test of a dechristianization of the world." This dechristianization, however, "will be a Christian victory" (68/54). In several places in *Le toucher*, Derrida "speculates," in his own words, "rather freely" about Nancy's project even though, by his own admission, he has only been familiar with the title of the project (68/54fn). The deconstruction of Christianity, he comments later in the text, "appears to be a task so difficult, so paradoxical, almost impossible, always in danger of being exposed as a Christian hyperbole" (249).[25]

In *Rogues* Derrida provides details about the dissimilarities between deconstruction as he sees it and other similar projects, among which one could include Nancy's deconstruction of Christianity. In addition to pointing out the contrast between deconstruction and critique, Derrida demarcates deconstruction from Heideggerian *Destruktion*. A destructuring of the history of metaphysics, *Destruktion* undertook a more "originary" reinterpretation of *logos*, yet in Derrida's opinion it never opposed logocentrism (R 206n/173fn). Another reason why deconstruction is not to be mistaken with Heideggerian *Destruktion* is that it never took as its goal "the objectifying form" of a diagnosis (206/174). Deconstruction could not be identified as signaling "the end of metaphysics," for it never associated itself with themes such as "after" or "post," "completion," "surpassing," "overcoming (*Überwindung*)," or the end (206/174). The "closure" of metaphysics, which does not signify the end, does not enclose something by the name of "metaphysics" in general and in the singular. Rather, Derridean deconstruction is "inscribed, undertaken, and understood in the very element of the language it calls into question" (206–207/174). Derrida emphasizes what in *Le toucher* he refers to as the Lutheran legacy of Heideggerian deconstruction (*destructio*), "this Christian (Lutheran, Pascalian, Hegelian, Kierkegaardian, Marxian, etc.) memory" that can never be forgotten when one reads Heidegger (LT 74).[26] "The theme and word *Destruktion*," Derrida further writes, "designated in Luther a desedimentation of instituted theology (one could also say ontotheology) in the service of a more originary truth of Scripture" (R 207n1/150n14). Despite his great respect for this tradition, Derridean deconstruction "does not belong, in any way, and this is more than obvious, to the same filiation" (207/174).[27] Finally, acknowledging his debt to Aristotelian aporia and the Kantian antinomies, Derrida acknowledges "the privilege" that the deconstruction he favors grants to "aporetic thought" (207/174).

In the ninth and tenth sessions of the first year of the *Death Penalty* seminar (1999–2000), Derrida distinguishes Nancy's venture from the mode of reading that since the 1960s he has named deconstruction. Linking the overarching themes of his seminar, perjury and pardon, Derrida notes that Christianity is the religion that calls itself and is in its very essence the "religion of a forgiveness of sins" (DP1 333/244). "This singularity of a religion of forgiveness," he points out, is inseparable from "the Passion, thus from the death of God, of the son of God, of God the Father made man as sacrifice and redemption of sins" (333/245). "This idea of forgiveness," Derrida comments, cannot easily be dissociated "from some death of God" (the death of God, of course, being "a Christian theme par excellence") or "from his resurrection or redemption" (334/245). In this way, Nancy's project of the deconstruction of Christianity, Derrida writes, is "the very thing [*la chose même*], business, and initiative of Christianity" itself (334/245). After all, what else could a deconstruction that "overcomes itself as it is carried out, that sublates itself" (using Nancy's own description in "The Deconstruction of Christianity") be, but "a Christian deconstruction" (334/245)? After all, Christianity, for Nancy, is what has been in a state of self-overcoming, a state that belongs to its very inner logic.

One can think another deconstruction, a deconstruction that does not sublate or overcome itself, what in a parenthetical remark during the session Derrida calls "a radically non-Christian deconstruction" (DP1 334n/245n6). He wonders whether "to self-deconstruct" has to mean "'to ask forgiveness' or to pass through the ordeal of forgiveness" (334/245). In *The Death Penalty* seminar, the indemnity of the unscathed, posed as the question of religion in "Faith and Knowledge," also emerges as the question of the death penalty. What both religion and the death penalty have in common, Derrida notes, is a similar concern: "'to come out' *unscathed* ['sortir' *indemne*] (344/254). Derrida deems "a deconstruction of death," even though necessary, to be insufficient since it involves a precomprehension of the meaning of death—which itself rests on the determination of the instant of death, the supposedly objective knowledge of what separates life and death. It is not enough to deconstruct death in order to assure one's salvation, Derrida maintains, since as a result of the deconstruction of death nothing (neither life nor death) walks away, escapes, or "comes out unscathed [*ne sort pas indemne*]" (328/241).

But how do we understand "to come out unscathed"? In session 10, Derrida explains that indemnity—providing a further gloss on a crucial term in "Faith and Knowledge"—can either mean "*being-unscathed* (that is, safe, sound, intact, virgin, unhurt, *heilig*, holy)" or "*being-indemnified*, that is, rendered once again unscathed, made unscathed, that is, paid, reimbursed by the payment of a compensation, redemption, by the payment of a debt" (DP1 344/254). The death penalty's "calculating decision," Derrida remarks, by "putting an end to life, seems, paradoxically, to put an end to finitude" (349/258). It seems to affirm its power over time, to master the future, and to protect itself against the irruption of the other (349/258). This calculation, mastery, and decidability, however, are phantasms. The finality of the end of finitude "is to produce the phantasm of this end of finitude, thus the other side of an infinitization" (349/258). "A calculating decision on the subject of our death cherishes the dream of an infinitization and thus of an infinite survival" (349/258). We desire or dream of giving "ourselves death" and to infinitize "ourselves by giving ourselves death in a calculable, calculated, decidable fashion" (350/258). This "phantasm of infinitization at the heart of finitude, of an infinitization of survival assured by calculation itself," Derrida believes, is "one with God" or with "the belief in God, the experience of God, relation with God, faith or religion" (350/259).

Since the trajectory of Western philosophical thought is inseparable from Christianity's path and since the closure of metaphysics entails its own self-overcoming, it is Christianity, and its major tenets such as resurrection, incarnation, creation, and eternal life, that require further thought and deconstruction. Derrida's later writings on "religion" demonstrate that the very thing to be thought is not simply Christianity but rather the unscathed. Furthermore, Derrida shows that the desire for being unscathed, safe, and intact—religion's desire—is bound to fail: for what desires to be safe and intact is auto-immune.

Death

3

Derrida Is the Death of Death

... *"adieu" tu m'abandonnes, pourquoi m'as tu abandonné, reviens, mais tu ne revient pas, tu ne peux pas revenir, revenant* ...

—Jacques Derrida, *Idiomes, nationalités, déconstructions*

Death

Death, the most inscrutable torment that afflicts human beings or a brute fact whose enormity refuses comparison with anything else, is that "unthinkable" whose reality is totally impenetrable.[1] The impossibility of adequately answering the question "What is death?" perhaps indicates the folly of raising it. It exposes us to the total "immeasurability" of something that we can never have an experience of (Dastur 5/4). It is not for no reason that Levinas described it as an "enigma," "a pure question mark," nay a "scandal." Death is "absence par excellence" and the dead disappear "absolutely" and "irreplaceably" (9/9).

The medical establishment and institutions in modern Western societies view death as the end of an organic existence. It is treated as a natural phenomenon that is organically observable, physiologically describable, and biologically explainable. Historians who have noted the transformation of views of death in Western societies explain that death has become demystified and medicalized, in order to mollify it and its effects, while mourning has been psychologized and individualized. Since Plato, philosophers have pondered this daunting subject, yet they have done so with a view to neutralizing and conquering it. If philosophical discourse has been a discourse on mortality, on the fact that we are mortal creatures who are finite and who die, it has been at once a recognition of mortality as well as a denial of death. If philosophy has presented itself to itself as that discipline that prepares one for and accepts death,[2] it has done so in order to ultimately overcome it and gain access to immortality.[3] Philosophy's intimate relation to death, accepting the separation of the body from the soul, is parallel to the foundational role of death in Christianity, which instituted a conception of temporality and human existence oriented toward the "End Time" and the Last Judgment. An eschatology (*eschaton*, extreme, last) as well as a teleology, Christianity, with the invention of the "afterworld," has as its ultimate goal triumph over death and gaining access to another life in another realm. At the "end time," also known as "end times," "end of time," "end of days," "last days," or "final days," world events are said to achieve a final climax. The significance of death in Christianity, which owes its prominence to the pivotal role played by the death of Christ, is of a piece with the unconditional affirmation of life and disdain for death in Christian societies. The expected attitude toward death is heroic fortitude and what is admired is serenity, equanimity, self-control, and stoicism in the face of it.[4]

In reflections on death from Plato to Seneca and Montaigne, from Spinoza to Hegel and Heidegger, philosophy has not unsurprisingly placed an emphasis on the death of the individual, on what Heidegger termed my "own," proper death. It is not until Levinas urged a change of focus from viewing death as *my* death or the concept of death to the death of the other that philosophy specifically turned its attention to and considered the other's death as a singular death distinctive from that of the self.[5] Yet, adhering to the adage made famous by Montaigne, philosophy has maintained its self-definition as the best preparation for learning how to live by learning how to die.[6] Philosophers have steadfastly affirmed the "virile" ideal of the philosophical death—teaching us how to die while facing death without searching for or being comforted by a thought of the afterlife.

Giving priority to the existential interpretation of death in *Being and Time*, Heidegger argues that the cultural, historical, and anthropological interpretations of death are insufficient not only because they all assume a precomprehension of death—as Derrida comments, these approaches "must *already* know what *death* means" (A 57/45)—but because they do not think death fundamentally enough. Thus, Heidegger argues for the priority of an ontological account of death that precedes all the ontic accounts. Levinas brings a novel approach to this perennial question in *God, Death, and Time*, drawing inspiration from the writings of Bergson, Fink, and Bloch.[7] In two lecture courses that were taught in 1975–1976 but were published as one text in 1993, Levinas seeks to counter the dominance of the Heideggerian interpretation of death. He describes death as "the non-response [*sans-réponse*]" (17), calling it "an irreversible" (16) that "exceeds thought" (130). For Levinas, death is "not of the world," is not somewhere in time, but belongs to a time beyond consciousness (129). In contrast to the tradition and opposed to Heidegger, Levinas wants to think death starting from time, as a function or modality of time (129). Drawing on Bergson and Bloch, Levinas is interested in the meaning that death confers on the future. Time as duration means that the future is open and nothing is definitive (65). Most notably, referring to Eugen Fink's less well-known *Metaphysik und Tod*, Levinas writes that "there is no genre of death"; each death is "a *first* death [première *mort*]" (105).

Derrida's approach to the question of death, in comparison to the philosophical tradition, has been absolutely singular. Even though there are many references to death in his writings, there exists no "concept" of death *as such* or a univocal meaning of death in his work. There are deaths—multiple deaths—yet each death remains singularly unique. There has been a resistance in Derrida's work to the notion of "death itself," for death is not one. If, as Geoffrey Bennington claims in "R.I.P.," "death is the only subject of philosophy" (62) and "philosophy is organized around or towards death," then Derrida's work is "the death of death," death as the engine that has driven philosophy, death as the crutch it relies on to uphold its virility, self-importance, and pathos (64). As Bennington writes of Derrida in the same place, "one evaluation of his early work," which may also be said of his later work, is "the simultaneous confirmation and displacement of the philosophical thinking of death or of philosophy as a thinking of death" (64).

In *Aporias*, the text in which Derrida broaches the question of death more "directly" than elsewhere, he declares, as if he were throwing his hands in the air, that "one knows perhaps neither the meaning nor the referent of this word" (A 49/22). Throughout his work, death has been associated with, among other things, irrevocable absence (without any pathos); disappearance (the relation to death as a relation to my disappearance in general is discussed in *Voice and Phenomenon*); technology, technicity, and the machine (the space of death is related to repeatability, the automatic, to technique, and to the machine); the image (OG 100), and so on. While Derrida has shown that every use of a proper name or the pronoun "I" entails death, this "death" is indifferent to "real" death. Death has been variously described as the name of a secret, as only possible as impossible (like the gift, love, friendship, the other, etc.) and designated as a shibboleth, an awaiting (oneself and each other), a nonpassive endurance, an experience of nonpassage, an aporia, and an event. Derrida has equated the purity of life or purity in general with death. Absolute safety, absolute immunity, and that which desires to be perfectly intact, thus being closed off from the outside, are all linked with death. So is the lack of any risk-taking, which leads to no future. Death—that which is nonphenomenal, in other words, what cannot be phenomenalized or come to appear—radically escapes all presence. In its coming, death, like the ghost, is without horizon (for a horizon is a limit, a border, a boundary). It "names the very irreplaceability of absolute singularity [*l'irremplacable même de la singularité absolue*]" (A 49/22). However, the "complication" or paradox about death is that "everyone's death [. . .] is irreplaceable," yet "nothing is more substitutable" than death (49/22). It is said only "*one time each time* [une fois chaque fois], *indefinitely* only one time [une seule fois]" (49/22).

The Proper Is Stronger than Life and Death

It is not until the penultimate section of "To Speculate—on 'Freud'" from *The Post Card: from Socrates to Freud and Beyond*, his reading of Freud's *Beyond the Pleasure Principle*, that Derrida comes to the question of death. And it is not until late in Freud's text, Derrida comments in the section entitled "Paralysis," that Freud mentions death, for there has been "dead silence about death [*silence de mort sur la mort*]" (PC 376/353). It is also starting from *Beyond the Pleasure Principle* that Freud employs Eros to inscribe his new theory of drives within the philosophical tradition of Plato's *Symposium* and the Aristophanes myth. Freud employs Eros in his last writings to connote the whole of the life drives in opposition to the death drives.[8] In the course of his reading of *Beyond the Pleasure Principle* Derrida zeros in on "the strange relation to oneself that is called the relation to the proper [*rapport au propre*]" and determines that "the law of the proper," "the law of oneself as proper," seeks its own, proper propriation. Derrida's reading demonstrates that, for Freud, the proper only wants to die in its own manner and arrives at death at its own pace (381/359).

In the subsection entitled "Couriers of Death" of "Paralysis," Derrida explains, Freud "advances a hypothesis about the nature of the drive in general and perhaps even about organic life in general" (PC 376/354). There is an "attribute [*charactère*]," he goes on, "inscribed in every drive and perhaps in all organic life." Freud defines this trait, this attribute, as follows: "It seems, then, that a drive [*Trieb*] is an urge [*poussée, Drang*] inherent in the organism [*habitant au-dedans de l'organisme*] aiming to the restoration [*Wiederherstellung*] of an earlier state of things . . . it is a kind of organic elasticity [or] the expression of an inertia inherent in organic life (36, mod.)" (376/354). In Freud's hypothesis "the programmatic writing, the writing which formulates the 'attribute,' is confounded [*se confond*] with the hypothesis of a force, an urge, a driving power [*puissance pulsionelle*]" (376/354). "This force of the attribute is written" as force in opposition to another force from the outside, "a counter-force" (376/354). "The force of inscription organizes the field in a network of differences of forces. The living," Derrida surmises, "is nothing other than this differential [of forces]" (376–377/354). This "external" force is what is commonly called nature.

The *Umweg*, the detour (initially encountered in the first chapter of *Beyond the Pleasure Principle* when the reality principle, in a never certain return to itself, imposes a detour in order to defer enjoyment), here "would defer/differ not with the aim of pleasure or of conservation . . . but with the aim of death, or of the return to the inorganic state" (PC 377/354). For Freud, it is a matter of return to the organic state, always leading back, going back, coming back (*revenir*) to death. Derrida notes that the detour is "not a derivative type of path or step. . . . a narrower or stricter definition of the passage, it *is* the passage" (377/354, emphasis added). In other words, the *Umweg*, the detour, *différance*, is the passage. "(The) *Weg* (is) *Umweg*" (377/354).

So, in Freud's judgment, "The end of the living [*la fin du vivant*], its aim [*but*] and term [*terme*], is return to the inorganic state" (PC 377/355). We could say "the evolution of life" constitutes nothing but "a detour of the inorganic aiming for itself," what Derrida calls "a race to the death" (377/355). This death is "inscribed as an internal law and not as an accident of life" (377/355). Thus, it is life that "resembles an accident of death or an excess of death, in the extent to which it 'dies for internal reasons [*aus inneren Gründen*]'" (377/355).

Freudian speculation results in two observations: "The driving detour in its conservative form, the conserver of the drive, is a *partial* process" (PC 378/355). There are "component drives [*Partialtriebe*]." The final sense of these "component drives" of conservation is that their movement *tends* to insure that the path (*Weg-Umweg*) toward death, the path of death, corresponds to internal, "immanent" possibilities. "The component drives are *destined* to *insure* that the organism dies *of its own, proper death* [sa propre mort], that it follows its own, proper path toward death. That it arrives by its own step at death [*eigenen Todesweg*]" (378/355). What the component drives do is to help dying one's own death, to help "that for which death is a return to the most proper [*à ce que la mort soit un retour au plus propre*]" (378/355, trans. mod.). "The organism (or every living organization, every 'corpus,' every 'movement') conserves itself, spares itself, maintains itself via every kind of differentiated relay, intermediary destination [. . .] Not in order," Derrida explains, "to keep oneself from death [*se garder de la mort*], or to maintain oneself against death [*ou contre la mort*], but only in order to avoid a death which would not return to itself [*qui ne lui reviendrait pas*], in order to cut off a death that would not be its own or that of its own" (378/356, trans. mod.).

The drive of the proper, then, proves to be the most significant drive. As Derrida explains, "The drive of the proper would be stronger than life *and* stronger than death," because "neither living nor dead, its force does not qualify it otherwise than by its own, proper drivenness [*propre pulsivité*], and this drivenness would be the strange relation to oneself that is called the relation to the proper [*rapport au propre*]: the most driven drive [*la pulsion la plus pulsive*] is the drive of the proper, in other words the one that tends to reappropriate itself" (PC 379/356). Ultimately the movement of reappropriation is the most elementary, the most forceful, the strongest: "The movement of reappropriation is the most driven drive. The proper of drivenness is the movement or the force of reappropriation" (379/356). What the proper demonstrates is "the tendency to appropriate oneself" (379/356). Yet, it is worth noting, the "expropriating structure" prevents reappropriation from closing on itself—"the proper is not the proper, and if it appropriates itself [*s'approprie*] it is because it disappropriates itself [*se désapproprie*]" (379/357). "Life death," Derrida remarks, "are no longer opposed in it" (379/357).

We have seen that for Freud the organism wills to be in charge of its own death, to die its own death. The proper dies at its own pace, tempo, rate, and speed—in its own way. The organism "wishes to die only in its own fashion [*nur auf seine* Weise *sterben will*]" and the component drives are there to assist it to die properly (PC 381/358). In Derrida's view, Heidegger's *Eigentlichkeit*, "a certain quality of the relation to the proper" alongside Freud's thinking of *Todestrieb* (381/358) is "pronouncing the law of life-death [*la-vie-la-mort*] as the law of the proper" (381/359). Rather than life *and* death or life *or* death, Derrida comments, a law of the proper seeks its "own, proper propriation" (381/359). "One must auto-affect oneself with one's proper death (and the oneself [*le soi-même*] does not exist before all else, before this movement of auto-affection), make certain [*faire que*] that death is the auto-affection of life or life the auto-affection of death" (382/359, trans. mod.).

Aporias

Is death an end? Is life, confined to its finite limits, restricted within its borders, a border that must not be exceeded? In *Aporias* Derrida famously examines the various ways of conceiving a border or a frontier while attending to views of death as crossing a line, stepping over or across a limit. Death "takes a figure," Derrida writes, "it has a privileged form [*schème*], the crossing of a line (between existence and non-existence)" (107/58). In fact, it seems impossible to think about death otherwise. English words signifying death, such as "decease" and "parting," convey the idea of departure and separation, while in French *trépas* (from the twelfth-century *trespas*, passage, *trépasser*) has a sense of passing away (*dépassement*) or transgression.[9] It would be impossible to give an account of or to summarize all the strands weaving through *Aporias*, Derrida's condensed, intense engagement with the philosophical (or ontological understanding) and "bio-anthropo-thanato-theological" notions of death. Each needs to be explored in scrupulous detail. In this chapter, especial attention will be paid to "the end" and "the experience of the aporia."

At the beginning of *Aporias*, a talk first delivered in 1992 at the third Cerisy conference devoted to his work, Derrida writes that death has very often been represented as a limit, an end (*finis*), a frontier, but also as a voyage, a departure, or the passage through a frontier or the crossing of a border, a line, a voyage between the here and the beyond. But, he asks, can death be reduced to crossing a line, "to a departure, to a separation, to a step, and therefore to a *decease*?" (A 22/6). He chooses as his point of entry accounts by Diderot and classical authors such as

Seneca and Cicero, while attending to the terminology being used by Seneca and Cicero to refer to death. Derrida begins "*by the end*," "by the ends or confines [*fini*]," that is "the term, the edge, limit, the border, most often that of a territory or of a country" (22/5). In the little-known essay "Essai sur la vie de Sénèque le philosophe," Diderot praises Seneca for bringing to light how human beings forget their own mortality by wasting so much of their time on mediocre tasks. In *De brevitate vitae* Seneca urges humans to order their life properly and to not give their time away.[10] In what, according to Derrida, amounts to "a rhetoric of borders" what is in question in Seneca's text is the property of one's life, especially the lines that delimit the right of property to one's life (18/3). *De brevitate vitae* is "a treatise about the tracing of traits as the borderly edges" of what *belongs to one* (18/3). In his *De finibus* Cicero, always attentive to Greek and Latin and justifying his translations, having originally translated the word for "the border" as "the extreme," "the ultimate," or "the supreme," now renders it as "the end [*la fin*]" (21/5).[11] Derrida notes that all the propositions about death that he has discussed involve a certain *pas* [step, not]: "*Il y va d'un certain pas*," it is the matter of a certain step, a certain not (23/6). What the *pas* involves is "the line that terminates all determination, the final or definitional line—*peras*" (24/7). The Greek word *peras*—term (*terme*), synonym of the Greek word *terma*, end or limit, extremity—leads us to *peran*, beyond, on the other side, which, in turn, take us to *peraō*, I traverse by penetrating, I cross through, I cross over life's term (in Aeschylus), and passing the final limit (in Sophocles) (25/7).

But what is "to pass the term of one's life [*passer le terme d'une vie*] (*terma tou biou*) (Sophocles, *Oedipus the King*)?" With this "'I pass [*je passe*]' (*peraō*)" we are placed on "the path [*voie*]," Derrida writes, "of the *aporos* or the aporia, the impracticable or refused, denied passage, what can be something else, the non-passage" (A 25/8). How are we to interpret this nonpassage, Derrida wonders, if we are to not read it, like the common interpretation does, as barred or impossible passage? The "non-passage," Derrida notes, can be something else: "the event of a coming or of a future advent [*venue ou d'avenir*]" does not any longer have "the form of the movement that consists in passing, traversing, or transiting. It would be the 'coming to pass [*se passer*]' of an event that would not have the form or the appearance of a *pas*: in sum, a coming without *pas* [*une venue sans pas*]" (25/8). The untranslatable *Il y va d'un certain pas* can be received in more than one way. Once the figure of the step is refused, "the edge-line [*le passage de la ligne*] is threatened," the indivisibility of the line and the identity of the two sides become problematic. One could argue, of course, that they have always been problematic (30/11).

The aporia, a "not knowing where to go" is "the *experience* of nonpassage" (A 31/12). Drawing an analogy to the questions he posed about Heidegger's vulgar concept of time in "Ousia and Grammē," Derrida says that the aporia he is presently examining is an experience other than opposing from both sides of an invisible line a nonvulgar concept to the so-called vulgar concept. More accurately, the aporia is "a traversal without line and without a divisible border" (35/15). Faced with the aporia, Derrida's intention is to try "to move [*me mouvoir*] not against or out of the impasse but, in another way, *according to* another thinking of the aporia, one perhaps more enduring" (32/13). The *experience* of the *aporia* (yoking together in one phrase two words that speak of the passage and the nonpassage) is to be thought of "as endurance or as passion, as interminable resistance or remaining [*restance*]" (42/19, trans. mod.). Among "the multiple figures of aporia" (44/20) that Derrida examines (for example, the impermeable nonpassage, the impasse without limit, the impossible, etc.), what is at stake with death is "not the crossing of a given border" but rather "the *double concept of the border*" (40/18). This way of approaching the aporia of death does not allow for a passage or step. "There is no more path [. . .] no more movement or trajectory," no more a passage across (47/21). "Not even the *non-pas*," this aporia would be "the deprivation of the *pas* (the privative form would be a kind of *a-pas*)" (50/23).

Is it possible to experience the aporia? (65/33). Derrida asks: "*What takes place* [ce qui arrive], *what comes to pass* [ce qui se passe] with the aporia?" (65/32). Is it to undergo it, pass through it, to be immobilized before it? (65/33). What is being questioned here concerning what takes place also involves "the event as that which arrives [*ce qui arrive*]" at the edge, the border, or threshold (65/33). "What is the event that most arrives [*l'événement le plus arrivant*]?" (66/33). "What is the *arrivant* that makes an event arrive [*fait arriver un événement*]?" (66/33). Does death happen or arrive at the threshold? What is the *arrivant*? (66/33). That which makes the event arrive, the *arrivant* is what "does *not* cross a threshold separating two identifiable places" (67/34, italics mine) but "affects the very experience of the threshold itself" (66/33). What is a threshold? A threshold is that which is supposed to mark the indivisible limit between two identities, concepts, or territories or to demarcate the limit between an inside and an outside.

Since the *arrivant* has no identity yet, "its place of arrival is also de-identified" (A 68/34). It is on this "essentially most difficult to delineate border [*au fond la plus difficile à tracer*]" that Derrida "is tempted to read Heidegger" (68/35, trans. mod.). This border "will always keep one from discriminating among the figures of the *arrivant*, the dead [*du mort*], and the *revenant*" (68/35). Without a frontier that can be clearly delineated, where identity is called into question, it is impossible to differentiate between the figures of the one arriving, the dead, and the returning ghost.

Among the outcomes of Derrida's analysis in *Aporias* we can list the following two features: 1) Originary mourning limits the preference for any priority to be given to either "my death" (Heidegger) or "the death of the other" (Levinas) (111/61). As Derrida writes, the contamination of the proper results in the death of the other thus becoming again "first." For, the death of the other, that is, the death of the other in "me" is the only death referred to in the syntagma "my death" (133/76); 2) Parallels can be drawn between death and the event: both are unpredictable, radically other, lack a horizon, and come as an absolute surprise. As Derrida had already written in *Of Grammatology*, "The relation to the other and the relation with death are one and the same opening" (OG 265/187).

Marranos

"*Death* is always the name of a secret, since it signs the irreplaceable singularity," Derrida declares (A 130/74). It is toward the end of *Aporias* that Derrida makes this association between death and the secret. Death names what is recognizable, publicly known, with a common name. It "puts forth the public name, the common name of a secret, the common name of the proper name without name" (130/174). Death, the name of an all too common event, not hidden but out in the open, nonetheless names a secret. It is a secret because what it refers to is always an absolutely singular event that cannot be phenomenalized, brought to presence, unveiled, or revealed. "It is therefore always a *shibboleth*"—a custom, principle, belief, or behavior distinctive of a particular class or group of people, the use of or inability to use which reveals one's party, nationality, orthodoxy—"for the manifest name of a secret is from the beginning a private name, so that [*faisant*] language about death is nothing but a great history, great story of a secret society [*une grande histoire de société secret*], neither public nor private, semi-private, semi-public, on the border between the two; thus also a hidden religion of the *awaiting* [*s'attendre*] (oneself as well as each other), with its ceremonies, cults, liturgy, or its Marranolike rituals"(130/74). A secret society, then, but this (not so) secret society, this "hidden religion," would be the society of those marked by, touched by death. Derrida refers to the awaiting one as a Marrano, a Marrano not as historically defined by belonging to a distinctive cultural heritage but "a universal Marrano." Death would then be the story of all those awaiting "Marranos" telling a secret that cannot be told.

Derrida further links death with the secret in *A Taste for the Secret* (1997), his series of conversations with Maurizio Ferraris, when he notes, "Clearly, the most tempting figure for this absolute/secret [*quest'altro segreto*] is death, that which has a relation to death, that which is carried off by death [*la morte porta con sé*]" (TS 52/58). For death is that which is, like the secret, nonthematizable and nonsharable, resistant to the daylight of phenomenality. The secret disrupts all transparency and consensus. There can be no consensus on the subject of death except that the singular is the singular, the other is the other. As secret, it is absolute—*ab-solutum*, detached from every bond. And like the secret, what can be shared is not a content. Derrida remarks that even though "the relation to death is a privileged dimension of this experience of the secret, *but I imagine that an immortal would have the same experience*" (58). Even for an immortal, this secret—death or the experience of death—would be "sealed" and "concealed" (58).[12]

Side

There is no *other side*, Derrida writes in *H. C. for Life, That Is to Say . . .* his wide-ranging reading of the work of Hélène Cixous. Commenting on "the strange and insistent use" that Cixous "makes, on her side, of the word 'side'" (H. C. 35/29) and finding a proliferation of references to the word "side [*côté*]" in her work, Derrida asserts that if pressed as to where he locates her work, he would always find her on the side of life. As for himself, he "will not be on her side" (28/20). "I, who always feel turned toward death [*tourné du côté de la mort*]," he writes wistfully, "I am not on her side [*je ne suis pas de son côté*]" (40/36). From the beginning of the text he asks himself what a "side [*côté*]" is or what a side means (33/27). Not only does he no longer know which side he is on, he admits he no longer knows "what a side is" (28–29/21). Yet Derrida nonetheless finds himself always on her side, "too much on her side" (28/21). Reflecting on questions of life and death raised in Cixous's writings, Derrida writes that in her work he can only find one side. For Cixous, Derrida remarks, "there is only one side and not two, and that side is that of life" (40/36). This is because she does not consider death to be a "side": "death is not a side, it is a nonside [*n'est pas un côté, c'est un non-côté*]" (40/36).

The term "side" suggests the taking of sides, taking up a position, one side in relation to or opposed to another. Yet going counter to the popular phrase in the American vernacular—"there are two sides to everything"—which affirms a certain belief in the homegrown variety of democracy, Derrida observes, "Life has no other side [*n'a pas d'autre côté*], if there is only one side [*qu'un seul côté*] [. . .] then the latter remains undecidable" (H. C. 50/47). Since this undecidable is necessarily the place of decision, this "can only be *for life* [*pour la vie*]" (50/48). "Because it is undecidable, one can only decide and settle only for life. But life, which is undecidable, is also, in its very finitude, infinite. What has only one side—a single edge without an opposite edge [*un seul bord sans bord opposé*]—is in-finite [*in-fini*]. Finite because it has an edge on one side [*bordé d'un côté*], but infinite because it has no opposable edge" (50/48).

Derrida refers to it as "this strange logic of the edge without an opposite edge, a unique side [*étrange logique du bord sans bord opposé, d'un côté unique*]" (H. C. 53/52). This unique side "is certainly the side that is dissymetrically turned toward the other, oriented, exposed, or held to the other [*tenu à l'autre*]" (53–54/52). "This remains a unique side without another side, and this would be life itself" (54/52). Derrida adds that death is in no way denied, "but it is not a side, it is a nonside" (54/52). "No more edge [*bord*] for me," Derrida bemoans. "No more death, maybe, since life has no opposite edge, but no more edge at all [*plus de bord du tout*]" (51/48). Thus, he is left to contend with the fact that he "would have no side at all" and that he does "not know where to put" himself (51/49). If "there are not two sides, Derrida writes, then, consonant with a differential thinking without opposition, "there is no side, and that is the undecidable" (72/75). "Life *for* life (and not a Heideggerian being-for-life)," then, "is therefore nothing else than a living of death [*vivre la mort*], but yes, still living, death, living it for oneself, for the other, and for life" (83/89). He notes that later he will call it "living for the sake of living [*vivre pour vivre*]" (83/89).

We die in the end, too quickly (H. C.).

I promise you in me to carry you in me. If you ever were to hear this promise, "it will only be in me, in my heart," in my heart of heart.[13] *(BSI, 2).*

Resurrection

4

Nancy's Resurrection

Finalement, j'aimerais mieux une vraie résurrection classique.

In the end, I would prefer a real classical resurrection.

—Jacques Derrida, quoted in Jean-Luc Nancy, "Reste, viens"

Resurrection, a central tenet of Abrahamic religions, in Christian worship denotes the return to life of Jesus Christ after the ascension to heaven of the body of light, the glorious body, while eternal life refers to continued life after the resurrection of the dead.[1] Traditionally, both these notions have been considered as forms of salvation (*salut*) of the saved after death. As hope for a "second chance" at life and as refusal of the finality of death, the question of salvation after death has often been raised as a matter of faith. In his later work Jean-Luc Nancy has explored the themes of "resurrection" and "eternal life," notions classically associated with a thinking of the hereafter, allowing him to delve into what he terms "a beyond of death" (Ad 128/88). What particularly interests Nancy is "the life of the dead," a life withdrawn from time, in the world outside the world. Entertaining a relation to "the outside of time," this "life" takes place—a "place" nonetheless—in an unnamable region. Nancy finds his observations about this beyond of death, about the dead one and the temporality specific to it, to belong somewhere between thought and sensibility, leading him to "a conduct that exceeds knowledge, wisdom, and consciousness" (137/95).

Resurrection

Judging by Nancy's various writings on resurrection, it would not be too far-fetched to suggest that he conceives of resurrection as part of the deconstruction of death. What he calls "the resurrection of death" is a deepening of death, an uprising, a "raising [*relèvement*]," a "lifting [*soulèvement*]" (NMT 33/18). While Nancy considers the "historical" resurrection of the dead as a "fantastic" operation, he views the resurrection of death as its transformation. In various texts published in the first five years of this century and collected in *La Déclosion*, Nancy goes on to redefine all the terms involved in or associated with resurrection in its Christic form or what Derrida labels "classical resurrection." Indeed, the deconstruction of resurrection could possibly be read as a response or rejoinder to Derrida's remarks on resurrection in *Le toucher, Jean-Luc Nancy*. In that text, Derrida praises Nancy's work, "the probity of his signature," and his exactitude—a word that he credits Nancy for "reinventing" and "reawakening"—a word that he believes is "rather new—like a resurrection" (LT 17/8).

Nancy's first contribution toward rethinking a notion of resurrection for philosophical thought was a short text, *Noli me tangere*, published in April 2003. While discussing how a host of classical painters have depicted the famous scene from the Gospel of John and the "resurrection" announced in it, *Noli me tangere* undertakes to resuscitate a notion of resurrection. A few months after its appearance and approximately a year after Blanchot's death in February 2003, Nancy presented a text entitled "Blanchot's Resurrection" as the opener for a series of papers at the Pompidou Center in 2004 devoted to Blanchot bearing the same title. This essay was later included in Nancy's book *La Déclosion* (2005) in which he devoted two chapters to Blanchot.

In Nancy's view, resurrection, rather than a return to life or a process of regeneration, signifies a reconfiguration of death and dying (NMT 32/17). Discussing the resurrection of Christ, he claims that resurrection is not "a resuscitation [*réanimation*]" but "the infinite continuation of death that displaces and dismantles all the values of presence and absence, of animate and inanimate, of body and soul" (73/44, trans. mod.). Contrary to its dominant interpretation throughout Western history, in Nancy's reading, resurrection is not a "reincarnation" or a "reanimation [*reviviscence*]" (33/18).

Nancy presents what he refers to as "the nonreligious meaning" of resurrection as "the departing into which presence actually withdraws [. . .]. Just as it comes, so it goes: that is to say, it *is* not" (NMT 29/15). Resurrection is described as "the uprising [*surrection*], the sudden appearance of the unavailable, of the other and of the disappearing [*le disparissant*] *in the body itself and as the body*" (29/15, trans. mod.). Death is thus not won over or "vanquished," but is "immeasurably extended [*étendu*], shielded [*soustraite*]" from being simply "a mere demise" (30/16). Referring to Christ, Nancy writes, this is because "He dies indefinitely," he is the one who does not "cease to depart" for his "presence is that of a disappearance [*la disparition*] indefinitely renewed or prolonged" (31/16). "He is departing for the absent [*il part pour l'absent*]," Nancy elaborates, "for the distant, the remote" (31/17, trans. mod.).

Nancy does not consider resurrection to be in any way a "dialecticization" or a mediation of death, and he is careful to stress in *Noli me tangere* that the "raising [*levée*] of the body is not a '*relève*' in the sense given to this word by Derrida to translate the Hegelian *Aufhebung*" (NMT 33/18). He deems it "incommensurable with every representation of a passage into another life" (34/18).[2] Instead, appealing to the etymology of *anastasis*, Nancy describes resurrection as "an uprising [*soulèvement*]," "a stance [*une tenue*] before death" (33/18), "a standing upright [*se-tenir-debout*] before and in death" (34/18).[3] What is affirmed in *anastasis*, then, is not only "the stance" but also "the reserve, [the] *restraint* [la retenue]" (33/18). As a much more earthbound and mundane affair, resurrection "designates the singularity of existence," for "everyone resurrects, one by one and body for body" (76/46, trans. mod.). Moreover, *anastasis* "does not come from the self, from the subject proper"; it is not something that the self does but "comes to the self from the other or arises from the other within the self" (35/19). Thus, the statement "I am resurrected" does not signify the accomplishment of an I but rather denotes a passivity. This is why Nancy can claim that "I am dead" and "I am resurrected" say the same thing (35/19).

Nancy expands his thoughts on resurrection when he reflects on Blanchot's work, particularly his first novel, *Thomas the Obscure*. In "Blanchot's Resurrection" Nancy claims that the motif of resurrection in Blanchot's *récits* is "indissociable" from death and "dying" (Déc 135/89). In this essay he introduces a distinction between "resurrecting the dead [*ressusciter les morts*]" and "resurrecting death [*ressusciter la mort*]." To resurrect the dead, he explains, would be to bring the dead back to life, making "life reappear" where death had put an end to it. This would be nothing but "a prodigious, miraculous operation," involving a supernatural intervention in the laws of nature (135).[4] However, what Nancy refers to as "the difficult, strange and obstinately evasive thought of resurrection" (144), constitutes "an entirely other operation" than the traditional notion of resurrection (136). If resurrecting the dead is "a miraculous operation" and if the Lazarus of the Gospel is "a character of a miraculous story [*récit*]" (138), then, for Nancy, resurrection does not speak of a fantastic event or spectacle. This "miracle" is not a nature-defying operation or fabulous event that exceeds common sense—for the latter would be the work of the Hegelian negative (142).

Resurrection does not escape death or "come out of it [*ne sort d'elle*]" but forms, Nancy claims, "the extremity and truth of dying" (Déc 135). It "goes into death [*elle va dans la mort*] [. . .] sinking irremissibly into it, to resuscitate death itself" (135/89). Nancy locates a source for his interpretation of death, dying, and resurrection in Blanchot in a passage from the first version of *Thomas the Obscure*, where the sole reference in Blanchot's oeuvre to the expression *mort ressuscité* occurs in chapter 8 (137/91).[5] If, in Nancy's reading, it is death that is resurrected, then the subject is "neither 'the resurrected one' nor the corpse" but death itself—"'death resurrected,' as stretched out on the corpse and so raising it without sublating it [*le dressant sans le relever*]" (138). Hence, resurrection cannot be deemed as an escape or exit from death, but rather what Nancy calls "an upright stance."

Nancy describes the story of Thomas in Blanchot's first narrative not as "a crossing through [*traversée*] of death" but designating "death itself as a crossing [*traversée*], as transport and transformation"—a passage not to elsewhere but "from itself into itself" (Déc 139/93, trans. mod.). In his reading of *Thomas the Obscure*, Nancy writes that "the space of resurrection, the space that defines it and makes it possible, is the space outside sense [*hors du sens*]" (140/93). In this space outside of sense, anteriority and posteriority have no "chronological value" but point to "an outside-of-time [*un hors-temps*], as much interminable as it is instantaneous, eternity in its essential subtractive value [*valeur de soustraction*]" (140–141).[6] The "subtractive value" of eternity, it seems, is meant to be understood as its removal from time. If, as Nancy writes in *Noli me tangere*, everyone resurrects, then "the space of resurrection," this outside-of-time, referred to in *La Déclosion*, belongs to all those who die (140).

Nancy takes up Derrida's objections to his portrayal of resurrection in "Consolation, désolation" and glossing the notion of resurrection discussed in his previous essays asserts that *anastasis* would designate nothing other than "redress [*redressement*] (*anastasis*)," a "raising up [*levée*] (and not sublation ['*relève*'])."[7] In French *redresser* is "to set upright, to straighten (up)" but also "to rectify," while in English "to redress" has a sense of "to remedy, restore, rectify, put right, set right, balance out." *Redressement* as an "adjustment" or "recovery" may be Nancy's attempt to remedy and rectify a tired traditional notion. Elaborating on the relation of *salut* to the one who is dead in "Consolation, désolation," Nancy reserves safety for the dead one, arguing that it is the dead one who is intact and safe.

Transformation of Death

In a chapter entitled "Rilke et l'exigence de la mort" in *L'espace littéraire*, Blanchot notes that, for Rilke, dying "will not be to die, but to transform the fact of death" (EL 189/146). Blanchot, whose writings on death serve as a source of inspiration for Nancy, specifies that the shift in Rilke's thought from a personal death to the "transmutation" of death "is only accomplished in us by death itself" (192/148). Indeed, "in this readier [*plus prompte*] death resurrection is expressed, the joy [*l'allégresse*] of a transfigured life" (189/146). Blanchot writes a bit further on of an "inward conversion," "a purification of death by death," a death to which no authentic relation is possible (195/150). By turning toward things, he avers, we learn "to feel the movement of transmutation and, in this movement, to transmute transmutation itself, to the point where it becomes the purity of death purified of dying" (200/154). Yet we soon realize that we "need to start from the depth of death in order to turn toward the intimacy of things" (201/155). Blanchot wonders whether Rilke may be judged to be "idealizing" the "ordeal of dying" in order "to purify it of its brutality" (201/154). Still beyond its "very accommodating extreme" that has its "reassuring side [*côté rassurant*]," he notes, there is also "a fearful side [*côté effrayant*]" (201/154). "If death's true reality is not simply what from the outside we call leaving life [*quitter la vie*]—if death is something other than its worldly reality, if it eludes us, turning always away—then this movement makes us sense its profound unreality: death as abyss, not that which founds but the absence and the loss of all foundation" (202/154, trans. mod.). (Note here Blanchot's displacement of the Heideggerian *Abgrund*. Perhaps, we can say that death itself is not an abyss, but *each and every* death is abyssal. Then, death would not be the absence of *all* foundation but the absence of *a* foundation *every* time.)

This movement of transmutation, Blanchot comments, is infinitely linked to the "metamorphosis" that "not only steers us toward death but also infinitely transmutes death itself, making of it the infinite movement of dying and of the one who dies the infinitely dead, as if in death's intimacy it were for the latter a matter of dying always more [*mourir toujours plus*], immeasurably—of continuing inside death to make possible the movement of transformation which must not cease" (EL 205/157, trans. mod.). It is in this way—if one were able to overlook Blanchot's pathos-ridden language—that it may be possible for Nancy to read resurrection as the transmutation or transfiguration of death.

In "The Space of Death," part of his chapter on Rilke, Blanchot quotes from a letter the poet sent to his Polish translator, Witold Hulewicz.[8] In an aside Blanchot comments that the popularity of this letter shows the tendency of substituting poetry with ideas in prose. Blanchot begins this section by quoting from Rilke's letter: "Death is that side [*coté*] of life that is not turned toward us, nor do we shed light upon it" (EL 169/133). At the end of the passage quoted by Blanchot, Rilke writes, "There is neither a here [*en deçà*] nor a beyond" (169/133). Calling death "this region [*cette région*]," in the following subsection, entitled "The Other Side [*L'autre côté*]," Blanchot further expounds: "Thus it would be what essentially escapes us, a kind of transcendence, but of which we cannot say that it has value and reality, about which we know only this: "that we are 'turned away from it' [*nous en sommes 'détournés'*]" (EL 170/133). Why, one might ask, are we "turned away"? We are turned away because of "our limits." We are limited beings who when looking in front of us cannot see what is behind. "When we are here, it is on the condition of renouncing the over there [*là-bas*]" (171/133, trans. mod.). It is the limit that "makes of us beings who are turned away" (171/134, trans. mod.). It is important to realize that "the other side" is not a beyond and death is to be found on the same "side." What "the other side" is, is the *other* of this side as well as being an other *side*. What is also significant is that, in our relation to death, we are turned away from it.

Blanchot's reference to the other side, which Nancy makes no mention of, alludes to Heidegger's discussion of death in §49 of *Being and Time*. Opposing all metaphysics of death, which is interested in the beyond, that is, in the other side (*Jenseits*), Heidegger reminds the reader that our methodological point of departure should be from this side (*das Diesseits*), "the point from which we can start" (A 99/53). "The decision is taken *here*"—an "irrecusable" and "uncontested" decision, according to Derrida (99/53). As Derrida observes in *Aporias*: "It is on this side, on the side of Dasein and of its here, which is our here, that the oppositions here and over there, this side and beyond, can be distinguished" (98/52). For Heidegger, this is "immediately justified" because one cannot do otherwise. Derrida does not find this choice of starting point so obvious or so unassailable and notes the enormity of "what is *being decided*" here (100/55). Heidegger "neutralizes the interest for the other side of a beyond" opposed to this side (102/55). But, rather than placing the blame on Heidegger's decision to privilege "this side," Derrida says that it is the very definition of "the originary and underivable character of death, as well as the finitude of the temporality in which death is rooted" that forces Heidegger to decide from here, "from this side here" (102/55). Accordingly, this demonstrates the "primordiality of being-toward-death" leaving us with no choice but to start from this side" (102/55). As a mortal, Dasein can only decide from his mortality.

As we have seen, Nancy's depiction of death shares several features with Blanchot, who describes death as "the absolutely foreign" (EL 162/128). While the latter defines death as the absence and loss of all foundation, Nancy labels the abyss as the place that the dead one is already *in*. Dying, which Blanchot calls the transmutation of death or a purification of death by death, is to continue inside death, going deeper within it. In Nancy's view, it is in resurrection that death is extended—one goes deeper and deeper into death.

THE DECONSTRUCTION OF DEATH

Nancy's essay entitled "The Deconstruction of Christianity," his first foray into what he calls the "operation" or project of deconstruction, can be read as an almost boastful, self-satisfied, triumphant manifesto on Christianity.[9] Nancy wonders whether the "Jew-Greek" that Derrida refers to in his essay "Violence and Metaphysics" is not really "the Christian." It is in this essay that Nancy originally argues that the Christian or Christianity is "the very thing, the thing itself [*la chose même*]," to be thought

("DC" 504). Christianity is itself and by itself in a "state of overcoming [*dépassement*]," Nancy asserts. This "*self-overcoming* [autodépassement] is perhaps very profoundly proper to it; it is perhaps its most profound tradition" ("DC" 505). Since Christianity is inseparable from the West, then "*all* our thinking is through and through Christian" (506); hence, "the modern world is itself the becoming of Christianity" (507).

As Nancy puts it, he is being guided by "the motif of the essence of Christianity as opening: the opening of the self and the self as opening" ("DC" 508). He proceeds to say of deconstruction that it "belongs to a tradition, to *our* modern tradition" (511). Undoubtedly, Derrida must have bristled at this "our (*nous*)." (*Qui nous?*) It is also Nancy's contention that the "operation" of deconstruction is itself traversed through and through by Christianity (511). Thus, it must be said, he contends, that deconstruction "is itself Christian" and "the gesture of deconstruction" can be found only within Christianity (512). It is Christian because Christianity is, from its inception or "originally [*d'origine*]," deconstructive (512). Since deconstruction means "*démontrer*, to reveal, to show, to disassemble," then the deconstruction of Christianity would be an "operation of *désassemblage*, disassembling and dismantling, focusing on the origin or the sense of deconstruction (512). Nancy then goes on to provide his assessments of some of the other creeds of Christianity, such as the Gospel, the "good news," kerygma, evangelism, Christology, incarnation, faith, sin, and so on (513). In several texts devoted to the deconstruction of Christianity, collected in *La Déclosion*, he expands on the assessment expressed in his article "The Deconstruction of Christianity," presenting his views on numerous themes such as atheism, monotheism, the messiah, belief [*croyance*]—which is linked to the spectacular and marked out from faith [*foi*]—the miraculous, the extraordinary, sacrifice, the spectral, the dead one, time outside time, the abyss, nothing, the safe and the intact, death as a departure, and so on.

Derrida first refers to Nancy's project, still in its infancy, in *Le toucher, Jean-Luc Nancy* (2000), his tome celebrating the work of Nancy. He also discusses Nancy's work and alludes to his project in interviews, seminars as well as in his publications, many times without directly mentioning him. In *The Death Penalty* seminar, without naming Nancy, Derrida shows his resistance to the idea of talking about death as a genre. Toward the end of the ninth session of the seminar, Derrida summarizes his observations on "the subject of death, the question, what is death?" (DP1 323/237). He wonders whether it is necessary to think death first before thinking the death penalty as a question derived from it, as philosophy in its entire history has done, or should things be the other way around? In his evaluation of the relationship of philosophy as a discipline to death, he remarks that all philosophies of death presuppose a "pre-comprehension of the meaning of the word 'death'" (323/237) and place a reliance on "the alleged objective knowledge of what separates a state of death from a state of life" (324/238). This knowledge is based on "the supposed existence of an objectifiable instant that separates the living from the dying" (324/238). The "simple idea" of this sharp limit, he claims, organizes all these meditations on death, even that of a deconstruction of death, which he links to Heidegger as a predecessor to Nancy (324/238). Every calculation on the subject of death assumes "alleged access to this [so-called objective] knowledge," supposing "the possibility of calculating and mastering the instant of death" (324/239).

Derrida, however, does not find the deconstruction of death to be sufficient. It is not enough to deconstruct death because "death is not one" (DP1 328/241) and "death in the singular no longer exists" (327/241). The deconstruction of death is insufficient because such a deconstruction "must not serve, on the pretext of dissolving the unity or the identity or the gravity of death," to "banalize" or "relativize" the death penalty (344/253). It is not enough to deconstruct death, even if it is necessary, "in order to survive," "to assure one's own salvation" (344/254). It is not enough to deconstruct death because after the deconstruction of death, not only death but life will not come out unscathed. This deconstruction is a wish to master finitude, a wish to be indemnified, a desire to be immune and unscathed. However, what wishes to come out unscathed is auto-immune. In fact, Derrida remarks acidly, nothing will come out unscathed from the deconstruction of death.

(As an addendum to Nancy's previous writings on death, already mentioned, and echoing some of the sentiments already expressed in *Noli me tangere*, it may be helpful here to open a parenthesis on his use of "parting" and "departure." As part of the continuing series of talks called "Little Dialogues," given to an audience of children, Nancy presented a talk under the title of *Partir—le départ* (Leaving—departure), which was published in 2011.[10] Discussing the title given to the gathering, in his talk Nancy notes the occurrence of etymologically related words such as *partir, disparition, part, partage*, and *partition*. The words of this family, he explains, come from the Latin *pars* and *partire*, which means to divide, to separate. The latter, he adds, was the second meaning of *partir* in French, which is no longer in use. It is ourselves that we divide or share, Nancy glosses. He points out a connection to the word "somewhere [*quelque part*]," by saying that when "we die a part of us remains somewhere." It is "an area [*une partie*]," a place, where something of the dead one "remains" (Pa 14–15).

Contrary to the teaching of most religions, Nancy asserts, the dead do not go anywhere (Pa 27). They do not go to another place, site, or to another world. In fact, they go "nowhere [*nulle part*]" (27). "A part of those who are dead, in us, with us, remains somewhere" because those who remain "are all a part of those who have left" (28). It is "in this way [*sous cette forme*]" that we can keep them (28). Those who have died have not gone anywhere but "have left the world" (28). Yet "non-visible traces of their presence and their departure" exist everywhere (29). We ourselves know that we are "always about to leave [*en partance*]" and "we are human because we are *en partance*," outward bound, due to leave, about to leave (29–30).

Religious representations of what is beyond death seek to reassure us, but there can be no real representation of death (Pa 36). From the point of view of the dead one, she has not left because she does not exist elsewhere. She has simply died and disappeared—which is not necessarily departing (42). Nancy admits that we often say that dying is departing, but we are mistaken. For there to be a departure, there must be somewhere that we are going, and yet in the case of death this is not the case (42). We are always taking our leave, departing, departing for this nowhere, "entering into the movement of leave-taking [*entrer dans le mouvement de partance*]" (46). "We leave without return [*partir sans retour*]" and we never arrive (27). In an expression of what some may interpret as utter resignation or nihilistic despondency, he declares: "Death is nothing at all [*rien du tout*] (56). There is nothing to say about death, nothing to do" (56). I now close this parenthesis.)

Eternal Life

In his improvised remarks at the closing of an international conference devoted to Blanchot, held a month following his death in 2003, Nancy mistakenly invokes the notion of "universal life [*la vie universelle*] (*sic*), which he attributes to Spinoza. In his comments pronounced directly following Derrida's presentation, "Maurice Blanchot est mort," which discussed, among other things, the notion of death in Blanchot's writings, Nancy refers to a phrase, "joyous death, aleatory [*la mort joyeuse, aléatoire*]," taken from Blanchot's *The Infinite Conversation*.[11] This joy, a liberation from the necessity of death, Nancy explains, is nothing less than an alleviation (*allégement*), "a life alleviated from life [*une vie allegée de la vie*]," a relieving from life defined (as classical philosophy defined it) as self-relation or auto-affection ("FC" 629). This "alleviated life [*la vie allegée*]" does not exclude another life, Nancy states, but is secretly linked to "the universal life of Spinoza, perhaps even also that of Leibniz, [. . .] that of Spinoza which is not at all a life that excludes the death of individuals" (630). This life, Nancy further glosses, by no means excludes death, but "includes these deaths in it without sublating them" (630).

In response to an invitation to attend the International Documentary Film Festival in Marseille in 2005, Jean-Luc Nancy sends a letter to Jean-Pierre Rehm apologizing for not being able to be there in person. In this letter, Nancy provides an illuminating explanation of his debate with Derrida regarding the question of resurrection and eternal life.[12]

> The long exchange that Jacques and I had regarding "resurrection" [. . .] was, neither for him nor for me, a matter of a phantasmatic belief in the return of the dead. It was a matter of much more: of understanding what the eternity that Spinoza said we feel and experience as ours, means for us. Eternity, which is, the outside of time. Not what always endures but precisely what does not last at all. The vanishing instant in its disappearance—the inscribed trace in its very effacing [. . .]. The great thoughts of resurrection are never fantasies of bodies come back to life. They are precisely thoughts without image. What resurrects, what sets upright the stretched-out body on the earth and soon combines with it, is the absence of image.[13]

SPINOZA

Nancy's reference to Spinoza and eternity in the letter to Rehm is thought-provoking and worth detailed exploration. Even though "eternal life" is not considered as a concept that belongs to the philosophical tradition, it is a major tenet of Christian belief, which is centered on the resurrection of Jesus from the dead.[14] In the New Testament, "eternal life" may be defined as the blessed life freed from death or continued life after death.[15] The first biblical reference to eternal life is in Daniel 12: 1–2. It appears in the New Testament forty-three times. In 1 Corinthians Paul states that eternal life cannot be obtained without resurrection. In the Synoptic Gospels (Matthew, Mark, Luke) and the Pauline Letters, eternal life is a future experience, whereas in the Gospel of John eternal life also pertains to the present. It can be possessed "here and now" by those who have accepted Christ, passing "from death to life." We are given assurance of eternal life instead of being provided with a description of what it would entail.[16]

Rather than referring to the Bible, Nancy initially appeals to Spinoza for an elaboration of the notion of eternal life. Even though no explicit reference to "eternal life" can be found in Spinoza's texts,[17] the notion of "la vie éternelle" attributed to him has been widely discussed by a number of Spinoza's French interpreters.[18] The pervasiveness of the notion of "eternal life" in Catholic France may have served as an influence on the translations and interpretations of Spinoza.[19] According to one interpretation, the eternal life of the mind is the feeling and experience that we are eternal. This experience of eternity is to be distinguished from survival and immortality. In the view of another interpreter, eternal life, being the eternal idea by which God conceives the essence of our body, is described as the idea that we *are* eternal, not that we *have* eternal life.

A few examples from major interpretations of Spinoza should suffice to give us a sense of what Nancy may be referring to as eternal life. In 1893 Victor Delbos devoted a chapter of his *La problème morale dans la philosophie de Spinoza et dans l'histoire du spinozisme* to the notion of "La vie éternelle."[20] In chapter 9 Delbos writes that Spinoza's doctrine "profoundly transforms" Aristotle's "theory"—in which *nous* or pure understanding (*l'entendement pur*) is eternal—thus aspiring to affirm the eternal life of the individual (193). In each of us, Delbos writes at the end of his chapter, God reveals to himself and to us the "intimate union of infinite Being and our finite individuality that indissolubly constitutes our salvation and the Glory of God in eternal life" (199).

According to Ferdinand Alquié's introduction in *Le rationalisme de Spinoza*, Spinoza can be distinguished from all other Western philosophers such as Malebranche, Leibniz, Berkeley, Hume, and Kant, because by following Spinoza's doctrine one can attain "eternal life [*la vie éternelle*]" and beatitude (*beatitudo*).[21] In a brief commentary, Alquié writes, Spinoza takes up a very classically "religious" position at the same time as he vigorously refuses the idea of the existence of the soul after death.[22] At times, according to Alquié, Spinoza speaks of the endurance of the soul without relation to the body when he declares that once the body is destroyed, something of the soul remains (*remanet*) that is eternal: *Mens humana non potest cum corpore absolute destrui, sed eius aliquid remanet, quod aeternum est* (*Ethics* V, 23). Elsewhere, Alquié notes, Spinoza holds that eternal life is not the survival of the soul after the body, that eternity cannot be defined by time and the soul can only be said to endure if it envelops the body (183). Spinoza uses the word "existence" to designate the life of the soul without relation to time (V, Proposition 23, Scholium). An idea is necessarily given in God (*donner en Dieu, in Deo datur idea*) that expresses the essence of such and such a human body "under the species of eternity" (V, 22). But it does not follow, Alquié argues, that I am myself eternal. "This is why," he says frustratedly, "the Spinozist doctrine of eternity is so difficult to understand" (186).[23]

Marxist literary critic and student of Althusser Pierre Macherey, in his interpretation of Spinoza, *Introduction à L'Ethique: La cinquieme partie*, is of the view that Propositions 21–23 of Part V of the *Ethics* clear the way for the conditions of an eternal life of the mind (*âme*).[24] Having already stated in Definition 8 of Part I at the beginning of the *Ethics* that eternity "cannot be explained by duration or time [*per durationem au tempus explicari non potest*]," Spinoza reemphasizes in Part V that "eternity cannot be defined by time or have any relation to time [*nec aeternitas tempore definiri, nec ullam ad tempus relationem habere potest*]" (V, Proposition 23, Scholium).[25] What, then, allows the human mind to elude the conditions of time and duration? Spinoza introduces "duration of the mind without relation to the body [*mentis duration sine relatione ad corpus*]" in Proposition 20 and develops the idea of the eternity of the mind (*âme*) in Proposition 23. In the latter Proposition he states, "We do not attribute to the human mind [*âme*] any duration that could be defined by time" (119). In addition, he notes, "the human mind cannot be absolutely destroyed with the body, there remains something eternal in it [*sed ejus aliquid remanet quod aeternum est*]" (Proposition 23) (127). As Macherey explains, there remains "something eternal [*quelque chose d'éternel*] that concerns the essence of the mind [*qui touche à l'essence de l'âme*]" (*mens*), because its functioning has structurally no relation to the duration (*durée*) of the body (129). Thus, "we feel and experience that we are eternal [*Nous sentons et expérimentons que nous sommes éternels*; *sentimus experimurque nos aeternos esse*]" (V, Proposition 23, Scholium) (131).[26]

This is a genuine experience of eternity. The eternity to which the mind accedes via this experience, Macherey notes, is an actual eternity (132). Thus this "something eternal that remains" should not be interpreted in terms of survival or immortality, in other words, as indefinitely prolonged duration, but "concerns the proper life of the mind [*la vie propre de l'âme*]" (133). Eternity does not describe "a possible state," Macherey explains, but refers to "actual practice [*pratique effective*], here and now" (203). This allows Macherey to expand the Scholium of Proposition 23 in his commentary as: "we feel and experience (in the present) and we feel and experience (always in the present) eternal [*nous expérimentons et nous sentons (au présent) que nous sentons (toujours au présent) éternels*]" (203). The second half of Part V of the *Ethics* (Propositions 21–41) explains that "beatitude consists at first of seeing things *sub specie aeternitatis*, from the point of view [*au point de vue*] of eternity" (199). In agreement with Martial Gueroult, Macherey writes that *sub specie aeternitatis* should not consistently be translated in a restrictive sense as "sous une espèce d'éternité" (133).[27]

Alexandre Matheron devotes his article, "La vie éternelle et le corps selon Spinoza," to an explication of Proposition 39 of Part V, which he translates as "Qui a un corps apte à un très grand nombre de choses a un esprit dont la plus grande partie est éternelle" (27).[28] This could be rendered as: "He who has a body that is capable of a great number of things, has a mind [*esprit*] whose greatest part is eternal" (this translation would be closest to Edwin Curley's but is not exactly verbatim).[29] For Matheron, Proposition 23 displays that the eternal idea by which God conceives the essence of our body is nothing other than our mind (*esprit*) (35). There is "*something eternal* in our mind itself" (35). However, Matheron notes that this does not prove that "we have an *eternal life* [*une* vie éternelle]." This eternal idea refers only to "the idea that we *are*" and not "the ideas that we *have*" (35). If the Propositions that follow (24–28) show that we have eternal ideas, then, Matheron asks, where can we draw the notion of eternity from? Since eternity cannot be explained by duration, he suggests, this idea can only come to us from "the aspect of ourselves that *is* the eternal idea of our essence" (37). To conceive the essence of a thing from the aspect [*sous l'aspect*] of eternity [. . .] is to conceive the thing itself, as real, starting from [*à partir*] the essence of God" (38).

By Nancy's own admission, the inspiration for a thought of eternal life in his own writings comes from a reading of Spinoza, but the notion of "eternal life" that Nancy attributes to Spinoza hardly appears as such in Spinoza's own writings. The only reference to *vita aeterna* in the *Lexicon Spinozanum* is to the "Annotations" to the *Theological-Political Treatise*. Annotation 5 reads: "It is clear from Mark 10.21 that to win eternal life it is not enough to keep the commandments of the Old Testament" (262).[30] In referring to eternal life Nancy may very well be following the French tradition of commentary on Spinoza, which has employed this notion with roots in the New Testament.

However, eternal life may be a reference to the late biblical period notion of "everlasting life [*chayei olam*]" (Daniel 12: 1–2).[31] In his important book on belief in the afterlife in Jewish thought, Spinoza's thoughts on immortality and their possible influence on his *cherem* or expulsion, *Spinoza's Heresy: Immortality and the Jewish Mind*, Steven Nadler further explains that Daniel's conception of "the final judgment seems to involve immortality as the proper reward for the righteous" (48). Nadler comments that there exists no single Jewish doctrine or unified view of the immortality of the soul (44). The existence of contradictory viewpoints with no unanimity among Jewish doctrines, he believes, makes it impossible to find a unified view. There is no unambiguous reference in the Torah to an immortal soul.

It is worth bearing in mind that a metaphysical dualism between mind and body is absent in the Torah: the *nefesh* (sometimes translated as the "soul" or "spirit"), the whole individual being, thus the identity of the person, seems to be essentially bound up with the body (44). The existence of Sheol, apparently an underground resting place for the dead, is mentioned for the first time in Genesis 42: 36 (45). To be sure, the conception of Sheol changed over time as theological belief and external circumstances changed. The later Proverbs states that Sheol was populated with *rephaim*, "shrunken ones," usually translated as "shades" or "ghosts" (45). When a person dies, he or she simply dies and has become one of the *rephaim* in Sheol, there is no hope of a return to life: "The dead will not live again, those long in their graves [*rephaim*] will not rise" (Isaiah 26: 14) (47).

Even though the Apocrypha have "no authoritative status in the Jewish canon," they afford some insight regarding views about the afterlife (in particular, the apocalyptic works such as 1 Enoch) (49). As Nadler writes, "The doctrine of the resurrection of the body will become a standard," indeed a nearly unanimous nonnegotiable belief (53). In later Hellenistic Jewish thought, the soul or *nefesh* (or, in some cases, *ruach*) survives as a conscious being with memory and contemplates its eternal condition (55). Spinoza's views on the postmortem persistence of the soul (the word "immortality" occurs only once in the *Ethics*), for Nadler, can be considered as simply "the logical culmination of what the medievalists Maimonides and Gersonides claimed about the soul and immortality" (95).[32] It should be noted that it is impossible to avoid the inevitable historicist gestures that an account, such as the one previously given, entails.

Nancy's Eternal Life

Aside from the letter to Jean-Pierre Rehm and his remarks at the Blanchot conference, Nancy also appeals to a notion of "eternal life" on several other occasions. In a chapter in *Adoration*, the second volume of his "Deconstruction of Christianity" project, Nancy refers to "eternal life," this time without directly relating it to Spinoza or providing any textual references (Ad 37, 129, 131).[33] In his chapter "In the Midst of the World," he writes that the eternal life is "not indefinitely prolonged life, but life withdrawn from time [*soustraite au temps*] in the very course [*dans le cours même*] of time" (37/23). If the life of ancient mankind were a life measured by its time, Nancy observes, Christian life lives in time, "the outside of time [*vit dans le temps le dehors du temps*]" (37/23, trans. mod.). This characteristic has an "intimate relation" to what Nancy calls "adoration," which he characterizes as "a relation to the outside of time (to the pure instant, to the cessation of duration, to truth as interruption of sense)" (37). Thus, "Christianity," in Nancy's definition, is "life in the world outside the world [*la vie dans le monde hors du monde*]" (37). To have faith would be "to believe in a beyond of death [*croire à un au-delà de la mort*]" (128/88, trans. mod.). For Nancy, belief is to be understood as "a weak knowledge [*un savoir faible*], a sort of supposition," but faith is assurance, "trust in the strongest sense" in other words, a trust that can never be justified (128/88, trans. mod.).

In a letter to the filmmaker Hugo Santiago, published in the chapter "Complements, Supplements, Fragments" of *Adoration*, Nancy attempts to clarify topics that he first broached in *Noli me tangere*. In this reworking and rethinking of terms first invoked in Derrida's *The Beast and the Sovereign, 2* (to be discussed more fully in chapter 7), Nancy in his letter to Hugo Santiago uses his own, at times ontological, terminology while developing an interpretation of Spinoza.[34] He writes that there can be no representation of death: while the dead person can be represented, the "I" who was alive cannot be. In death, "I" disappear (Ad 128/88).

The other who is dead is unreachable. In his letter Nancy explains that he wanted to put forward a different sense of resurrection, a sense unlike the common definitions of *anastasis* as rebirth, regeneration, and a new beginning to life (Ad 129/89). Resurrection, for Nancy, is not a simple beginning anew in "another life," which would only be a projection of the life that has been lived by the dead one. He associates this projection with "hallucination," linking it with "the phantom and the apparition, etc." In contrast, Nancy describes *anastasis*, the "raising" of the body, as a "tipping up [*basculement*]" or a rising up of sense (129/89). He is searching for a "contact point [*un point de contact*]," Nancy says, between thought and sentiment or sensation, a kind of perception that he distinguishes from the "hallucinatory perception of the phantom" (130/90). As soon as I name the dead one, Nancy comments, I grant her another life, "the other of life [*l'autre de la vie*] in the world of the living, that is, the life of the dead [*la vie des morts*], and therefore still a life" (131/90, trans. mod.). Nancy's eternal life of the dead one is still a life, but a life outside time—"the life of the dead" (131/90). Nancy claims that he is "touching on a region" that "seems to me to be suspended between representation, thought, sentiment, and sensation"—a region he is unable to name (131/91). He goes on to explain: "This life of the dead is at the same time their non-life, the pure ceasing of their being as 'I,' *and* the life whose imprint is in us and continues living there with a life that cannot be reduced to representation" (131/91). This life is "what I know and feel of the presence, allure, and voice of the dead one [. . .] a living trace" of the other "incorporated in me" (131/91, trans. mod.).

At this point, Nancy finds himself "between pure thought and representation" (Ad 131/91). "I am in a sensibility" that is neither strictly speaking mine nor that of the dead one (who feels nothing any longer) but is "the sensibility of our meeting [*la sensibilité de notre rencontre*], of what we lived through together" (131/91, trans. mod). Perhaps one should not submit the dead entirely to death, Nancy asserts. Thinking *death* while also thinking *the dead*, Nancy believes that the dead are "well and truly in the world, in molecules or atoms caught up in different combinations" (132/91). They are linked together in what Freud called the id (*ça*) (132/91). Thus, the dead one "still lives such a life [*vit encore de cette vie*]" made up of all the relations that she was a part of (132/91, trans. mod.). For, Nancy believes, "*relationships* do not die [les *rapports* ne meurent *pas*] and, after all, what is "at stake" is "relation [*rapport*]" (132/92, trans. mod.). To think this, Nancy says, taking a page out of Derrida's book, is to be concerned with the phantasm.

Nancy's aim, he reveals, is to think "an utterly other site [*un lieu tout autre*]," a place completely other, perhaps the site alluded to by Derrida in his last words ("I love you and I am smiling at you wherever I might be [*d'où je suis*]") (Ad 133/92, trans. mod.). In Nancy's view, Derrida's phrase may have implied a "wherever" and "perhaps 'nowhere'" (133/92). A completely other place, but nonetheless a place. The dead may no longer be here, Nancy continues, but "we live, we survive 'our dead' [*nous survivons à 'nos morts*']" (133/92). This is nothing but, Nancy writes, with a nod to the use of "awaiting" and "approach" in Derrida's *Aporias*, "the continuation of relation, and it can be the awaiting [*l'attente*] and the approach [*l'approche*] of a happy encounter [*retrouvaille*] in an unheard-of place [*lieu inouï*] and according to an unknown mode of being [*un mode d'être inouï*]" (133/92). (Nancy's reliance on a notion of being, existence, or life for the manner in which the dead one appears cannot go unremarked here.) Is this the same thing as saying that the dead one "remains" or "survives"?

Juan Manuel Garrido's *Chances de la pensée: A partir de Jean-Luc Nancy* may provide a helpful explication of Nancy's views.[35] Garrido notes that Nancy's project of the deconstruction of Christianity is a philosophical investigation of the conceptuality and genealogy of Christianity in order to reinvent new philosophical possibilities (76). Using examples from three of Nancy's texts, "Psyche," "Sur le seuil," and *Noli me tangere*, Garrido argues that the "idea" of 'eternal life'"—but why is it an "idea"? Could any term be more classically metaphysical than an "idea" or a "concept"?—is found in the interpretation of Freud's dead Psyche, the dead body of the virgin in Caravaggio's painting or again in the interpretation of "the idea of resurrection."[36] " 'Eternal life,' " Garrido explains, "is nothing other than the mode of being or appearing of the one who is dead," in other words, of "the one who has ceased to be and to appear" (11). The dead one (*le mort*) is the one who has "ceased to be 'I [*je*]' [. . .] the one who has lost the self [*le soi*]" (40). Yet the dead one does not represent death as a general essence (40). "The other—the dead one—is not an other ego [*moi*], an other like me [*l'autre comme moi*], the living other, the other perceiving body or the existing other" (41). It "is neither living nor non-living, neither stone, nor animal, nor human [. . .]. It is to be found nowhere in this world or in another world" (41). In fact, it simply cannot "be found" (41). "The dead one quite simply 'is' not; that is, it does not *live*" (41). She is neither in a "here" nor in a "there." She comes to speak to us "from where she may be: outside every site, outside locality itself, outside space or time." It is only from some "over there [*là-bas*] that an *other* worthy of the name comes and can speak" (41). Perhaps, Garrido adds, "we are entrusted to the task of rethinking 'life' itself beyond being, in the figure of a dead one [*un mort*]" (42). "Not as being, appearance, comprehension or perception, presence or representation—but as the inaccessibility of the other" (42). This reference to life echoes Nancy's thinking in *Adoration* of "another life"—"the life of the dead" (Ad 131). "Of the dead one," Garrido continues, "we only have traces" (43). The dead one " 'is' in a time that will have already preceded the presence of all expression [*verbalité*], process, flux, or becoming" (43).

Nancy's marginal notes on Alfonso Cariolato's text, *"Le Geste de Dieu" Sur un lieu de l'*Ethique *de Spinoza*, a book based on a phrase from Spinoza ("God's gesture [*Dei nutu*]"), may substantiate Garrido's interpretation.[37] Nancy comments that the "body that feels eternal" is not 'never ending [*sempiternel*],' not of unlimited duration, and not immortal, but separated from duration [*separé de la durée*]."[38] "The dead one 'rises [*se redresse*]' against all that seeks to summon it into [*faire venir*] the flow of time—the flow of perception, meaning, care, project, history, future, living, speaking, being, the world" (43). It " 'stands upright [*se redresse*]' in the midst of the world against the world and outside the world. The 'life' of the dead one is being-outside-the-world [*être-dehors-le-monde*]" (43). Our life, however, cannot be eternal—it is "infinitely mortal" (44).

Toward the end of the chapter "Complements, Supplements, Fragments," Nancy states that he is searching for "what passes between the two regimes" of thought and sentiment, his remarks being "concerned with affect and not the concept" (Ad 133/92). For, what he is searching for is affect, and indeed, "affect is relation" (133/92). In thinking about the dead one we are led to think—with a thinking that is "also poetic"—and with a sensibility that feels "the continuation of relation," "the unheard-of place where my unheard-of being, which will no longer be 'mine,' *will be back among* 'its own' [retrouvera *'les siens'*]" (134/93). Nancy is fully aware that everything we feel is felt in time whereas affect is, by definition, related to life and can be interrupted by death. Thus, it seems, there can be no affect as far as the dead are concerned. Yet we are affected, Nancy claims, just where affect should not be possible. Nancy also admits that "all of this, I know and I say it again, is untenable for both thinking and sensibility" (136/95). Moreover, Nancy is also attempting to think a conduct that exceeds thinking, a thinking that is sensibility. We conduct ourselves [*nous tenons*] [. . .] in a *conduct* [*une* tenue] that exceeds knowledge, wisdom, and consciousness" (137/95).

We have seen that Nancy affirms the Spinozist reading of eternity as eluding the conditions of time and duration. Eternal life, he maintains, is what belongs to the dead: the dead one is safe from any harm and, as dead, has eternal life. And by extension, the resurrected are also eternal (since, according to Nancy, we all resurrect). Salvation is there for the dead one who belongs to a time outside time—the time of the dead. This time is also, Nancy contends, the time of Christian life in the present and the future. As he points out, Christianity is "a relation with the outside of time," "the life in the world outside of the world," in the same way that eternal life is (Ad 37/23). In contrast, Juan Manuel Garrido in his provocative book reserves eternal life only for the dead one. Eternal life—the mode of appearing of the dead one—allows us to rethink life in the figure of the dead one, the inaccessible other.

Would it be a strange hypothesis to suggest that Nancy's notion of "eternal life," his remarks in the "Complements, Supplements, Fragments" chapter of *Adoration*, and other related texts, are a reading of Derrida's seminar *The Beast and the Sovereign, 2*? Nancy is not thinking a new life but life anew, life withdrawn from time. Outstretched in an almost unthinkable relation to the outside of time, Nancy is exploring the other of life—the life of the dead. Finding himself in an unnamable region between thought and sensation, a site or "place" akin to the id, in which there is a relationship between atoms and molecules linked together, Nancy's thought is a probing of what it means to believe in a beyond of death. To assess Nancy's "poetic" thinking, I will turn in the final chapter to a more detailed examination of Derrida's thoughts in *The Beast and the Sovereign, 2*, about what he labels the phantasm of "dying alive."

Since "I have no certain knowledge whether or not there can be spirit, spectral survival [la survie spectrale] in the living dead [la mort-vivant] or after death" then, I will always be telling myself a story, I will be making as if "and yielding to the phantasm according to which all is not over and in which moreover so-called death does not consist in an end" (BSII 236–237/163–164).

Survivance

5

The Desire for Survival?

> ... *le fantôme n'étant ni mort ni vivant, ou bien mort-vivant mais sur-vivant* ...
>
> —Jacques Derrida, "De l'écrit à la parole"

The provocation that has presented itself as "the desire for *survival*" has garnered much critical attention as of late. Foregrounding a notion of desire in Derrida's work, Martin Hägglund's *Radical Atheism* has presented his work as describing, representing, or calling for a "desire for survival."[1] Yet it needs to be asked whether what Derrida calls survival, or *survivance* as he prefers to refer to it in his later work, is something that can be *desired*. Is not surviving, or survivance, in addition to referring to the finitude of a mortal being also a structural feature of, for example, writing, the date, and the name? In *Radical Atheism* Hägglund asserts, "Derrida himself did not provide a systematic account of his notion of desire, and it has remained unexplored by his commentators, but I will argue that it is altogether crucial for his thinking" (32). Embarking upon "a sustained attempt to reassess the entire trajectory of Derrida's work"—no small feat—in *Radical Atheism*, Hägglund refutes a notion, which Derrida never endorsed or promulgated, of "an ethical or religious 'turn'" in his thinking" (1). Using as his pivot the notion of desire, Hägglund expresses a need for a systematic account in order to provide an inventory of what is and what is not desirable.[2] Since what has traditionally been designated as desirable, the absolute being of God or the immutability of the soul, fails to meet Hägglund's criteria, he provides an alternative:

"everything that can be desired is mortal in its essence" (111). Life, on his account, is "essentially mortal, which means that there can be no instance" that is immortal, as immortality is equated with an existence uncontaminated by time (8).[3]

According to Hägglund, what is desired is in its essence finite, which seems to designate the opposite of infinite and is thus something that terminates, ends, or dies. Employing a Lacanian definition of desire inspired by Plato, Hägglund takes desire to be an attempt to attain fullness. In the account of desire (*epithumia*) in the *Symposium* Socrates declares that the desiring subject "desires what it does not have" (Griffith) or "lacks [*endeés*]" (Lamb) (200b) and wants "to continue to possess in the future what he possesses now" (Griffith) (200d).[4] As Diotima tells Socrates, what is mortal tries to be everlasting and immortal. This "love [*eros*]" with a view to "immortality [*athanasias*]," also translated as "desire for immortality" (Griffith), is how a mortal being partakes of (Lamb), or tastes (*metexei*) (Griffith), immortality (208b). For Lacan, the lack of fullness—the fact that desire cannot be fulfilled—is what gives rise to desire. What is ultimately desired, Hägglund reasons, is the desire for survival and not the desire for immortality. Thus the desire to survive is the desire to live on as a mortal being—hence Hägglund's relentless refutation and refusal of immortality and insistence in favor of a "radical atheism."

Hägglund approaches his reading of Derrida, which he opposes to those providing a "theological account" of Derrida's work, from the perspective of the problem of atheism.[5] Taking issue with traditional atheism in his crusading fervor and zealous denial of the existence of God and immortality, Hägglund aims to strongly rebuke those critics who write about Derrida from a "religious framework." Stating that there is nothing beyond mortality and that life is "essentially mortal" (an oft-repeated phrase), Hägglund argues that "the so-called desire for immortality," displays an "internal contradiction" with a desire that "precedes it and contradicts it from within" (1). In fact, the desire for immortality disguises "a desire for survival" (1).

In Hägglund's view, the notion of survival defines life as "*essentially mortal*" (48) and inherently divided by time (33). He defines "to survive" as "to remain after a past that is no longer and to keep the memory of this past for a future that is not yet" (1). (Isn't this a very classical and conventional definition of "to survive"? Would one need to appeal to Derrida to come up with such a definition?) He argues hyperbolically—

although one cannot but think here of the tone of an advertising slogan or a religious exhortation—that "every moment of life is a matter of survival" (1). Hägglund's notion of "survival" is, at best, a Nietzschean affirmation of mortal being, rejecting the desire for anything that exceeds or transcends finite human life. Life, for Hägglund, is predicated on the idea that it may come to an end at any moment (pathos or panic?). The fact of living should then be an affirmation of finitude. It is hard to see how this account differs from classical existentialism, peddled for decades in American philosophy departments urging young minds to take up the virtues of *carpe diem*. Why would we need Derrida to tell us what Nietzsche, Heidegger, Sartre, and others seem to have told us already—unless Derrida is saying something else entirely?

Presenting a purely formal account of Derrida's work shorn of subtlety, elegance, and complexity, Hägglund, like a good analytic philosopher, points out inconsistencies, incoherences, fallacies, and logical contradictions in Derrida's readers and interpreters, finding "untenability" and incompatibility everywhere. Providing a systematic account of Derrida's notion of desire, an account that Derrida himself did not provide, and developing arguments in directions deemed by Hägglund as "crucial" for Derrida's thinking (82), Hägglund seeks to explicate "the logic of deconstruction" (as if there is such a thing, as if deconstruction is simply a logic, and as if a younger generation, who may have never heard of Gasché and Bennington, who meticulously laid out the logical intricacies and [infra]structural aspects of Derrida's thought, is in need of being instructed about its logical operations). Hägglund, who seems to mistake deconstruction's task as simply providing systematic accounts, treats deconstruction, according to Michael Naas, as "a discourse of ontology or epistemology," restricting deconstruction to merely ontological claims.[6]

Displaying a dogged attachment to mortal life and a tenacious opposition to all that is immortal or resembles it, Hägglund is adamant that as human beings we live on by remaining "subjected to temporal finitude" (2). His privileging of temporality can be discerned throughout *Radical Atheism*: for Hägglund, everything in Derrida seems to follow from "the constitution of time" (In what sense of *follow*? Come after? Logically proceed from? And why just time and not space as well?[7] In what sense does "the structure of the trace *follow* from the constitution of time"? [1]). Hägglund refers to "the trace structure of time" (9), but why is Derrida said to have had an insight simply into "the trace structure" of *time*? Nothing is exempt from "temporal finitude," Hägglund argues (2–3), yet all he seems to understand by "the time of mortal life" is the fact that we are "finite," that is, that we die (2). This is how we are to understand the statement that immortality would annihilate the time of mortal life.[8]

What is surprising is that in none of Hägglund's work, whether in *Radical Atheism* (2008) or in subsequently published texts, is there a mention of the notion of "radical atheism" in Derrida's own work.[9] In "Penser ce qui vient," a talk initially given at the Sorbonne in 1994 following the publication of *Specters of Marx* and published a year before Hägglund's book, during the course of thinking about the event and what comes, Derrida raises the notion of "radical atheism" when he asks himself whether he is an atheist or a radical atheist.[10] Derrida broaches the topic of an atheism, not as a personal conviction that can or cannot be shared, but an atheism or a secularism (*laïcité*) or some kind of "structural agnosticism" that characterizes a priori every relation to what comes and who comes (Pcq 21). Derrida's atheism differs from Hägglund's, whose atheism is fervently in opposition to religiosity or any belief that bears a resemblance to it. For Derrida, as he explains in "Penser ce qui vient," to think the future is to be able to be an atheist. However, even if his atheism is a "structural" atheism, Derrida wonders whether he is not a "singular" atheist "who remembers God and who loves to remember God" (21). In his brief remarks Derrida states that he would like to think further about "a hypermnesic atheism" that brings together the messianic promise, revolutionary spirit, the spirit of justice, and emancipation. For, the concept and thinking of the political is, for Derrida, inseparable from this singular atheism (23).

In what follows, I would like to pursue several elements or themes of Hägglund's discourse of "radical atheism"—a discourse that has gained in popularity and purportedly represents the new way of reading Derrida—namely, desire, finitude, immortality, and survival, in order to examine in more detail his interpretation of Derrida's work.

Desire

There are many instances where the word "desire [*désir*]" appears in Derrida's texts, but can it be said that desire as such is an "operative concept" in Derrida's work, as it is, for example, in Lacan? Admittedly, there is no such thing as a "Derridean term," a term that exclusively belongs to his discourse, as Derrida has revisited certain terms that he originally had put into question ("experience," would be an example). However, Derrida has resisted returning to certain sedimented concepts belonging to the history of metaphysics in a way that Jean-Luc Nancy has not had the compunction to do.

The usage of the term "desire," which commonly denotes a wish, a want, or an inclination for what is beneficial, useful, and so on, is very complex in Derrida's writings and does not lend itself to easy summarizing. When asked about the role of desire in his thought, he disclosed:

> What bothers me with the use of the word "desire," and I have often tried to avoid it, is that where the word appears in writers such as Lacan, and well before him too, it tends to be defined as part of the structure of the subject: of the soul, the psychological or the psychoanalytic subject [. . .]. My concern was to develop a differance whereby desire was not seen as a matter of consciousness. If there is desire, it is *because* there is difference. This psychologism, this anthropologism bothered me.[11]

In another interview, entitled "Dialanguages" in *Points* . . . , Derrida comes close to providing a description of desire when he tells his interviewer, Anne Berger, "I rarely speak of loss, just as I rarely speak of lack, because these are words that belong to the code of negativity, which is not mine [. . .]. I don't believe desire has an essential relation to lack. I believe desire is affirmation."[12] In *Given Time* Derrida comments further on the distinction between desire and need while considering Aristotle's discussion in *Politics* of chrematistics and economy, remarking on "the supposed finiteness of need and the presumed infinity of desire" (GT 200/158). In the same text, responding to the question "Why desire [*désirer*] the gift?"(19/8), he asserts that this would be possible only according to "the measureless measure" of the impossible, as the gift is another name for the impossible (45/29).

In his early writings, Derrida writes about "philosophical desire"— philosophy's desire (M 321/269) or the desire of metaphysics: references abound to the desire (*désir*) of logocentrism and the metaphysics of presence for the transcendental signified (OG 71/49), the desire (*désir*) or wish to believe in the remaining of the thing itself (VP 117/89, new trans.), the suspicion of writing as a "perfectly coherent desire [*désir*]" of ethnocentrism (OG 161/110), and to the desire of and for reason (*la raison du désir et le désir de la raison*) (in Kant) (TP 45/38). One can also find references to metaphysical desires that Derrida puts into question, such as "the desire for the origin [*le désir d'origine*]" (OG 345/243), the desire (*désir*) for presence (OG 206/143), the desire (*désir*) for the center (411/280), the desire (*désir*) for a "centered structure" (WD 410/279), "desire of the proper [*un désir du propre*]"(GT 36/22), "the desire to exclude the stranger [*le désir d'exclure l'étranger*]" (SM 273/172), as well as the "desire for the archive [*désir d'archive*]" (AF 38/19) and the "archive's desire [*le désir ou le mal d'archive*]" (AF 52/19). Other times, the appearance of the word refers to a concept in a thinker's writings, for example, the notion of desire in the work of Hegel (*Glas* 23a, 33a), Nietzsche (Ep 46–48), Levinas (WD 147/xx), or to Fukuyama's usage of Hegelian desire (SM). *Sauf le nom* speaks of "the desire of God [*le désir de Dieu*]" (ON 103/80), the desert as "the proper place" of *desire* [*le propre lieu du* désir] (103/80), and characterizes "God as the other name of desire [*Dieu comme l'autre nom du désir*]" (103/80). In *The Beast and the Sovereign, 1*, Derrida treats extensively the notion of desire in the writings of several authors: Lacan, Deleuze, Flaubert, Valéry, and D. H. Lawrence. On other occasions, desire is accompanied by another term in a pair, as in the desire and the disorder of the archive (*le désir ou le trouble d'archive*) in *Mal d'Archive* (AF 128/81), or the terror and desire of being buried alive in *The Beast and the Sovereign, 2*. It seems one would be hard-pressed to find many places where Derrida uses the term for his "own" purposes.

While the references in the earlier texts cast a suspicious eye on the notion of desire, in his later works Derrida is more likely to use the term favorably. For example, in *Psyché: Invention de l'autre* he comments on the desire for invention (Psy 34–35); in *Donner le temps* he writes of the desire to think and to give the impossible (GT 52/35), in "Faith and Knowledge" he writes of "an invincible desire for justice" (FK 31/18); in *Echographies*, he refers to what he calls "exappropriation," where "it is necessary" that I try to make what I desire mine, while it remains other enough for me to desire it (E 125/111); in *Sauf le nom* he writes of the desire of God (*désir de Dieu*), double genitive (ON 18–20/37) and the desire of the desert ("the desert as the other name, if not the proper place, of *desire*") (ON 103/80); and in *The Death Penalty* seminar he notes that the death sentence is desired "as desire itself" (DP1 339/249). It would be safe to say that the way desire functions in these Derridean texts does not adhere to any traditional concept of this term, whether Platonic or psychoanalytic, and would have to be assessed contextually and carefully read in relation to a notion of need.

Finitude

Throughout his early writings, from an appraisal of "originary" or "primordial" finitude in Husserl in *The Problem of Genesis in Husserl's Philosophy* (1953–194) (PG 171n91/98n91, 257n8/163n8) and *Introduction to Husserl's Origin of Geometry* (1962) (OrG 108/105–106; 151n1/138fn164) to an investigation of the thinking of Levinas, Freud, Husserl, and Heidegger in various essays in *Writing and Difference*, Derrida engaged with the thought of finitude. Yet, given what Rodolphe Gasché in *The Tain of the Mirror* refers to as "Derrida's persistent critique of the notion of finitude," Derrida cannot simply be branded as a thinker of finitude since the latter has meaning only within the philosophy of presence.[13] In fact, the very idea of finitude is derived from the movement of supplementarity, Derrida tells us in the essay "Freud and the Scene of Writing" in *Writing and Difference* (WD 337/228). In *Of Grammatology* he describes *différance* as "something other than finitude" (OG 99/68) and in *Voice and Phenomenon*, published the same year, he informs us that we cannot think *différance* within the opposition of the finite and the infinite (VP 114/87). As late as *Le Toucher, Jean-Luc Nancy* (2000), a voice in Derrida's text half-jokingly, some would say sarcastically, refers to Nancy's notion of touching or *le toucher* as simply a thought of finitude: "Touching is finitude, period [*Le toucher, c'est la finitude, un point c'est tout*]" (LT 160).

Thus Derrida's thinking of *différance* is not simply a thinking of finitude, whether radical or not, whether temporal or not, but a thinking together of the finite and the infinite. In "Derridabase" Geoffrey Bennington refers to "the inextricable complication of the finite and the infinite that *différance* gives us to think" while admitting that "the terms 'finite' and 'infinite' function in a disturbing way in Derrida's texts."[14] Bennington, commenting on the notoriously difficult and misunderstood phrase (what he also refers to as "a line" or "a slogan, a motto, a maxim, a sentence, even perhaps a witticism" [75]) "infinite *différance* is finite" from *Voice and Phenomenon* (VP 114/87), observes in *Not Half No End* that the infinite and the finite are "wrapped in a paradoxical relation."[15] This indicates that the thinking of the infinite and the finite cannot be simply reduced to oppositions and that their complex and intricate relation would have to be carefully unfolded and explained.

Granted, Hägglund may be making efforts in this direction by describing *différance* as a thought of "infinite finitude" (220fn14). Yet this notion, which is insufficiently developed, combined with his vociferous defense of and emphasis on finitude—however radical—still places the *stress* on a certain notion of finitude. Perhaps Hägglund's inspiration comes from Derrida's tangential question in "Violence and Metaphysics" when he asks, "Can one think 'spurious infinity' [*le "faux-infini"*] as such (*time, in a word*)"? (ED 176/120, my emphasis). Hägglund appeals to "Violence and Metaphysics" to explain the difference between spurious and positive infinity and to show how *différance* is a form of nontotalization that contests a notion of positive infinity, as the latter reduces or "sublimates" the trace. Contrary to the Hegelian true or genuine infinity (*Unendlichkeit*), which is an all-embracing totality, Derrida's thinking of infinity is non-Hegelian. Even though Derrida's thinking of the trace, the text, and the infinite substitution of quasi-transcendental terms or nonconcepts have been compared to a form of infinity, Derrida's infinite is not any form of endlessness.

Here it would be worth briefly referring to some of the central historical sources of the relation between finitude and infinity. The thought of what has been called "positive infinity," according to Rodolphe Gasché, begins with Plato, culminating via Spinoza in Hegel's theology of the absolute concept as logos.[16] Spinoza rejected the conception of the infinite that represents it as an amount or series that is not completed, while Hegel also argued against spurious infinity for a genuine notion of infinity. For Hegel, the true or genuine infinite, associated with reason, is unconditioned and self-contained whereas the bad infinite, associated with the understanding, is the merely endless. Spurious infinity (*das schlechte Unendliche*), "the indefinite, a *negative* form of infinity," associated with an infinitist metaphysics, is only another form of the finite (ED 175/119). True infinity includes itself and its other. As he writes in the *Science of Logic*, true infinity must be an infinite that "embraces both itself and finitude—and is therefore the infinite in a different sense from that which the finite regarded as separated and set apart from the infinite."[17]

It is true that, for Heidegger, finitude (*Endlichkeit*) is temporal finitude. Neither infinite nor immortal, Dasein exists as finite, exposed to its end. Dasein does not have an end (*Ende*), but "exists finitely" (SZ 378/329).[18] As *Being and Time* demonstrates "primordial time is finite"

(379/331), while infinite time is derived or secondary. Primordiality, then, is not infinity. It is in his reading of Kant in *Kant and the Problem of Metaphysics* that Heidegger demonstrates that man is finite.[19] Finitude is the source of the understanding of Being and of all "infinity."[20] Furthermore, from *The Concept of Time* (1924) to "Time and Being" (1962) Heidegger distinguishes the thinking of time from the thinking of eternity. In contrast to the theological problematic of eternity, to think time is not to think eternity. The finitude of Dasein does not mean that it will die one day, but that it exists as dying. Finitude is connected to the limit, but for Heidegger the limit is not that at which something stops but that from which something begins. An echo of Heidegger's emphasis on finitude as temporal may be found in Hägglund's stance. According to Hägglund's reading of Derrida, with mortality comes temporal finitude, which initiates the desire for "mortal survival." Thus, the "radical atheist" is driven by the desire for mortal survival.

Immortality

Radical Atheism and subsequent publications set up an opposition between mortality and immortality, in which "the desire for immortality" is contrasted with the mortal condition, thoroughly and unapologetically lived in time. What causes Hägglund's ire and draws his criticism is a conception of immortality, which he associates with religiously inclined interpreters of Derrida, as perfect and indivisible, not situated in time and having no relation to an outside. In contrast, Derrida is portrayed as espousing a thinking of radical finitude. So caught up is Hägglund in opposing or fighting those he sees as conservative religious advocates that he falls back on traditional conceptions of immortality and eternity in the history of Western thought as discrete concepts and neglects to consider how mortality and immortality have been treated in Derrida's own work. Not only is there no clear-cut opposition or demarcation in Derrida's writings between immortality and mortality, as Hägglund would like to have it, but also Derrida's is a thought of the strange, paradoxical imbrication of mortality and immortality. Immortality is not a state reserved for the deathless but rather it is only the dead who become immortal.

However, before turning to his treatment of immortality, it would be helpful to very briefly see how immortality has been treated in the Western tradition. It has been shown by a number of scholars that as early as Heraclitus, mortality and immortality were not considered to be rigorously separated or demarcated from each other. Marcel Conche in his commentary on Heraclitus's fragment 162 argues that, for Heraclitus, "the mortals [*thnetoi*]" and "the immortals [*athanatoi*]" are not treated in separation from or in opposition to each other. In fact, immortality is thought by Heraclitus *in relation* to mortality.[21] There is an undoubted affinity between this fragment and certain mystic doctrines associated with the Orphic or Pythagorean tradition, indications of which may also be found in Empedocles's *Katharmoi* or "Purifications." From Homeric survival where the name and the renown of heroes who had shown valor in battle would be remembered and memorialized, Pericles's funeral oration bestowing immortality on patriots, the Pindaric *threnos* or lament for the dead and its related eschatology, to the Empedoclean *daimon* and the thought of the preexistence of the soul and its transmigration into other beings, and the Orphic and Pythagorean beliefs about asceticism and inner life, notions of immortality in Greek thought are inseparable from the development of a notion of the *psuchē* or the soul. The Platonic notion, where the soul constitutes one's real being in the interior recesses of each individual, is a late development in Greek thinking. For Plato, the *psuchē* is immortal, permanent, and unchanging, detaching itself from the body at death, while the living body is considered to be insubstantial and illusory. It is not until later that the pagan concept of immortality becomes contaminated by the Christian idea of resurrection.

Perhaps the notion of immortality in the Western tradition would best be considered in the context of survival, as a form of survival, as Derrida once did in *Aporias* (1993) when he referred to "the theme of immortality like that of any form of survival [*survie*] or return [*revenance*]" (A 103/55–56). While considering Heidegger's account of Dasein's relation to death and assessing the relationship between mortality and immortality in *Aporias*, Derrida writes that Dasein remains immortal, in other words, "without end [*sans fin*]," in the sense of *verenden*, and imperishable in its originary being-to-death. As Dasein, I do not end, I never end (76/40–41). In fact, Derrida will write later on, underscoring the inextricable relationship between mortality and immortality and the necessity of not thinking them in opposition to each other, "only a living-to-death can think, desire, project, indeed 'live' immortality *as such*" (102/55). He adds that in fact one cannot "think being-to-death without starting from immortality" (103/55). More importantly for a consideration of Hägglund's work, Derrida emphasizes that "the theme of immortality like that of any form of survival or *revenance* . . . is *not opposed to being-toward-death, it does not contradict it*, it is not symmetrical with it, because it is conditioned by being-toward-death and confirms it at every moment" (103/55–56, my emphasis).

Dead—Immortal

In order to further examine Derrida's thinking of immortality and its complicated relation to mortality, I would like to turn to one of his texts, *Demeure—Maurice Blanchot*, in which he pursues a probing, intricate reading of what he names "immortality *as death*" (D 89/69, author's emphasis). In the midst of a meticulous and painstakingly close analysis of Blanchot's *L'instant de ma mort*, the "auto-biographical" account of the narrator's close call with death, in *Demeure*, Derrida refers to a stark phrase, what he calls a "sentence without sentence [*phrase sans phrase*]": "Dead—Immortal [*Mort—immortel*]" (86/67). Two words held together and separated by a *tiret long*, "a sole line [*un seul trait*]" of "union and separation, a disjunctive link [*liaison disjoignante*]" spanned by an abyss (86/67). In what follows I would like to comment on Derrida's description of this phrase and suggest that it can be used as an example of how he treats the question of immortality. Even though it is embedded in a text devoted to a close reading of a narrative, one could argue that Derrida generalizes this notion, as he often does when it comes to something that appears to be absolutely singular (like one's own language in *Monolingualism of the Other*, for example), to provide an account of "immortality *as death*" (my emphasis). It will become clear that Derrida does not ever believe in a clear opposition between immortality and mortality or finitude, and his reading of mortality and immortality does not conform to any traditional definition.

Blanchot's text *L'instant de ma mort* ostensibly consists of an account provided by the narrator about a witness, who may be the narrator, involved in certain events leading to the experience of being almost executed. Even though the reader may wish to assume that the text is the account of the narrator-witness—and much of the structure of the text seems to lead one to believe this—it is important to note that, as Derrida writes, there is a "null and uncrossable" distance between the one who says "I" and the "I" of the young man of whom he speaks and who is himself (D 84/65). In other words, the reader must not forget that not only does a distance separate the narrator from the witness and from the signatory of the text but that, more significantly, the aim of Derrida's text is to show that there is "an essential compossibility" between testimony and fiction" (49/42).[22]

I would like to focus my attention on a couple of passages in this notoriously elliptical narrative in which the young man, about whom the narrator writes, and the female members of his family are forced by the invading troops to leave their home, preparing to face a firing squad. As the young man pleads to have the members of his family, all female, be spared, he ends the sentence mentioning their long, slow procession suggesting that death had already taken place, that it had already happened. Death has already arrived because it is "inescapable" (D 79/62–63). It is an experience from which one is not "resuscitated . . . even if one survives it" (79/63). For "one can only survive [this death] without surviving it" (80/63). Yet this survival should not be mistaken for a resurrection. In Derrida's view, the entire scene mimics and displaces the Passion, the Resurrection, and absolute knowledge. There can be no knowledge, for in "the life without life of this survivance" all knowledge would tremble (80/63).

Blanchot then makes a reference to "the encounter of death with death," perhaps the encounter between what has already arrived and what is going to come (D 82/64). The two deaths meet, a death that is "both virtual and real," at the tip of the "instant" (82/64). Death "has come to pass insofar as it comes; it has come as soon as it is going to come" (82–83/65). Death thereby "encounters *itself*" in this "arrival of death at itself" (83/65). This death that never arrives and never happens to me, Blanchot observes, is the event of an "unexperienced experience [*expérience inéprouvée*]" (quoted in D 83/65).

Not only is death not an event that can be experienced but also one death cannot replace the other: the one who says "I" cannot take the place of the young man he has been, substitute or speak for him or relive what has been lived, and consequently is not capable of describing this very "odd experience" or what he felt at that moment. Nothing but death separates the two "egological identities" (D 85/66). The young man who is "offered unto death" is described as "Dead—Immortal" (86/67).

Derrida glosses the state of the young man as: "Dead and yet [*et cependant*] immortal, dead because [*parce qu'*] immortal, dead insofar as [*en tant qu'*] immortal (an immortal does not live), immortal from the moment that [*dès lors que*] and insofar as [*en tant que*] dead, although and for as long as [*tandis que et aussi longtemps que*] dead; because once dead one no longer dies . . . one has become immortal" (D 86/67). This is because, as Derrida explains a little further on, "an immortal is someone who is dead [*c'est un mort*]," for only "someone who is dead can be immortal" (86/67). What has happened to him is "immortality, with death and as death at the same instant" (86/67). The immortals are dead, but this immortality, Derrida explains, is "not a Platonic or Christian immortality in the moment of death or of the Passion when the soul finally gathers together as it leaves the body, having already been at work there in philosophy according to the *epimeleia tou thanatou* of a pre-Christian *Phaedo*" (86–87/67). Rather, it is in the instant of death, in death, that "immortality yields to [*se livre*] an 'unexperienced experience'" (87/67). Death arrives "where one is not yet dead in order to be already dead, at the same instant" (86/67–68). At the same instant, I am dead *and* not dead. "I am immortal because I am dead: death can no longer happen to me" (87/68).

Blanchot designates this experience as "the happiness of not being immortal or eternal" (quoted in D 89/69). Even though "dead—immortal" may appear to be the reverse of the preceding description, it does not, Derrida notes, in the least signify eternity (89/69). The condition that Derrida describes in *Demeure—Maurice Blanchot*—that of one who is dead and yet immortal, dead because immortal, and dead insofar as immortal—is far from designating what has been understood as immortality in the Western tradition. "The immortality of death is anything save the eternity of the present" (89/69).[23] For what Derrida designates as "abidance [*demeurance*]" "does not *remain* [*reste*] like the permanence of an eternity" but rather "is time itself" (89/69). Not timelessness or eternity of the present, but the time of an interminable lapse (*laps*) or interval. Not an ongoing or perduring state of timelessness, abidance (*demeurance*) would be an awaiting, a waiting for, a withstanding, an enduring, a bearing patiently. To abide somewhere is to sojourn or to continue in a place. What Derrida draws out of Blanchot's text is what he describes as a "non-philosophical and non-religious experience of immortality as death [*l'immortalité comme mort*]" (89/69). This experience "gives [*donne*] . . . the happiness, this time" of being neither immortal nor eternal (89/69). In "the immortality of death," there is "a bond without bond, the disjointing [*désajointement*], the disadjusting [*désajustement*] of a social bond [with other mortals] that binds only . . . to death, and on condition of death" (89–90/69).

Returning to the narrative of *The Instant of My Death* we find that "at that instant," death happened to the young man. But death had already taken place. The moment that the young man had begun to wait for "the final order" of "Fire," he had left the world, "dying before dying, not for another world, but for a non-world beyond life, not for a transcendent beyond or the beyond that religions and metaphysics tell us about, but for a here-below without world [*ici-bas sans monde*], for a beyond here-below [*un au-delà ici-bas*], a without-world [*un sans-monde*] from which he who is already dead already returns [*déjà revient*], like a ghost [*comme un revenant*]" (D 91/70–71). Like a ghost that returns.

The young man who has left the world for a non-world is not beyond this world or transcendent to it. Far from it. He is without world, in this non-world here-below. His being without world signifies that he is already dead. The dead one is not elsewhere but here-below. Rather than a transcendent beyond, the beyond here-below is a beyond here from which the already dead returns. Survival or *survivance*, then, is a ghostly returning, *revenance*.

The reference to immortality as death in *Demeure—Maurice Blanchot* hearkens back to Blanchot's ruminations on mortality and immortality in "Literature and the Right to Death," which are taken up again by Derrida in *The Death Penalty, 1*, seminar of 1999–2000. In the fourth session of that seminar, while discussing the writer's role and literature's relation to revolution, Derrida sheds further light on the notion of death as the impossibility of dying or on sur-viving as dying by citing Blanchot's famous phrase from "Literature and the Right to Death": "As long as I live, I'm a mortal man, but when I die, by ceasing to be a man, I also cease to be mortal, I am no longer capable of dying, and my impending death horrifies me because I see it as it is: no longer death but the impossibility of dying" (DP1 174/119).[24]

The Impossibility of Dying

It would be instructive here to look at Blanchot's early interpretation of Kafka, particularly in the essays "Reading Kafka" (1943), "Literature and the Right to Death" (1948), and "The Language of Fiction" (1949), all published in *The Work of Fire* (1949), in order to draw out themes from Blanchot's reading and to show the force that a reading of these essays has exercised on Derrida's thinking of mortality and immortality. It cannot be underestimated how uncannily consonant Derrida's terminology—motifs such as "buried alive," "survival," among others—and conceptualization are with Blanchot's. Derrida's affinity with, and development of, Blanchot's reading of Kafka would have to be stressed here.

There is no end, there is no possibility of being done with the day, Blanchot declares in "Reading Kafka." Such is the truth that Western man has made "a symbol of felicity" (PF 15/8). He has tried to make the fact that there is no end "bearable by bringing out [*en dégageant*] the positive side, that of immortality, a survival that would compensate for life." But, rather than compensating for it, "this survival [*survivance*] is our life itself" (15/8). We do not die but we do not live either, as Blanchot writes. "We are dead as we live [*nous sommes mort de notre vivant*], we are essentially survivors" (16/8). Even though death "ends our life," Blanchot stresses, "it does not end our possibility of dying" (PF 16/8). "Dying," here as well as in Blanchot's other writings, is understood intransitively as an ongoing process while one is living. It is also worth recalling that in a later text *The Writing of the Disaster*, Blanchot, referring to the "passivity" of dying (Ec 29), describes dying as "without power" (67). In Hegel, death is "at work [*à l'oeuvre*]," linked with the power of negation (76), whereas for Blanchot, dying is associated with "non-power" (81). Dying "outside of oneself [*hors de soi*]" (50) is "without goal"—like thinking (67).

In "Literature and the Right to Death" Blanchot observes that when we die, we leave death behind. To die is to be absent from one's own death. It is the loss of death, "the loss of what in it and for me made it death" (PF 325/337). As alive, I am dying, but "when I die, I cease to be mortal. I am no longer capable of dying" (325/337). My ability or capacity for dying dies or ends with death. After death, dying is no longer possible. Death, then, occasions the impossibility of dying. Certain religions have taken this impossibility of death and have tried to "humanize" it by calling it "immortality" (325/337). This means that by losing the advantage of being mortal, I also lose the possibility of being man. "To be man beyond death" is "to be, in spite of death, still capable of dying, to go on as though nothing happened" (325/337). Other religions call this "the curse of being reborn [*la malédiction de renaissance*]" (325/337). Blanchot explains: "You die because you have lived badly, you are condemned to live again, and you live again" (325/338). In dying, by being "really dead," you become "a truly blessed man" (325/337–338). According to Blanchot's reading, Kafka inherited this idea from the Kabbalah and Eastern traditions. Whether, strictly speaking, it is understood as reincarnation or not, it nevertheless involves a kind of transformation or metamorphosis. Blanchot illustrates this wryly and succinctly with a description that the readers of Kafka would be familiar with: "A man enters the night, but the night ends in awakening [*conduit au réveil*], and there he is, an insect" (PF 325/337–338).

Blanchot comes back to this idea in "The Language of Fiction" (1949), reiterating that Kafka "probably under the influence of Eastern traditions seems to have recognized in the impossibility of dying the extreme curse of man" (PF 87/81). Since "man cannot escape unhappiness," by not being able to "escape existence," it is in vain that he heads toward death because "he dies only to survive. He leaves existence, but only to enter the cycle of metamorphoses" (PF 87/81). Thus, as Blanchot formulates, there can be "no actual death in Kafka, or more exactly, there is never an end" (87/81). This is perhaps because Blanchot, similar to Levinas, believes that one cannot exit existence. The thought of the "impossibility of dying" is derived from the interminability of existence—like the Ancient *apeiron* existence is without beginning or end. Thus, Blanchot comments, most of "Kafka's heroes are engaged in an intermediate moment between life and death" (87/81). Blanchot observes that this strange condition of "the dead who do not die" is expressed by Kafka in a couple of stories, "The Hunter Gracchus," in which the Black Forest Hunter is alive *and* dead, and "The Guest of the Dead." Defining ambiguity, wherein "assertion and negation are in continuous threat of reciprocity," Blanchot describes the ambiguity of the condition that he calls being "*buried alive*" in the following way: "death that is life, that is death as soon as it survives [*dès qu'elle survit*]" (89/84). One dies, only to survive. If death is not a possibility, then life can only be described as the ambiguous survival of a "death that is life, that is death." An examination of Blanchot's thought has shown that rather than depicting a death-bound finitude, the condition that Blanchot terms "buried alive" or survival speaks of the complex and entwined relation between life and death.

The Desire for Survival?

The survivance that Derrida writes about is far from *my* desire to survive. As one of the two always survives the other, it could just as easily refer to the survival of those who survive *me*. This sur-vivance, which will be discussed further in the next chapter, is a "survival that is neither life nor death pure and simple" (BSII 193/130). For, life and death are not proper selfsame structures, but each is *haunted by the other*. Bound up with spectrality, sur-vivance is an originary trace anterior to the distinction between life and death. An excess, an overabundance, an extravagance, *sur*-vivance is a "lapse" of time that "lasts" interminably. But this "lapse" is the very structure of what has been called existence, Dasein. Thus, "survival is indeed that of the living dead [*mort vivant*]" and what survives is a living dead (*un mort vivant*) (193/130).

6

For a Time

The Time of Survival

les morts vivent

—Cicéron, *L'amitié, Laelius de Amicita*[1]

Les morts ne sont pas morts, ou ne sont pas tout à fait morts

—Paul Valéry, preface to James G. Frazer's *La crainte des morts*[2]

. . . never forever, but for a long time.

—Jacques Derrida, "Biodegradables"

What is the time of "for a time"? How long does survival last? How long is "for a time"? Less than an eternity, but not forever—for a time.

In his comprehensive, instructive, and probing book *Miracle and Machine: Jacques Derrida and the Two Sources of Religion, Science, and the Media*, Michael Naas patiently and thoughtfully analyzes what he dubs a great philosophical text on religion, namely, Derrida's essay "Faith and Knowledge" published in 1996.[3] Naas's book, itself a major work on Derrida's thought, scrupulously guides and informs the reader about the structure and details of the "Faith and Knowledge" essay, which Naas calls "Derrida's most direct and ambitious attempt to answer the question of the nature of religion in general and its relationship with science and the media."[4] Unlike the so-called guides that have proliferated to meet the demands of academic presses, who themselves seem to have almost abandoned the thought of publishing probing intellectual research, Naas's *Miracle and Machine* is a genuine guide. Patiently explicated, expertly explained, demystifying without losing any sense of the complexity of Derrida's thought, *Miracle and Machine* discusses the structure, architectonics, and typography of "Faith and Knowledge," skillfully laying bare its why and wherefore, demonstrating how its form, style, and format reflect the theses within it.[5]

With nine chapters, an introduction; a prologue; an epilogue; an analysis of Don DeLillo's novel *Underworld* woven in as a subtext, as a supplement; four substantial "Observations" on Kant, Hegel, Bergson, and Heidegger; and a detailed timeline of Derrida's publications between 1993 and 1995 at the end of the book, Naas's *Miracle and Machine* masterfully brings together a macro- and microscopic reading, proceeding from the conditions and the context of the arguments of the book to the most minute details of its language and writing, in order to demonstrate the very complex stakes involved in the question of "religion." In addition to explicating an undoubtedly complex Derridean text—complex in its structure and its construction, its language and its thinking—following the logic of exemplarity, Naas's book also functions as a guide to the intricacies of a deconstructive reading, steering and gently instructing the reader as it carefully proceeds. In its sweep and detail, in the clichéd phrase that I find impossible to avoid here, it is not possible to do this work justice.

Naas shows "Faith and Knowledge" to be an "at once improvised and highly constructed" text full of repetitions, doublings, and moments of duplicity. Demonstrating the duplicity inscribed into the very form of "Faith and Knowledge," in the two words of the title, naming the two sources of "religion," the two forms of religion, the dogmatic and the true, the division of the book into two sections (fifty-two sections composed of two sets of twenty-six), the two times and places of its writing: first, its presentation at a small, informal gathering on the island of Capri, Italy, in February 1994 and then, its writing at Laguna Beach, California, in April 1995), the two, at least two, kinds of "writing," the spoken and the written, the two forms of typescript or font, the further division of the text into the bolded and the nonbolded, Naas also shows that Derrida's arguments do not proceed in a logical and linear fashion but are scattered throughout, progressing nonetheless by a constant doubling back to its themes and motif.

Even though Derrida's arguments are not made in a straightforward fashion, it is Naas's contention that we can isolate three main theses underlying "Faith and Knowledge." Naas isolates them in a chapter (that he must have had great fun titling) called "Three Theses on the Two Sources and Their One Common Element." According to Naas, these express: the fundamental duplicity of religion, the fundamental conflict between science and religion, and the fundamental complicity of religion and science (65). While I am not able to pursue the full details of these topics here, I can highlight the focus on elementary trust, reliability, or trustworthiness (*fiabilité*).

Among the discussions that I found illuminating and that I greatly learned from in *Miracle and Machine* are: the treatment of the question of *salut, salut* as salvation or as safety (50–52) and *mondialisation*, the process of becoming worldwide (58) in chapter 2; the discussion of the miracle as being coextensive with elementary faith (93–94) and testimonial faith's conditioning of every social bond as an interruption, as an interruptive unraveling (94–95, 97–99) in chapter 3; the theme of breath (*souffle*) (110–114), the connection between the machine (118) and faith, showing that it is the machine that makes possible the faith that opens up a future (120) in chapter 4; the experience of the secret (127), in particular its relation to Christianity as a religion of internalization, of the virtualization and spectralization of the body of Christ in the Eucharist, explaining the divergent uptakes by the Abrahamic religions of what took place and was said between YHWH and Abraham, as well as the specificity of Islam's attachment to the untranslatable letter and its resistance to mediatization and translation (131) in chapter 5; the penetrating examination of the most desert-like *khōra* and the rethinking of "religion" itself on the basis of another social bond, the one that first opens up, and interrupts in opening up, every community (195) in chapter 6; the consideration of "the ellipsis of sacrifice" (207) and the discussion of how when the specter of life-death is repressed the phantasm of pure life takes its place (225) in chapter 7—and I haven't even mentioned yet the grenade and the pomegranate seeds in chapter 8.

Rather than engaging in a mechanical exercise of summary here, I would like to submit to scrutiny Naas's discussion of an important theme raised at the end of his book, that of survival or living on (*survivre*). I would like to take the opportunity to think through a most pressing thought invoked in chapter 9, entitled "The Passion of Literature: Genet in Laguna, Gide in Algiers." There, Naas takes up the unusual juxtaposition of two writers who were important for Derrida during different phases of his life: Gide especially during his youth, and Genet, who played an important role in Derrida's work, certainly since the composition of *Glas*. Toward the end of chapter 9, after speculating about the role played by these writers in "Faith and Knowledge" and presenting a hypothesis about their presence at the end of the essay, Naas turns to Derrida's views regarding death and the acceptance of death.

Examining the notion of "the end" in the Western tradition that Derrida is reading, Naas remarks that in this tradition the end is never quite the end. For there is always something that comes after the end, "something like an afterlife or an afterworld, some kind of life everlasting" (263–264). What about Gide of *Fruits of the Earth*, the *Journals*, or even *The Immoralist* may have appealed to Derrida, Naas writes, is his "unconditional embracing of life in the here and now, on earth and in this world, rather than sacrificing this world and this life to some beyond" (264). Bringing together his discussion of Gide with Derrida's "final words," words scribbled on an envelope, as he says, near the end of his life and read aloud by his son, Pierre Alferi, at his gravesite in Ris-Orangis, Naas concludes that in their "emphasis on this world, this finite world," both Derrida and Gide issue a plea not to sacrifice this world for the promise of another world.

Naas explains that Gide's reference to the very common expression *de l'autre côté*, on the other side, very much like Nietzsche's thought, eschews an otherworldly religion or ethics, for what is promised on the other side of life, and encourages the celebration of the joys and riches of this world. One may wonder how to distinguish a thought embracing the wonders of *this* life from other competing discourses on finitude such as Nietzschean tragic finitude, or a certain embrace of carpe diem by the existentialists, for whom Gide was a favorite author. Of course, such a belief, as Naas rightly worries, can lead to the neglect of "the 'other side' that is to be found on *this side*, that is of the other world *within this world*" (267). He will go on to explain what he means by this other side within this world.

Having already referred to the appeal that Derrida makes to the phrase *de l'autre côté* in chapter 3, Naas writes that for Derrida there is already "another side to this 'other side,' not some other world beyond this world but an 'other side' or an 'other world' within this world" (267). This "other side" is "not some other world to which I might gain entrance after death but [rather] the inner sanctum of the other, to which I can have no access" (267). For this reason, Naas writes, there is "another *other world*," but not one "above or beyond this one but another world 'within' the world, an infinitely other, nondialectizable, nonsynthesizable world 'within' this one" (268). And this thought becomes most poignant with the death of the other.

At this juncture in his chapter, Naas admits that it would be difficult not to want to pose the question, the question that many readers of Derrida may have been wondering about, about whether Derrida himself believed in another world or in an afterlife. Quoting Derrida's own statements about his own death, for example, the one in *A Taste for the Secret* when he said, "I do not believe that one lives on post mortem," Naas says declaratively that "Derrida did not believe that we live on somewhere else or that we live again; he did not believe in another world; in a world 'on the other side' of this one" (270). Glossing this further, Naas observes that "while we are not resurrected for another life or in another life, 'we' do sur-vive or live on *for a time* after death through the traces we produce and the marks that make us visible to others. . . . 'We' begin sur-viving or living on from the moment we are born" (270, my emphasis). This surviving is, as Derrida wrote in *Archive Fever*, "the surviving of an excess of life" over itself (AF 96/60).

While the nouns *survie* and *survivance* have existed in the French language since the sixteenth century (n. f. 1544) and the seventeenth century (n. f. 1606) respectively, the use of the verb *survivre* goes back to the eleventh century (1080). Both nouns refer to the state of the person who survives someone, to living after life, and to the fact of surviving, while the verb *survivre* signifies "to remain alive after someone; to still exist after someone or something has died or disappeared; to last or to continue longer than; to escape a violent and collective death, to survive a catastrophe; continuing to live after something unbearable."[6] A recent text of the French art critic and historian Georges Didi-Huberman, *Aperçues* provides a very insightful analysis of the use of the words *survie* and *survivance*.[7] Discussing his reference to *survivance* at an Aby Warburg conference in London, Didi-Huberman notes his preference for *survivance*, rather than "survival," as a translation of Warburg's notion of *Nachleben* (207).[8] He refers to the employment of the term "survivals" by social anthropologist Edward B. Tylor (1871) in *Primitive Culture*. Examining customs and beliefs that maintained their function and meaning, Tylor contrasted them with those that had both lost their usefulness and were not well integrated with the rest of culture. The latter he called *survivals*. Even though Tylor held a Darwinian evolutionary point of view, in Didi-Huberman's interpretation of Tylor, what is culturally transmitted is not simply what has subsisted in the tradition, but *Nachleben* also concerns more discrete and more disruptive objects, more symptomatic of the culture.

Didi-Huberman then points out that the French language introduces a "division [*division*]" that is "unknown" or "unrecognized" in English (208). In French one only speaks of *survie* when someone has escaped death, for example, someone who has escaped or survived a massacre, a famine, or an accident. The one who has survived was never dead. He was the most "adapted" (*plus "adapté"*) and has survived, outlived (*survecu*). If he were dead and he appeared to us as living, Didi-Huberman points out, we would say that he was *ressuscité* (resurrected) or *rené* (reborn), not that he *survecu* (survived). The word "survivance" is employed for things, ideas, and images—never for beings that may have escaped death or who were resurrected, revived (*ressuscité*).⁹

The rather mysterious notion of *survivre* and *survivance* make an early appearance in Derrida's work. In one of its first instances, in "Freud and the Scene of Writing," it emerges in relation to writing (*l'écriture*), which is described as a "surviving trace [*trace survivant*]" (WD 331/224). Later in "Circumfession" writing is again portrayed as that "intense relation to survivance" (Cir 178/191). In *Shibboleth*, the 1986 text devoted to Paul Celan, "the signature of the date" is designated as capable of "surviving and calling the disappeared or the deceased [*appeler le disparu*]" (Sh 59/32), while in *Memoires—For Paul de Man*, from the same year, we learn that the name "*already survives*" the name holder, bearing his death each time it is pronounced (MPD 63/49).

Survivre is not survival after death. It is not, as it is commonly defined, to continue or to remain alive after someone or something or to live after and endure the loss of something invaluable and precious. Neither does *sur-*, as Derrida explains in the second volume of *The Beast and the Sovereign*, indicate superiority, supremacy, height, altitude, or highness above life. "It does not add something extra to life any more than it cuts something from it" (BSII 194/131). *Survivre* does not refer to a state of life after demise ("the afterlife"), but to a reprieve, an afterlife that is *more than* life or more life *still*. Both *more life* and *no more life*, it is itself a life-after-life or life-after-death—a temporal extension of life in the form of a reprieve.

"Des tours de Babel" (1985), Derrida's contribution to a collection of texts dedicated to Maurice de Gandillac, eminent translator and Derrida's professor, focuses on Benjamin's "The Task of the Translator" (1923).[10] In that text, Benjamin uses two words, *überleben*, in order to refer to life postmortem, and *fortleben*, to designate the continuation of life and the living on of works of art. The French translation, by Gandillac himself, uses the same word *survie* to render both words. Derrida writes regarding translation, the focus of Benjamin's text: "Sur-vival [*survie*] gives a surplus of life [*un plus de vie*], more than a surviving [*plus qu'une survivance*]. The work does not simply live longer, it lives *more and better* [plus et mieux], beyond its authors means" (214/203). He argues that the work has "a structure" of "survival," with the translation assuring the survival of a text (217/206).

In an interview given in the mid-'80s Derrida further explains that *survivre* is not a matter of survival in the sense of posterity.[11] Surviving, rather, treats this "strange dimension" of *plus de vie*, both "more life" and "no more life."[12] In the interview Derrida uses another expression, *plus que vie*, more than life, to add to his descriptions of what he means by *survie*. So, he remarks that for him *survivre* is a matter of both *plus de vie* and *plus que vie*. In response to a question about translation Derrida refers to the relation between the original text and the translated text as an *augmentation*. Translations, he explains, produce augmentations or new textual bodies. This augmentation is precisely *sur*vivance, not in the sense of merely allowing the original to survive but allowing it to have another life, as it were, in another language, a more invigorated, perhaps even richer, life. In *Mal d'Archive* Derrida describes surviving in a similar way, referring to "the surviving of an excess of life" (AF 96/60).

The most extensive treatment of the originary notion of *survie* occurs in "Survivre," which originally made its first appearance in English in 1979 as "Living On: Borderlines," and was later published in French in *Parages* (from 1986 again). Just as *Aporias* is an examination of the question of death and the purported separating-line between life and death, "Survivre" is concerned with the instability of edges, borders, and boundaries that "join: separate" and mark the spacing between. For the most part, a reading of Blanchot's narrative *L'arrêt de mort* (both "death sentence" and "suspension of death")—although such a description would be a simplistic reduction and diminish the complexity and richness of this text—"Survivre" is a rumination on a survival and a ghostly return beyond the straight line of one's lifeline: "Survival [*survivance*] and *revenance*, living on and ghostly returning. Living on [*survivre*] goes beyond [*déborde*] both living and dying" (Par 153/134).[13] Living "beyond" one's death, *sur-vivre* is not life *after* death (a state of life or a continuation of life) but rather sur-viving, *more* life *still*. Derrida describes *sur-vie*, which Michael Naas renders as a "sur-life," "a surplus of life," for this "*more-than-life* [sur-vie]" marks a survival in the time of life (*une survie dans le temps de la vie*], in the form of a reprieve [*sursis*]" in which the survivor lives "more than a lifetime [*plus qu'une vie*)" in the short span of a few moments (Par 168/147, trans. mod.) (214).[14]

It is during a roundtable discussion on translation at a colloquium dedicated to two texts by Nietzsche and other related works ("Otobiography, Transference, Translation") that Derrida raises the notion of *survivre* in relation to Benjamin's work once more. There Derrida insists on Benjamin's statement that "the structure of an original is survival [*survie*]," what he refers to as *überleben*. A text is original "insofar as it is a thing, not to be confused with an organic or a physical body [*corps organique, un corps physique*] but rather a thing, let us say, of the mind [*une chose de l'esprit*], meant to survive the death of the author or the signatory, and to be above or beyond the physical body of the text, among other things. Benjamin has a certain number of sentences of the Hegelian type, Derrida remarks, to explain that "one must understand life—'*Leben*'—not on the basis of [*à partir de*] what we know in general about organic, biological life, but, on the contrary, on the basis of the life of the mind [*la vie de l'esprit*], that is, life that rises above nature and is in its essence *survival* [survie]."[15] "To understand a text as an original it is to understand it independently of its living conditions [*conditions de vie*] [. . .] and to understand it instead in its *surviving* structure [*structure survivante*]" (161/122). Derrida refers to Benjamin's alternative usage of *fortleben* and *überleben*, both translated as *survivre* in French, and clarifies that *überleben* means "above life and therefore survival in the sense of rising above life" whereas *fortleben* indicates "survival in the sense of something prolonging life" (161/122).

In *Politics of Friendship* Derrida writes that what is called *philia*, or friendship, begins with the possibility of survival. Friendship is a relationship that structurally necessitates that the friend "already bear my death and inherit it as the last survivor" (PFr 30/13). The friend bears, carries (*porter*) my own death (which is expropriated in advance). In a way, she is the only one to bear it. "*Surviving* [survivre]" would thus be "another name of a mourning whose possibility is never to be awaited," since mourning, its anguished apprehension, will have begun before death (31/13). One does not survive without mourning—without literally bearing or carrying this grief (*porter le deuil*) (30/31). For Derrida, *survivre* is "the essence, the origin, and the possibility, the condition of possibility of friendship" (31/14). The time of surviving thus gives the time of friendship. Such a time gives itself in withdrawing, it occurs through effacing itself. Its *contretemps* "disjoins the presence of the present" inscribing "intemporality and untimeliness [*intemporalité et intempestivité*]" in friendship (31/14). In giving time and taking time friendship "survives the living present" (32/15). For Derrida, this bereaved survivance is to be distinguished from the stability, constancy, or firm permanence of Aristotelian primary friendship (31–32/13). Friendship, as Derrida writes, is promised to "testamentary *revenance*, the haunting return, of a more (no more) life, of a surviving [*la revenance testamentaire d'un plus-de vie, d'un survivre*]" (20/3, trans. mod.).

In a late discussion with Jean-Luc Nancy and Philippe Lacoue-Labarthe in 2004, Derrida describes his feelings regarding the anticipation of his death. In his relation to the death to come, knowing that it will annihilate him, he acknowledges that there is beneath the surface "a testamentary desire" that "*something* survive, be left, be transmitted—an inheritance" that will not come back to him "but that, perhaps, will remain."[16] There is a feeling that haunts him about what will remain, not simply things that are in the public domain but also private things. This feeling, which he calls testamentary and is linked to the structure of the trace, is part of the experience of death (93).

In his last years, in published texts, seminars, and interviews Derrida publicly expressed his struggle with his so-called mortality, with the fact that he had come to terms with death or had to "learn how to die." For Derrida, the fact that he was not able to accept death did not mean that his fatal illness was met by a "refusal" to die, but rather that it caused a thoughtful consideration of how mortality has been defined throughout the philosophical tradition. Perhaps this "refusal" to learn to die, as every philosopher must learn to do in order to properly be a philosopher, was itself a "refusal," on the part of Derrida, of philosophy as a way of life that leads to the *soteria* of the soul and as a discipline or practice *of* and *for* death (and hence as a discipline for immortality). As demonstrated earlier, Derrida's thinking of survivance from the very beginning questioned the easy distinction between mortality and immortality. When, in his interview with Jean Birnbaum in 2004, initially published in *Le Monde*, he said that he was at war with himself or against himself, this was because he could not believe that death was simply an end.[17] If surviving begins before death and not merely after it, as it is commonly thought, then life itself *is* originarily survival: "life *is* living on, life *is* survival [la vie *est* survie]."[18]

As we have seen, *survivance* does not simply refer to what remains and endures for posterity nor does it signify surviving or somehow living on after death in an afterlife or life-everlasting in an afterworld, but the *sur-* in *sur-vivre* indicates "more living," *plus de vie*, a more than life, *plus que la vie*, in life.[19] For life and death, which are not separable as such, are themselves both traces of a *sur-vie* or irreducible survivance that dislocates the self-presence of the living present. The possibility of this *sur-vivre* does not wait for death "to make life and death indissociable," it comes in advance before death, to disjoin and dislocate the self-identity of the living present (BSII 176/117). The living present is divided, divides itself, between its life and its survival, bearing death within itself. Survivance, then, is or says the complication, the inextricable alliance of the dead and the living.

In the celebrated essay "La différance," originally a talk in which Derrida profitably exploited the unheard difference between *différence* and *différance*, he explains that "the ending *-ance* remains undecided *between* the active and the passive" (M 9/9).[20] *Différance* is "neither simply active nor simply passive, announcing or rather recalling something like the middle voice" (9/9). In the talk, Derrida also gives *mouvance* and *résonance* as an example to illustrate his point. In an interview with Raoul Mortley, he stresses that "Differance is productive [. . .] it is neither active nor passive. It is more of the order of the middle voice in Greek grammar, neither passive nor active."[21] Let us recall that in *Positions*, in response to a question posed by Julia Kristeva, Derrida says: "The activity or productivity connoted by the *a* of *différance* refers to the generative movement in the play of differences."[22] In the conversation with Mortley just cited, Derrida elaborates that the use of the suffix *-ance* "is a way of forming a noun on the basis of the present participle: *mouvance, souffrance*, these are neither activities nor passivities."

The notion of survivance and its complex temporality need to be thought in relation to *restance*. What is *remaining* and what is its relation to *surviving*? Both remaining and surviving are bound up with a certain spectrality, a ghostly returning (*revenance*) and haunting. Anterior to life and death, survivance makes life and death possible. Life and death "would themselves be but traces and traces of traces" of a survivance (SM 17–18/xx). Another name for a mourning, survival is never present. It dislocates the living-present, which divides itself, bearing death and what would survive it.

~

In chapter 9 of *Miracle and Machine*, "The Passion of Literature: Genet in Laguna, Gide in Algiers," Naas considers Derrida's beliefs on the so-called afterlife and survival. By tracing and underscoring Naas's use of the phrase "for a time" (one of them italicized by him) I would like to further explore the question of survival and its time. I do not claim any expertise in numerology, and in the wake of Naas's own book that makes a great case for the significance of all kinds of numbers in Derrida's "Faith and Knowledge," I cannot say anything erudite about this number of repetitions—five—except to point out his emphasis on the expression "for a time." My remarks or questions will have to do with how one is to understand this "for a time."

Commenting on Derrida's views about death and what may come after it, Naas stresses that Derrida's work from the very beginning argued for and demonstrated a logic of survival and living on (*survivre*), though this should not be mistaken for a belief in an afterlife. "Derrida developed throughout his work," Naas writes, "a singular thinking of survival or living on, a notion of the trace as what, in principle if not in fact, always survives the one who produced it or received it [. . .]. As soon as I utter or even read a trace, as soon as I make a mark, my death and my survival are implied therein, my death and the trace or mark that can always survive me *for a time*" (here I note the second appearance of the phrase "for a time") (271). In other words, the trace survives me: "while every trace—as finite—is threatened by forgetting, erasure, indeed by catastrophe or apocalypse, the trace in principle survives me" (271). However, Naas emphasizes, this powerful thought of survival is "a far cry from any kind of belief in an afterlife or in the immortality of the soul" (271).

"We begin living on already from the beginning, and 'we' continue to live on in these signs after our death," Naas writes (271). But how to understand this living on? When Derrida, in his final note read at his funeral, says, "I love you and am smiling at you from wherever I may be [*d'où que je sois*]," Naas emphasizes, "we are to understand living on as living on only 'in' these words," in the subjunctive and not in the indicative, as they are repeated or as they remain repeatable in others, for others—and only *for a time*" (271, author's italics, the third appearance of the phrase). "Living on 'in' these words," Naas clarifies, "is in the subjunctive, which denotes a mood of verbs expressing what is imagined or wished or possible, rather than in the indicative designating a mood of verbs expressing a simple statement of a fact or making a factual statement.[23] "We," of course, do not continue to live after death or survive our death, but "we" do live on in the "afterlife" of the words uttered, signs or marks made and traces left. So, only in the time of "for a time."

Derrida did not believe, Naas continues, in an afterlife or in an eternal or immortal life after death, conventionally understood, but "always only a finite and very mortal survival" (272). Here we could ask what a "finite" and "mortal" survival would be? If Derrida has been rethinking "finitude" from his earliest texts, combining a thinking of finitude with that of the infinite, "finite" and "mortal" cannot be taken as simply the end of a short, death-bound life on this earth, especially since in several other places, such as *The Beast and the Sovereign, 2*, Derrida links finitude with a *survivance* that is "neither life nor death pure and simple." There, writing of the alliance of the living and the dead, he states, "this finitude [. . .] is survivance" (BSII 193/130). A thought of *survivance* would then seem to require that the finite be thought in intricate relation to the infinite, as infinitely finite.

Naas very astutely notes that "it might be thought that this living on is something of a consolation in the face of death, solace in the recognition that, although we are not immortal, the traces we leave live on within the world in the memories of others, in the works available to others to read, hear, or experience, and so on" (272). Yet, Naas explains that Derrida's survival is, first, anything but a "personal" survival, "for the trace I leave behind is precisely not 'my own'" and second, that "with every death, including my own, there comes the end not of some individual within the world but the end of the world as such" (272). As Naas observes, Derrida rejects the thought that my death can be understood and situated dialectically within the horizon of other deaths. Derrida does not agree with the idea of a common horizon of death, for, death truly is "the end of the world." This end of the world should, no doubt, be understood in terms of the very notion that Derrida argued for in the preface to *Chaque fois unique, la fin du monde*, where he emphatically stated that the death of the other signifies not the end of *a* world but the end of *the* world itself.

Since Derrida did not believe that he would be going to another world, Naas writes, "there might be living on *for a time*, but certainly no afterlife" (272, my emphasis, fourth appearance). For, despite his genuine struggle and constant preoccupation with death, Derrida could not accept death. "He could not accept death," Naas comments, "because he—like all of us—had a certain *preference* for life" (273). (But this "preference for life," as we have seen in *H. C. for Life, That Is to Say . . .* , where Derrida also finds himself turned toward death, is not without its complications.) He could not accept death because he could not think or assimilate it; he could not accept it because he wished to question and thus rethink the concepts he had inherited from the tradition, in particular, those of redemption and resurrection. What we can say is that what he thought was in the end *on the side of life*. Derrida "simply could not accept death," Naas argues, "because to do so would be to accept nothing less than the end of the world" (273). Thus, the acceptance of (his own) death would be tantamount to accepting the end of the world. It is true that Derrida could not accept death in the sense of resigning himself to it. This he could never do, but he *did* accept death as the end of the world; he *did* know that death would be the end of the world. I will return to this at the end of the chapter.

Naas then writes that for Derrida there is living on but there would be no resurrection (274). With every breath one is already living on, surviving, not at all immortal but living on as absolutely mortal.[24] As Naas shows throughout the book, Derrida's thinking of the trace was always tied to a reflection on death and mourning, a mourning that starts from the very beginning. "Only insofar as work allows itself to be . . . uprooted, displaced, and translated, transplanted elsewhere, can it live on *for a time*" (274, my emphasis, fifth appearance). How do we take this emphasis again on "absolutely mortal"? Surely, this mortality is not that of a dying subjectivity or of a simple finitude. How would we reconcile the relation between mortality and a certain living on, surviving, remaining (*restance*), ghostly coming back (*revenance*), that is, a certain immortality? When in one of the first substantial treatments of the notion of survival in "Living On: Borderlines," Derrida remarks that in *L'Arrêt de mort* the living on (*survivance*) of the one who narrates (*le récitant*), who is a survivor, is also a spectral coming back, a ghostly return (*cette survivance est aussi une revenance spectrale*), what is the time or duration of this survival (Par 182/159)? Is its time only "for a time"?

Perhaps with his stress on the expression "for a time" Naas is emphasizing the provisional nature of survival and living on, survival for a time, in the same way that he argues in chapter 6, "'Jewgreek is Greekjew': Messianicity—Khôra—Democracy," that Derrida was not willing to give up the notion of the messianic "for the moment" (172). Or perhaps Naas wants to say that survival lasts "for a time," as in the duration of one's time, one's epoch. One way of reading the thought that one lives on "for a time" after one's death would be to say that the memory that others have of oneself lasts only *for a time*, only for one's time, for one's epoch, after which this memory naturally dissipates. In a wonderfully strange text entitled "'Dead Man Running': *Salut, Salut*," written in honor of the fiftieth anniversary of *Les Temps modernes*, Derrida comments on this very thought, on what you might perhaps call Sartre's overzealous belief in finitude. In this hastily written essay penned in the form of a letter to Claude Lanzmann, Derrida links epochalization, the fact that one's thought belongs to an epoch, to the process of sanctification, showing an alliance between the concept of epoch and the concept of salvation. For Derrida, this emphasis on epochalization is predetermined and overdetermined by the value of life. So, does memory just endure "for a time," the time of one's epoch?

Or perhaps, like the Homeric belief in the fame or reputation that outlasts the hero's lifetime, survival is akin to the living on of memory. This would, then, be something like a living on in posterity, the survival that posterity promises. For Homeric *kleos*, honor and glory is bestowed upon the hero who has died a glorious death and whose memory will live on. The hero's desire is to perform great deeds in order to transform his death into eternal glory. In the *Iliad* Hektor does not intend to die "without a struggle and some glory [*akleiōs*] or without some great deed" that is to be remembered.[25] The beautiful death (*kalos thanatos*), the glorious death (*eukleēs thanatos*), in the prime of youth leads to glory, virtually guaranteeing unassailable renown.[26] The logic underlying heroic honor is the need to be recognized as supreme, superior in rank, status, and valor and "to be famed 'among men-to-come [*essomenoisi puthesthai*; *hommes à venir*].'"[27]

Heroic striving has its roots in the will to escape aging and death, which amount to amnesia, silence, demeaning obscurity, and the absence of fame. By welcoming death and confronting it with valor, death is overcome as something to be feared. What matters most is being valued, honored, and recognized and by being glorified in a song of praise the hero is allowed to continue, beyond the reach of death, to be present in the community of the living, his life converted into legend and linked to that of other heroic individuals. In his analysis of "glorious death," Jean-Pierre Vernant notes that this *kleos*, of course, assumes the existence of a tradition of oral poetry that serves as a repository of shared culture and as societal memory. The hero who is praised in song is not only committed to memory, memorialized, remaining present in the memory for all "those to come" but also commemorated in the memorial tomb, the raising of a *sema*.

When Naas writes that accepting death is something Derrida could never do because it would be equivalent to accepting the end of the world, he appeals to Derrida's words in *Learning to Live Finally*: "We are all survivors who have been granted a temporary reprieve [*en sursis*]" in order to underscore the temporariness of this "for a time."[28] However, isn't the reprieve that Derrida is referring to here that of the duration of our life—the duration of our life itself as a reprieve—and not what happens *after* it? It is our life itself, the life that is riven with death and will live on, that Derrida considers as a temporary reprieve (273). When Naas remarks that in the preface to *Chaque fois unique, la fin du monde* Derrida made it very clear that "death—*in this case*, the death of the other—must be understood not as an event within the world [. . .] but as the end of the world itself," he surely intends to be understood that almost every time Derrida wrote about the end of the world, whether it was in *The Work of Mourning* or in *Rams*, it was always in relation to the other's death and with a stress placed on the death of the other, notwithstanding the complications he introduced in *Aporias* regarding the irrelevance of the primacy of "my death" or "the death of the other" in the polemic between Levinas and Heidegger.

The phrase "for a time" seems to place an emphasis on the finite. It seems to underscore that life is inevitably fleeting, transitory, and short-lived. However, one begins to wonder how one could reconcile this emphasis on a certain mortality and finitude with the thought of spectrality and with the thinker who wrote and kept on writing incisively, perceptively, insistently, and trenchantly in dozens and dozens of places about specters and ghostliness. Could Derrida's writings on matters of life, death, and spectrality be equated with and be considered on the same level as the stock, mechanical existential response of a certain finitude? Perhaps it is *infinite* survivance that is finite.

The death of the other is each time the end of the world. The other's death is the end of the world, the world envisioned as something that we commonly share. The death of the other is a reminder that what we call "the world," the fact that we believe that there is only one world, is the result of a tacit agreement, a shared history. For "the world"—whether the *kosmos*, the universe, or the globe—does indeed have a history, a history that requires to be told again. With the other's death so dies a certain concept of the world as *one world*. Each birth opens up and each death closes a "unique world" (E 138/123). The other's is "an other world" (138). And each death, each time, signals "another end of the world" (CFU 124/95). With each death the world disappears. Nevertheless, the "world" is "there," some will claim, assured of its certainty. Yet Derrida believed that what we call "the world" is the "indispensable assumption or presumption" of a "'credible' gathering" (an act of faith without knowledge), "the gathering of an infinity of worlds, possible and real" (IND 248). "The presumption of a community, of a gathering of this infinite dispersion of worlds," he stresses, is "faith itself" (IND 248).

An invocation of faith, Michael Naas's *Miracle and Machine* has the great virtue of causing the reader to wonder, helping us understand that this is what a marvelous event does. If Naas's book is miraculous work it is because he shows us that the miracle cannot be understood without a relationship to calculation, programming, and repetition. And the wonder is that to accede to the event of this miracle we have to pass via the machine, via all the repetitions and duplicities recounted and mapped out through the chapters of *Miracle and Machine*.

How long, then, does survivance last? Who can say how long "for a time"—the time of survival—is?

7

Dying Alive

The Phantasmatics of Living-Death

Dis, quand reviendras-tu?

—Barbara

Somewhere in the middle of session 5, almost at the midpoint of the second year of his ten-week seminar *The Beast and the Sovereign*, which turned out to be his last, Derrida provocatively declares: "if I were to say 'Robinson Crusoe' was indeed 'buried alive,' he was indeed 'swallow'd up alive' you would not believe me" (BSII S5 189/127). He insists that, contrary to what the readers of the novel would claim, "it is true, that really is the story [*récit*], the story itself, not what it tells [*raconte*]" (190/128). Robinson Crusoe was indeed buried alive. Derrida here makes a distinction between the conscious phenomenality or representation and the fantasmatic content that "happens, really did happen" (191/128). Using classical phenomenological terminology concerning intentional experiences, he provides a gloss: As if the noematic nucleus or kernel (*Kern*) of the phantasm "(being buried or swallowed up alive)" happened to him . . . virtually but irreversibly happened;" as if dying a living death, the material or the logical content, did happen to Robinson.[1] Robinson is "afraid of dying a living death, and so he already sees it happening, he is buried or swallowed alive, it's what he wanted" (191/129). Derrida raises the stakes further by provokingly stating that in fact, in the indicative, "it really did happen to him," dying a living death did happen to

"'Robinson Crusoe,' the narrative [*récit*] itself" (192/129). When Derrida refers to "*Robinson Crusoe*," he further explains, he has been naming a "fictional narrative [*récit*], that is also a journal, a travel journal, a confession, the fiction of an autobiography, an anthropological treatise, an apprenticeship in Christian prayer," and so forth (191–192/129). Thus, "the narrative entitled *Robinson Crusoe* and, within it, the character and the narrator, the author of the journal and the character that the author of the autobiographical journal puts on stage," are all living dead (192/130). Readers of the second volume of *The Beast and the Sovereign* may already be familiar with this seemingly outrageous declaration. Here I would like to explore a little further some of the consequences arising from Derrida's comments as well as discuss the intriguing confluence of three terms—the phantasm, dying alive, and survival—which would need to be considered and thought in terms of each other.

Derrida states that not only the narrative, but also the character named Robinson Crusoe, the one who speaks and the one keeping a journal, and so on, "might have desired that the book outlive [*survive*] them" (193/130). This living on or survival (*survie*), Derrida tells us, is that of the living dead. That which is living dead lives on, it sur-vives. Like any trace, a book is at once alive and dead, or neither alive nor dead. Thus each time we trace a trace, each time we leave behind a trace, a certain "machinality" or technicality, "the machination of this machine . . . each turn, each re-turn, each wheel" then "virtually entrusts the trace" to a "sur-vival," in which the oppositions of life and death, the living and the dead, has no relevance (BSII 193/130). Each time this living-dead machine is "a dead thing that resuscitates each time a breath of living intentionality intends it and makes it live again by animating it, like a "*geistige Leiblichkeit*," "a body proper animated, activated, traversed, shot through with intentional spirituality" (193/131).

Before discussing the important notion of survival, what Derrida increasingly refers to as *survivance*, it is necessary to turn to what he calls *the phantasm* of living death. Derrida proceeds to clarify his statement about the case of Robinson Crusoe by stating that since "dying a living death, in the present, can never really present itself, as one cannot presently be dead, die, and see oneself die, die alive, as one cannot be both dead and alive, dying a living death can only be a fantasmatic virtuality, a fiction" (BSII 192/130). Dying alive, then, is a phantasm. But what is a phantasm? What is a fantasmatic virtuality and how significant is it that Derrida can later claim that it "organizes and rules over everything we call life and death, lifedeath?" (192/130). Now, in Derrida's estimation this fantasy of being buried alive or swallowed alive, the terror and the desire of living death, is Robinson's "great organizing fantasy or phantasm [*le grand fantasme organisateur*] (terror and desire)" (176/117). To "disappear, leave, decease alive in the unlimited element, in the medium of the other" is the phantasm that animates Robinson (146/94):

> Robinson Crusoe's fundamental fear, *the* fundamental, foundational fear, the basic fear [*peur de fond*] from which all other fears are derived and around which everything is organized, is the fear of going to the bottom [*fond*], precisely, of being "swallow'd up alive."[2] . . . He is afraid of dying a living death [also "dying alive," *mourir vivant*] . . . thus of sinking alive to the bottom . . . He is afraid of . . . being swallowed or devoured into the deep belly of the earth or the sea or some living creature . . . That is the great phantasm, the fundamental phantasm or the phantasm of the fundamental. (122/77)

Derrida wonders if "the threat" of being eaten and swallowed by the other is "not also nurtured like a promise, and therefore a desire" (122/77). This is why he refers to Robinson's "terrified desire" as a "double phantasm" (146/93).

The Phantasm

"Dying alive" needs to be thought with the phantasm, *as* a phantasm. Now, as Derrida reminds us in *The Beast and the Sovereign, 2*, seminar, in Greek *phantasma* means both "product of the imagination and fantasy [*le fantasme*] or revenant" (BSII 200/136). The phantasm is a term belonging to the Platonic denunciation of *mimesis*, where the doubling of the model by the copy, the semblance, the appearance, the simulacrum, the ghost, or the phantom of the thing represents the false and the non-true. Already in *Glas* (1974), using the terminology of the phantasm, Derrida challenged the determination of difference as opposition or contradiction, which is indispensable to Hegelian discourse. In an interview subsequent to the publication of *Glas*, he wondered whether one can be satisfied with the common definitions of the phantasm, hinting at his own dissatisfaction with the "confused" and "less than clear or unambiguous" way that the term was being used (Poi 30/22–23). Philosophical discourse, he noted, "can no longer be assured of possessing a philosophical concept of the phantasm," of having a "knowledge" that "would control [*un savoir maîtrisant*] what is at issue in this word" (30/23). In his remarks Derrida further pointed out that the phantasm "eludes the philosophical grasp" such that it is "no longer a term in a conceptual opposition that arises from philosophy (originary/derived, real/imaginary, material reality/psychical reality, and so forth)." In more pensive, speculative comments he wondered what would happen if the phantasm were "coextensive with absolute knowledge?" (30/23). In a later interview regarding the phantasm in *Paper Machine* entitled "Paper or Me, You Know . . ." Derrida explains: "The word condenses all together [at once, *à la fois*] the image, spectrality, and the simulacrum—and the weight of desire, the libidinal investment of affect, the notions of an appreciation extended toward that which remains inappropriable" (PM 269/63). In his late seminar *The Beast and the Sovereign, 2*, Derrida states that he is again turning to the notion of the phantasm "to figure or configure" the very "contradictory," "inconceivable," or "unthinkable" thing called "living death" (BSII 218/149). He does acknowledge that he finds the thought of "dying alive" an impossible thought, which has no sense, defies sense and good sense, and is thus "unintelligible."

Rather than being considered as a phenomenon manqué, the phantasm, as Derrida demonstrates in *H. C. for Life, That Is to Say . . .* and elsewhere, needs to be interpreted in relation to the event. Rather than repeating the age-old philosophical gesture of being engaged in the partition and separation of the phenomenon from the phantasm, prying apart the phantasmatic from actual or external reality, it should be realized that the thinking of the phantasm each time requires a "*thoughtful analysis* of what binds and unbinds the appearing of the phenomenon, the *phainesthai*, insofar as it is indissociable from the *phantasma*, that is to say, both from the dream and the spectral phantom, of *revenance*, which *phantasma* also means" (H. C. 94–95/103). What makes the phantasm "almighty [*toute-puissante*]" is precisely this indissociability, this undecidability—it is *both at once* (192/130). The phantasm undoubtedly does not exist, it *is* not, instead, what must be emphasized is "what *happens* or *arrives* with [*ce qui* arrive *avec*]" the phantasm (H. C. 73/76). In order to attend to the relation of the phantasm to the event, to the event of the phantasm, which eludes the age-old philosophical distinction between actual or external reality and the phantasm, one must "analyze," as it will be shown, "the phantasm as much as produce the event, in the same twofold gesture [*geste dédoublé*]" (95/103).

As Michael Naas—one of the first interpreters to bring to our attention the notion of phantasm and provide a powerful interpretation of it—writes, "what must be emphasized is less the ontological status of the phantasm than its staying power . . . its regenerative power."[3] As Naas observes in "*Comme si, comme ça*: Following Derrida on the Phantasms of the Self, the State, and a Sovereign God," his article on "the nature of the phantasm in general in Derrida's work" (187–188), the phantasm should not be understood "in terms of truth and falsity, or image and reality, but in terms of power and affect" (200). What is necessary is "to take into account the force and tenacity" of the phantasm (192).

In "*Comme si, comme ça*," which later appeared as a chapter in his *Derrida from Now On*, Naas while stating that the phantasm belongs to the set of words or quasi-concepts such as specter, ghost, phantom, spectrality, fantomaticity, and haunting, would like to reserve for the phantasm "a rather special use and status in Derrida's work" (189). Examining three phantasms (which are also forms of sovereignty), those of the self, the nation-state, and God, Naas argues that the "deconstruction of the phantasm nonetheless remains for us an essential task" (188). In fact, he stresses, "deconstruction would thus be, first and foremost, a deconstruction of the phantasm, a deconstruction of any putatively pure origin, indeed, of any phantasm of purity and of any simple, seemingly self-evident or axiomatic origin, any indivisible, inviolable order" (191). During a discussion of the phantasm of sovereignty in Derrida's text entitled *Unconditionality or Sovereignty*, Naas adds: "The phantasm needs to be exposed and denounced not because it is untrue, false, or merely apparent but because it is so powerful it threatens the very freedom that makes it possible" (197). That the phantasm of indivisible sovereignty needs to be exposed and denounced there can be no doubt. However, if Naas is suggesting that the phantasm tout court or the phantasm in general needs to be denounced, we would have to ask whether "dying alive" is a phantasm like that of sovereignty, or of a pure origin, ipseity, uncontaminated presence, and the self-coinciding self, which would need to be exposed and denounced? In other words, if deconstruction is, as Naas argues, the deconstruction of the phantasm, would the phantasm of "dying alive" need to be deconstructed too or is the phantasm already deconstructive?[4]

The Phantasm of Dying Alive

So, in what way is "dying alive" a phantasm? Doubtless, it cannot be taken as describing a true or real occurrence—one cannot really die alive—but this phantasm has a very powerful effect. As Derrida emphasizes, the phantasm, even though it is traditionally opposed to the real, is "really [*effectivement*] more effective, more powerful, it is *really* [en effet] *more powerful* than what is opposed to it, whether good sense, reality or perception of the real, etc." (BSII 201/137). In fact, the perception of the real has less power or effectiveness than this "quasi-hallucination" (201/137). Robinson's phantasm is "more real, more effective for him, in its psychic reality, than what is opposed to it by or in the name of a reality principle" (201/137).

What, then, can be said of the phantasm of dying alive? The originary, spectral phantasm of "dying alive" is the contamination of two supposedly contradictory states or conditions. Since life and death as such are not separable as such, in other words, since death, and for that matter, life as such, is not a self-identical notion, the opposition of living and dying can no longer be strictly pertinent. The phantasm resists the "What is?" question regarding its ontological status. This is why the phantasm of dying alive—"to survive death while really dying"—is described by Derrida as unthinkable. Accordingly, a phantasm is described as "a certain 'as if' (an 'as if' in which one neither believes nor does not believe)," as if, perhaps "something could still *happen* to the dead one to affect the body" during cremation or the burial (BSII 217/149). Due to this undecidable structure, the only access or approach to the phantasm can be at the level of pathos.

The phantasm of dying alive describes the situation in which one allows oneself to be affected by this intolerable that goes beyond sense. As Derrida notes, "under the sign of this 'as if,' 'perhaps,' 'I do not know,' we allow ourselves to have an impression made on us, we allow ourselves to be *affected*" (BSII 217/149). What Derrida calls dying alive is "an affect, a feeling, a tonality of pathos, [where] we allow ourselves really to be affected by a possibility of the impossible, by a possibility excluded by sense" (217/149). The senses and good sense would indicate that dying alive and its affect or tonality be "excluded by what is often called the reality of the reality principle, i.e. by the impossible possibility that the dead one can be still affected [*le mort soit affecté*] or that we could still be affected by the dead one" (217–218/149). According to this reality, any "being-affected is interrupted by death"; in other words, there can be no affect without life, without sensibility (217/149).[5]

Yet, Derrida states,

> it is precisely because this certainty [KS: that there can be no life without sensibility] is terrifying and literally intolerable, just as unthinkable [. . .] as the contradiction of the living dead, that what I call this obscure word "phantasm" imposed itself on me. I do not know if this usage of the word "phantasm [*fantasme*]" is congruent or compatible with any philosophical concept of the *phantasma*, of fantasy or fantastic imagination, any more than with the psychoanalytic concept of the phantasm [*fantasme*], supposing, which I do not believe, that there is one, that there is only one, that is clear, univocal, localizable. (BSII 218/149)

At once situated between consciousness and the unconscious, simultaneously inside and outside, the phantasm is thus auto- and hetero-affective. If auto-affection, as Derrida formulates it in *Of Grammatology*, is a universal structure of experience and associated with life and all living beings, then the experience of the phantasm is simultaneously "auto-hetero-affective" (BSII 130–131/83), where the "nearest and the farthest, the same and the other, touch each other and come into contact" (124/78). For "the phantasmatic nature of what orients our desire and our terror, our experience (let's call it our Robinsonian experience) of the living dead," concerns "the simultaneously [*à la fois*] auto-affective and hetero-affective structure of the phantasm" (224/170). Put otherwise, the auto-affective experience of the phantasm, *my* phantasm, is irreducibly inhabited by hetero-affection.

So, we have surmised that dying alive is an all-powerful phantasm, but its "fictive or fantasmatic virtuality in no way diminishes the real almightiness [*toute-puissance*] of what thus presents itself to fantasy" (BSII 192/130). For, as Derrida writes, the phantasm is omnipotent and almighty, an almightiness that "organizes and rules over everything we call life and death, life death [*la vie la mort*]" (192/130). Derrida further elaborates: "This power of almightiness [*puissance de la toute-puissance*] belongs to a beyond of the opposition between being or not being, life and death, reality and fiction" (192/130). Then, the only possible access to or presentiment of death can be via or through the phantasm of dying alive since it is not possible to have a direct access to death, to death *as such*.

Thinking Death

To demonstrate this Derrida will accordingly take a detour through Heidegger's "The Thing" to show that thinking death *as such*, as Heidegger would wish, is not possible.[6] In session 5 Derrida turns to a "famous passage" in Heidegger's "The Thing" (BSII 182/121).[7] According to Heidegger, man alone dies. Human beings are called mortals (*Sterblichen*) because they "*can* die [sterben *können*]" (171/176). He comments that to die means "to be capable of death as death [*Tod als Tod*]." This capability, this ability, *Vermögen*, Derrida adds, is a power. This power is the "power of the as such," a being capable of the *as such* (184/122–123). Therefore, "access or relation to death is a being-able, a power (*Können, Vermögen*)" (183/122). Only man can die because only mortals are capable of death as death. "Such a power or potency defines the mortal, man as mortal," and "this power to have access to the *as such* of death . . . is none other than access to the ontological difference, and thereby to Being as Being [*l'être en tant qu'être*]" and not to "being as being [*l'étant en tant qu'étant*]" (BSII 184/123). Heidegger's aim is to suggest that man must now be defined not simply as a living being but as a mortal. This is why "rational living beings [*vernünftigen Lebenwesen*] must first *become* mortals [Sterblichen werden]" (171/176). This is what Derrida calls Heidegger's great lesson.

Derrida, however, finds himself deaf to this lesson. As he conveys in *The Beast and the Sovereign, 2*, access to death as such, access to dying properly speaking or to death itself, is not possible. We cannot *think* death as Heidegger believes. What the phantasmatics of living death suggests is that perhaps death *as such* is not something that can be *thought about*. If death *as such* does not appear to us, if our only possible access is not through thinking death, then it is only via a meditation on the phantasmatic that we can have access to it. And, conversely, any reflection on the phantasmatic must pass through the experience of living death, a "living death beyond life" (BSII 186/124). Derrida observes, thus putting into question the supposed difference between thinking and imagining, "perhaps thinking death as such, in the sense that Heidegger wants to give it, is still only imagination. *Fantasia*, fantastic phantasmatics [*fan-*

tastique phantasmatique]" (176/117). For, as Robinson knows, "we die alive anyway [*de toute façon on meurt vivant*]" (176/117).

The Intemporality of the Unconscious

Derrida turns to Freud's essay "The Unconscious" ("Das Unbewusste" [1915] SE XIV) where he situates the phantasm in "this place without place," at once "ubiquitous" and "unlocatable" between "the system of the unconscious and the system of conscious perception" (BSII 218–219/150). The phantasm's liminal location is due to the fact that the concept of each system is "inadequate" to account for it or for what Freud calls "phantasmatic formations [*Phantasiebilungen*]" (218/150). In section 5 of this essay, entitled "The Special Characteristics of the System Ucs.," Freud mentions that "the processes of the unconscious system are intemporal (*Zeitlos*) and are not ordered according to the consecutiveness of the temporal order" (221/151). As Derrida points out, this intemporality is also "an indifference to contradiction" (221/151). If we are to continue to dare to think what "phantasm ['*fantasme*']," dying a "living death or to *die in one's lifetime*" means, we have to remember this unlocatability, this intemporality of what is under question (221/151–152).

Timelessness in Freud's Writings

Numerous references to timelessness and the unconscious can be found throughout the Freudian corpus. The "Editor's Introduction" to *The Ego and the Id* in the *Standard Edition* provides a very helpful summary of the references to the unconscious in Freud's writings.[8] The unconscious is very briefly mentioned in the early works, such as *Project for a Scientific Psychology* (1895), *Studies on Hysteria* (1895), and *The Interpretations of Dreams* (1900), chapter 7. Apart from passing allusions in *The Interpretations of Dreams* and "On Narcissism," the first explicit mention of the timelessness of the unconscious is in a footnote added in 1907 to the last chapter of *The Psychopathology of Everyday Life* (1906): "The unconscious is quite [completely, in general—KS] timeless [*Das Unbewusste ist überhaupt zeitlos*]."[9] In the scientific meeting of the Vienna Psycho-Analytical Society that took place on November 8, 1911, to discuss "the supposed timelessness of the unconscious," Freud makes the remark about the unconscious that it "functions without the element of time."[10] He calls it "a system in which the element of time plays no role whatsoever" but displays "something that resembles 'spatiality'" (308). This permits us, he says, to infer "a sort of localization" (308).

The timelessness of the unconscious is further considered in section 2 of Freud's essay "The Unconscious" (1915): "The processes of the system *Ucs.* are timeless, i.e., they are not ordered temporally, are not altered by the passage of time; they have no reference to time at all. Reference to time is bound up, once again, with the work of the system Cs."[11] Freud also observes that "all of what is essential from childhood has been retained" in childhood memories (148). Freud describes the unconscious in *The Interpretation of Dreams* (1900) as "the true psychical reality [*eigentlich reale Psychische*]" because "it is as much unknown [*unbekannt*] to us as the reality of the external world [*das Reale der Außenwelt*]."[12] Our sense organs are just as incapable as the inadequate presentation of the data of consciousness. Moreover, the logic of temporal reality does not apply to the unconscious. In "Thoughts for the Times on War and Death" of the same year Freud observes that the unconscious does not believe in its own death: our unconscious "knows nothing that is negative, and no negation; in it contradictories coincide. For that reason it does not know its own death."[13] This is because the unconscious cannot acknowledge anything negative and death "has a negative content" (296). The structures of the unconscious are unaffected by the passage of time. All mnemic material (the original impression as well as the material's subsequent impressions) persists and is preserved.

Freud presents a summary of his views regarding the unconscious in *Beyond the Pleasure Principle* (1920): "We have learnt that unconscious mental processes [*unbewussten Seelenvorgänge*] are in themselves 'timeless [*zeitlos*].' This means in the first place that they are not ordered temporally [*nicht zeitlich geordnet warden*], that time does not change them in any way [*die Zeit nichts an ihnen verändert*] and that the idea of time [*Zeitvorstellung*] cannot be applied to them. These are negative characteristics which can only be clearly understood if a comparison is made with *conscious* mental processes."[14] *The Ego and the Id* (1923) sees the introduction of the term "das Es," the id, derived from the German psychiatrist Georg Groddeck and adapted by Freud. The reason for resorting to the unconscious is Freud's belief that the psychology of consciousness is incapable of solving the problems of dreams and hypnosis. The state in which very powerful mental processes or ideas "existed before becoming conscious [*Bewusstmachung*] is called by us *repression* [*Verdrängung*]."[15] He makes clear that "all that is repressed is unconscious, but not all that is *Ucs.* is repressed [*es bleibt richtig, dass alles Verdrängte ubw ist, aber nicht alles Ubw ist auch verdrängt*]" (287/18). After 1920 the categories of the Freudian theoretical apparatus undergo a change and the main properties of the system *Ucs.* reappear in the agency of the id. Freud will refrain from using the term "unconscious" in a systematic fashion and will from now on use the id in order to refer to the instinctual life or "the dark, inaccessible [*dunkle, unzugängliche*] part of our personality."[16] Described as "a chaos, a cauldron full of seething excitations [*einen Kessel voll brodelnder Erregungen*]," Freud explains, "the logical laws of thought [*die logischen Denkgesetze*] do not apply in the id," nor does the law of contradiction (73). "There is nothing in the id that corresponds to the idea of time [*Zeitvorstellung*]; there is no recognition [*Anerkennung*] of the passage of time [*zeitlichen Ablaufs*]" and "no alteration in its mental processes [*Verdrängung des seelischen Vorgangs*] is produced by the passage of time" (511/74). All its processes are dominated by the "economic [. . .] which is intimately linked to the pleasure principle" (74). He notes "the inalterability by time of the repressed" and further refines the descriptions of the id (74). In this paper Freud attributes unconsciousness to other portions of the mind (75). Now the ego is understood as a portion of the id. The unconscious contains more than the repressed; it includes all our memories, thoughts, and wishes, some of which can gain access to the preconscious and consciousness.

We can recapitulate Freud's views regarding the temporality of the unconscious by saying that there is no such thing as temporal order in the unconscious; the logic of temporal reality does not apply to the unconscious (succession may be replaced by simultaneity), a system in which the element of time plays no role whatsoever; the unconscious is inalterable by time, all mnemic material is preserved, *all* wishes, instinctual impulses, modes of reaction and attitudes of childhood are not destroyed but merely overlaid and persist; the unconscious believes itself to be immortal and thus fails to acknowledge the passage of time or mortality; and finally the law of non-contradiction does not apply to it.[17]

TIMELESSNESS IN DERRIDA'S WRITINGS

Derrida's earliest remarks on timelessness can be traced back to his introduction to Husserl's *The Origin of Geometry* (*L'origine de la géometrie*). There he writes that the objectivity of a geometrical truth would not be what it is without the pure possibility of an inquiry into a pure language in general. Without this possibility, it would become neither omnitemporal nor intelligible for all. In a note, Derrida explains that "'supratemporality [*Überzeitlichkeit*]' and 'timelessness' (*Zeitlosigkeit*) are defined in their transcendence or their negativity only in *relation* to worldly and factual temporality. Once the latter is reduced, they appear as omnitemporality (*Allzeitlichkeit*), the concrete mode of temporality in general" (OrG 70n1/77n75). Derrida underscores the relation of timelessness to a common conception of time in his "Freud and the Scene of Writing," writing that "the timelessness [*l'intemporalité*] of the unconscious is no doubt determined only in opposition to a common concept of time, a traditional concept, the metaphysical concept: the time of mechanics or the time of consciousness" (WD 318/215). If temporality is the temporality of consciousness, of philosophy, then *Zeitlosigkeit* can seem to be atemporal and non-linear only from the linear-progressive viewpoint of the time of consciousness. At the end of the passage Derrida adds, "We ought perhaps to read Freud the way Heidegger read Kant: like the cogito [*je pense*], the unconscious is no doubt timeless [*intemporel*] only from the standpoint of a certain vulgar conception of time" (WD 318/215).[18]

In his essay "Différance" in *Margins of Philosophy* Derrida labels the unconscious a "metaphysical name" because "the unconscious is not, as we know, a hidden, virtual or potential self-presence. It differs from, and defers itself, which doubtless means that it is woven [*se tisse*] of differences, and also that it sends out, delegates, representatives, proxies" (M 21/20).[19] There is no chance that it "exists," is "present," or is "itself" somewhere, and even less chance that it might become conscious. The unconscious is not a "thing" or "a virtual or masked consciousness." "This radical alterity as concerns every possible mode of presence is marked by the irreducible effects of the *après-coup*" (21/21, trans. mod.). And, "in order to describe traces," so as to read "the traces of 'unconscious' traces (there are no 'conscious' traces), the language of presence and absence, the metaphysical discourse of phenomenology, is inadequate" (21/20–21, trans. mod.).

I cannot bear it. "I don't have the heart." To dare to think the "phantasm" of the living-dead courage is needed. I do not have the courage, the courage "to bear the weight of this bearing (BSII 223/153). Should there be any courage, it could only be the courage of my fear.

The Phantasm and the Event

Derrida's reading of Hélène Cixous in *H. C. for Life, That Is to Say . . .* urges us to think the relation between the phantasm and the event. Since the phantasm eludes the grasp of the philosophical, it requires being thought at the limits. For Derrida, what is at stake in Cixous's texts is "a new logic of the phantasm and the event which, inseparable from a poetics of the event, takes into account an unheard-of, performative might, a mighty power of making-say [*faire-dire*] as making-happen or arrive [*faire arrive*] of the *might* [puissance] of the event," a might that a theory of speech acts cannot subdue or overpower (H. C. 73/77). And this is precisely what Derrida brings to bear on his reading of Cixous, a poetics of the event that "produces magically, miraculously, and quasi-mystically the very thing it nominates" (95/97). For Derrida, and for Cixous, it becomes a matter of "analyz[ing] the phantasm as much as produc[ing] the event, in the same twofold gesture [*geste dédoublé*]" (95/103). This is precisely what, Derrida believes, Cixous "continually puts to work [*fait travailler*]," the "production of a living event, which it brings into the world (95/103) . . . *while analyzing it* [tout en l'analysant]"—making and interpreting "indissociably" (95/104). There is no other "rule for reading" than, Derrida writes, to at once "make and to interpret while countersigning. If interpretation supposes analysis, that is to say, the *analuein* of the unbinding [*déliaison*] that unties, then *to make* or *do*, on the contrary, comes down to binding [*à lier*], to binding oneself [*à se lier*] and allying oneself [*se lier et s'allier*], to doing the contrary at the same time" (95/104).

Derrida's intention, he admits, was to prove that "the apparently subordinated might of the subjunctive was potentially mightier than that of the present indicative of the verb," that is, of the constative (H. C. 96/104). Here Derrida links a certain omnipotence, which he might be tempted to call "magic," to the im-possible, unpower, vulnerability, and death (98/107). A certain exploration of the performative force of the writing, Derrida claims, would display "the irrecusable effectiveness" of the *phantasmata* under consideration (98/108). To be sure, the distinction between the phantasm and the so-called actual or external reality is by no means "discredited" but "one would have to rethink it from this place [*repenser depuis ce lieu*] where it does not yet take place [*n'a pas encore lieu*]" (99/108). The border between the real and the phantasmatic, for example, between real seduction and the phantasm of seduction, is not yet secured. Along the same lines, while pursuing a reading of magic, animism, and omnipotence of thoughts in Freud's *Totem and Taboo*, Derrida complains that Freud places too much faith in the distinction between the real or the actual and the phantasm, acting as if the "effects of the affect" were not real events, as if the "as if" had no real effect (101/111). What Freud is displaying, Derrida believes, is an ignorance or dismissal of "the knowledge and power of language in general" (101/111). He seems unaware, Derrida comments, that "the effect, both affective and effective, of a performative is always magical in appearance. It always operates as if by an enchantment" (101/112). Freud introduces the thought of animism, a theory of being-for-life [*Belebtheit*] and then says very little about it in terms of anthropo-ethnological experience (*Erfahrung*). As Derrida recounts, Freud claims that "any people, as a people, any culture known and determined by experience has its own *Geistervorstellung*, a theory of revenants" (103/113). "There is no culture," Derrida states, "without *unheimlich* spectrality, without an organization of haunting" (103/113). Freud speaks of a *Belebtheit*, of which in Derrida's assessment, "we can say nothing by anthropological, culturalist, or ethnological experience, and which is not even a philosophical doctrine [. . .] but a quasi-originary *Belebtheit* that must announce itself to some pre-empirical or pre-positive experience" (103/113–114). According to Derrida, it is this experience that "writes and analyzes itself, maybe *experiments itself* [s'expérimente] each time that in the life and works of Hélène Cixous the mighty power of the 'might' is at work." This experience "puts this *Belebtheit* to work," "by provoking the event, by making-letting it happen [*faisant-laissant arriver*] before any philosophical, scientific, or cultural thesis on being as life or on the essence of the living" (103/114). "This experience of *Belebtheit*, which makes and analyzes the phantasm," is not a stance on the essence of being as life. Not an "entity [*étant*]," the life of this *Belebtheit* is rather "a mighty power of the 'might' without an other side, without a contrary" (103–104/114). "Death is neither unknown nor denied nor avoided," Derrida remarks, "it is simply not a contrary and another opposite side of living, a yonder or a beyond" (104/114).

Survivance

Let us turn from the deployment "this poetico-performative, the magical *might* [*puissance poético-performative et magique*]" to a number of crucial passages in session 5 of *The Beast and the Sovereign, 2*, on the question of survivance, in order to show the interrelation of the notions of dying alive, the phantasm, and survivance (H. C. 104/114). My remarks will be in the form of a commentary on these passages. We started out with Derrida's claim in his discussion of *Robinson Crusoe* that "a book the text of which is fiction in the first person, inserting into the living narrative quotations, inserts, inscriptions from a journal speaking in the first person," is both alive and dead. Each time a trace is left behind, whether gestural, verbal, written, and so on, a certain machinality consigns this trace to a sur-vival. Derrida further comments: "The book lives its beautiful death. That's also finitude, the chance and the threat of finitude, this alliance of the dead and the living" (BSII 193/130). What is most notable in this passage is Derrida's description of finitude. It has become very popular these days to speak about Derrida's work as espousing a radical finitude. What the preceding passage and the ones that follow make clear is that finitude is not to be considered as the being-toward-death or mortality of a living being called man or Dasein, but rather involves an alliance of the living and the dead. This thinking of finitude, rather than indicating the limit or termination of mortal life, leads to thinking a *certain* circle of lifedeath.[20] I will briefly turn to this *certain* circle at the end of this chapter.

Derrida proceeds to provide a further gloss on finitude, elaborating it as survival. This survival, however, despite the grammar of *überleben* or *fortleben*, as in the case of Benjamin, for example, discussed in *Memoires: For Paul de Man*, does not signify something that is "*above*" life" (BSII 193/131). Nor does it "add something extra to life" or "cut something from it" (194/131). It will be also recalled that since the "Différance" essay Derrida has consistently shown a preference for the *-ance* ending, which marks a suspended status between the active and passive voice. Like *différance*, *revenance*, and *restance*, Derrida expresses that he "prefers 'survivance' to the active voice of the active infinitive 'to survive' or the substantializing substantive survival" (194/131). Of the relation between finitude and survivance Derrida states: "I shall say that this finitude is *survivance*. Survivance in a sense of survival that is neither life nor death pure and simple, a sense that is not thinkable on the basis of the opposition between life and death" (193/130).

Derrida goes on to expound on what he is calling survivance by contrasting it with "lifedeath," a notion from the 1970s and '80s, which he discussed in texts on Freud (*The Post Card*), Nietzsche (*The Ear of the Other*), and Blanchot (*Parages*), where he considered and questioned prevalent notions of life and death: "No, the survivance that I am speaking of is something other than life death [*la vie la mort*] but a groundless ground [*un fond sans fond*] from which are detached [*se découpent*], identified, and opposed what we think we can identify under the name of death or dying (*Tod, Sterben*)" (BSII 194/131). Survivance is not quite lifedeath then but forms the abyssal base, the almost more "primordial" ground from which life and death arise, as it were. "It [*Ça*] begins with survival [*survie*]" (194/131). What Derrida refers to here as *ça*, besides grammatically designating the third-person, singular neutral pronoun "it," bears the traces of a reading of the psychoanalytic notion of *Ça*. Originally the French translation of Freud's *das Es* (SE: the id), *ça* for Lacan was conceived in linguistic terms as the unconscious origin of speech and was later equated with "the subject." With a nod to psychoanalysis, Derrida is referring to the abyssal ground without ground that is survivance as "it [*ça*]." *Ça* is survivance. Survivance, Derrida continues, "is where there is some other that has me at its disposal" (194/131). This other survivance is where the self is defenseless, when I am turned over to the other. I am survived by the other: "That is what the self is, that is what I am, what the *I* is, whether I am there or not. The other, the others, that is the very thing that survives me, structurally my survivor" (194/131). In a subtle rewriting, "the other" here is "the survivor of me," what is "called to survive me" (194/131).

As Derrida declares, "Like every trace, a book, the survivance of a book, from its first moment on, is a living-dead machine [*machine morte-vivante*]" (BSII 194/131). Every trace dies alive, is a living-dead machine that sur-vives. For there is survivance from the very first trace, from the very first breath.

Derrida comments:

> This survivance is broached from the moment of the first trace that is supposed to engender the writing of a book. From the first breath, this archive as survivance is at work. But once again, this is the case not only for books, or for writing, or for the archive in the current sense, but for everything from which the tissue of living experience [*le tissu de l'expérience vivante*], is woven [*tissé*], through and through. A weave of survival [*Tissage de survie*], like death in life or life in death, a weave [*tissage*] that does not come along to clothe a more

originary existence, a life or a body or a soul that would be supposed to exist naked under this clothing. (BSII 195/132)

The first thing to recall is that this survivance does not simply concern living experience or simply apply to what is living but is equally at work in writing, the book, the mark, the archive, or wherever there is a trace. We might then ask how to think this weave of survival? This weave is the interweaving of life with death or the intertwining of life and death, a meshwork, the texture of a fabric that would not be like clothing that covers a naked body or soul but that itself constitutes dying alive. Survivance is, Derrida writes, a weave, an interlacing of life and death in which the two can no longer be separable concepts or entities.

The Weave

The consideration of the notion of the weave is a long-standing matter in Derrida's writings. Recall that *texte* (derived from the Latin *textus*, meaning cloth, and from *texere*, to weave [*tisser*]) means cloth [*tissu*]. Rodolphe Gasché in *The Tain of the Mirror*, referring to "the problem of *symplokē*," the weave, as "a major *fil conducteur* in Derrida's writings," contrasts references in Derrida's work to a textual chain, a tissue of differences, textile, and texture with its classical treatment in Plato's dialogues, in particular the *Statesman* (*Tain* 97).[21] In Plato's dialogue the craftsmanship of the weaver is the leading paradigm for the activity of the true statesman even though the latter is shown to have a much more complicated task. Gasché shows that for Plato dialectics unites and unifies elements that are opposite, tying together strands that are diverse in nature with the aim of forming an organic whole (*Tain* 95). At the beginning of *Dissemination*, Derrida makes a reference to "a kingly weaving process (*basiliken symplokēn*) (306a), the activity of the true statesman (*politikon*). He notes that *symplokē* is essentially dialectical when he states: "dialectics is also an act of weaving, a science of *symplokē*" (Diss 122). In the *Sophist* Plato goes as far as calling *symplokē* "the very condition of discourse" (Diss 166). While acknowledging the importance of terms such as *Geflecht*, *Verflechtung*, and *Verwebung* in the works of Freud, Husserl, and Heidegger, Derrida's notion of the text—what he calls the tissue of differences of force, the system of referrals of difference or chain of differential referrals, the economy of traces, the texture of the text, or the text in general—differs from the classical *symplokē* in that it is not governed by the values of truth, totality, and unity.

Ground

What is of even greater interest is that Derrida follows the discussion of the weave with the mention of "the groundless ground [*le fond sans fond*] of this quasi-transcendentality of living to death [*vivre à mort*] or of death as sur-vivance" (BSII 195/132). The weave constitutes the quasi-transcendental condition of possibility and impossibility of life and death, forming a ground without ground for living death or dying alive. The phantasm of living death then has as its source, ground, or base (but a ground that is abyssal, an originary ground without ground) this tissue of survivance. Here Derrida seems to be pushing the thinking of the second of what, in the *Death Penalty, 2*, seminar, following Heidegger, he calls the two "accentuations" of the principle of reason, namely, the interpretation of reason that bears on sameness, the Same as Being and *Grund*.[22] It would no longer be a matter of thinking the famous Leibnizian dictum *Nihil est sine ratione* (Nothing is without reason) in terms of reason, or a thinking of being from beings or from that which is a being, but rather as being, that is, as ground (*Grund*).[23] Heidegger's interpretation emphasizes a history of Western thinking that thinks being as ground and not as *ratio* or cause.[24] This, for Heidegger, leads to a thinking of a ground of the ground, a ground without ground, a ground that is also an abyss. For, to the extent that being as such grounds, it remains without-ground—the fathomless. Being, then, "is" the abyss. I argue in chapter 1 and elsewhere that in various writings in his last years (i.e., in *Rams*; *Chaque fois unique, la fin du monde*; the *Death Penalty, 2*, seminar; and *The Beast and the Sovereign, 1*) Derrida furthers an elaboration of this second accentuation as far as possible, developing every other as a ground, whose death inevitably leads to an abyssal loss of ground.[25]

Following a discussion of the weave of survival at work from the moment of the first trace, Derrida then turns to a consideration of what we may call a "certain circle." Survivance belongs to this *certain* circle of lifedeath, a circle that by definition cannot be self-enclosed but rather is in excess of itself. As Derrida remarks in *The Beast and the Sovereign, 2*, seminar: "Living death beyond life, live to death, living death, etc. This is perhaps the same circle [*Vivre la mort au-delà de la vie, vivre à mort, mourir vivant, etc. C'est peut-être le même cercle*]" (BSII S5 186/124). Derrida immediately poses the question "What is that—the circle?" without providing an obvious answer. In a seminar taken up by the treatment of a series of circles, the details of the circle of dying alive, composed of the interweaving of *mourir vivant, survivance, revenance,* and *arrivance* (to which we could also add *restance*, in addition to *demeurance* and *demourance* from *Demeure* and *la mourance* from "Avances"), remain unexplored.[26] The question before us is this: How are we to think this *certain* circle—not cycle—if life and death cannot be rigorously separated, if death is not termination, and what is "beyond" life belongs to a returning circle of survivance whose intertwined elements are made up of dying alive, remaining (*restance*), arriving (*arrivance*), and ghostly returning (*revenance*), forming a ground without ground from which life and death are detached?

When Derrida writes in session 4 of *The Beast and the Sovereign, 2,* of the inseparability and indissociability of life and death, he refers to the logic of survival as "a survival of the remainder, the remains [*une survivance du reste, des restes*]" (BSII 176/117). Survivance is a remaining but not the remaining of a plenitude or an entity that is fully present and maintains itself. Survivance defies essence and any substantiality. Something remains, but this something is not a portion left over of something larger. It is not even a thing. Something survives in the crepuscular realm between life and death—not life or death themselves but what makes their distinction possible. To survive, to remain, is a spectral "mode of appearing"; it is to come back hauntingly. In *Mal d'Archive* Derrida recounts Yosef Hayim Yerushalmi's praise for Lou Andreas-Salome, who reports to have read in Freud's *Moses* a new form of "the return of the repressed." Yet this time not as "phantoms out of the past" but as, what one can call, "triumph of life." Survivance no longer means death and the return of the specter, Derrida comments, but the survival of "an excess of life that resists annihilation" (AF 96/60).

Survivance does not await "actual" death, nor does to sur-vive mean to escape death. We are all, structurally speaking, survivors. We die alive. In fact, everything, every trace, dies alive and what dies alive survives. And since we are always leaving traces, this allows something to remain, to live on. It will be recalled that a trace is the minimal structure necessary, or the constituting possibility, for there to be any difference. As soon as there is difference, referral to the other, or experience, there is a trace.

Each and every trace dies alive and thus sur-vives. Its very condition is to die alive, to be living dead. Since "dying alive," by definition, resists the tribunal of truth and reality, in other words, since we cannot really die alive, dying alive can only be a phantasm. And we are *affected* by this phantasm, this virtuality, a certain impossibility that organizes all that we call life and death. The phantasm of living dead or dying alive, then, calls to be thought with survivance.

As Derrida said in the interview he granted *Le Monde* in 2004, this sur-vival has nothing to do with one's will or intention but rather it is structural:

> The trace I leave to me means at once my death, to come or already come, and the hope that it will survive me. It is not an ambition of immortality; it is fundamental. I leave here a bit of paper, I leave, I die; it is impossible to exit this structure; it is the unchanging form of my life. Every time I let something go, I live my death in writing.[27]

One sur-vives one's own death. One dies alive, since the line between life and death cannot be rigorously demarcated and since the living-present divides itself (*se divise*)—it divides itself between its life and its survival—its specter leaves it and survives. The living-present bears death within itself and inscribes within its immediacy what would survive it (E 61). This makes each of us a survivor in reprieve (*en sursis*)—life itself has the temporality of a reprieve.

Perhaps an Other Time, Place, and Logic: Affect, the Phantasm, and the "As If"

We have already established that Derrida's later seminars mark a return to the notion of the unconscious. The time of "the world," what we call time, belongs to consciousness—it is *the time of* consciousness. And consciousness is presumed by life in "this world," which involves auto-affection. Interrogating phenomenology as a philosophy of life, from very early on, Derrida questioned the enigma of the concept of life and its relation to presence. Leaving aside for another occasion a discussion of the "torsions" and the rewriting that the notion of experience has gone through in Derrida's work, it can be said that life, conventionally conceived, is also bound up with experience.²⁸ Experience is lived experience, something that the dead cannot partake of. The dead one does not belong to the time of consciousness. What the dead one and the id (*ça*) share is that they both belong to a realm that is intemporal, that "intemporality" which Freud attributes to the unconscious.²⁹ In *The Beast and the Sovereign, 2*, Derrida comments that besides being intemporal, the id is also unlocatable. This unlocatability and this intemporality of what is under question may help us to think what the "phantasm ['*fantasme*']" of dying a "living death or to *die in one's lifetime*" might mean (BSII 221/151–152).

In *The Beast and the Sovereign, 2*, Derrida refers to "the possibility of another so-called logic of the unconscious" (BSI 146/101), while in his previous seminar, *The Death Penalty* seminar (2000–2001), presented before *The Beast and the Sovereign* but published subsequently, Derrida touches on another unconscious. In a digression, he takes time to affirm that the "unconditional im-possible (e.g. the gift, the pardon, hospitality, etc.)" does not fall under the purview of consciousness or self-presence and that he has always called attention to

> this aneconomy, to an other concept of the unconscious [*un autre concept de l'inconscient*], one that is precisely not determined through and through by self-preservation, conservation, by keeping [*la garde*], by memory, the calculation of a repression that never creates or destroys anything (nothing is lost, nothing is created, such would be, on the contrary, the axiom of Freudian conscious that I was calling into question by speaking of the im-possible, the un-conditional, the gift, forgiveness or hospitality; in this way, I was calling into question the logic—one that is, for that matter, incontestable and very powerful (it is the very force and principle of reason, reason since Freud)—of a certain economistic [*économiste*] concept of the Freudian unconscious that represses but forgets nothing: I was calling it into question in the name, not of a faithful memory, but of a certain radical forgetting [*un certain oubli radical*] that is no longer even repression. (DP2 232–233/172)

In the previously cited paragraph on the intemporality of the unconscious from the sixth session of *The Beast and the Sovereign, 2*, seminar, Derrida mentions a certain *Erlebnis*, "a 'conscious' or 'preconscious' 'lived experience'" belonging to the unconscious (BSII 220/151). He asks, how can a lived experience also belong to the unconscious? Naturally, such an experience that is "quite unintelligible, impossible even," defies sense and "logico-philosophical consciousness *qua* consciousness" (220/151). Derrida labels it "an impossible thought, a thought of the impossible" that would be a contradiction between two systems, one excluding contradiction and the other never hampered by it (220/151).

We need to remember the intemporality and the indifference to contradiction of the unconscious, Derrida says, if we want "to continue to dare to think what 'phantasm' seems to mean" (BSII 221/151). Freud situates the phantasm in a liminal position, in a *between*-place: "this place without place that is ubiquitous and unlocatable" somewhere "between the conscious and consciousness [. . .] between the system of the unconscious and the system of conscious perception" (218/150).[30] Appealing to Heidegger's sentiment already discussed in his seminar, that we should not be afraid of formal contradictions or so-called vicious circles, and also to Hegel, Derrida reminds us that these apparent contradictions augur "the beginning of thought" (221/152). To think the unimaginable and the incongruous and the zone in which this impossible affects us, we must think it as phantasm (217/149). For this thinking of affect requires "a certain 'as if,'" "'as if' something could still *happen* to the dead one" (217/149). Derrida further writes about this "impossible feeling":

> under the sign of this "as if," "perhaps," "I do not know," we allow ourselves to have an impression made on us, we allow ourselves to be *affected*, for this is an affect, a feeling, a tonality of pathos by a possibility of the impossible, by a possibility excluded by sense, by the senses and by good sense, excluded by what is often called the reality of the reality principle, i.e. by the impossible possibility that the dead one can be still affected or that we could still be affected by the dead one him- or herself, by the dead, by the death of the dead one itself, him or herself: just where this affection, this affect, this being-affected, everything seems to tell us, then, with an invincible authority, that this affection, this being-affected *of* the dead one or *by* the dead one is, precisely, interrupted, radically, irreversibly interrupted, annihilated, excluded by death, by the very sense of the word "death." There is no affect without life, no event without life, there is neither affect

nor event without sensibility, that power to be affected that is called life. (BSII 217/149)

This is precisely why we have to deal with a phantasm. To attend to this affect, we must begin to think radically anew what is meant by affect, the phantasm, and the "as if." Is being-affected "excluded by death"? Is there "no affect without life"? For "to transform death into annihilation" would be "to deprive the dead one of everything through which she can still affect, *from the outside, from some exteriority*, affect our sensibility in the a priori forms of sensibility, as Kant would say, namely time and space" (BSII 242/168, trans. mod., my emphasis). If the dead one is not annihilated, not reduced to nonbeing, as Levinas says, but is what no longer responds, if there is room "for some survival [*quelque survie*]," how to think this sur-vival, this survivance? (237/164). If we were to follow Derrida's recommendation, in order to reflect on "the acute specificity of the phantasmatic [*fantasmatique*]" what needs to take place is to "pass through" the "experience of living death [*la mort-vivance*] and of affect, imagination and sensibility (space and time) as auto-hetero-affection" (244/170).

Not simply "a commitment [. . .], an oath, a duty" (BSII 357/258), but also a "promise of fidelity" addressed to you (243/169)—"a declaration of love" (357/259).

"[She] preferred . . . to die while loving, to die while loving life, to die alive . . . to die in [her] lifetime, to die while preferring life, even to die from loving life" (DP1 374/277–278).

"For she knew these things better than anyone else: pain, anxiety, illness— and death. Art and laughter, when they go together, do not run counter to suffering, they do not ransom or redeem it, but live off it; as for salvation, redemption, and resurrection, the absence of any illusion shines like a ray of living light through all of [her] life and work" (CFU 136/173).

Notes

Prologue: Salut—A Spectro-Poetics?

1. Derrida's thoughts regarding "the world" cannot be separated from a criticism of globalization and cosmopolitanism. Bound up with a Christian heritage, rooted in Roman Latinity, globalization refers to "a certain oriented history of human brotherhood" that views the "globe" as a marketplace. See Jacques Derrida, "Globalization, Peace, and Cosmopolitanism," in *Negotiations: Interventions and Interviews 1971–2001*, edited and translated by Elizabeth Rottenberg (Stanford: Stanford University Press, 2002), 375. A more detailed discussion, which is not possible here, would have to take into consideration Derrida's use of *mondialisation* (1993); worldwide-ization, *mondialatinisation* (1996); and *altermondialisation* (2004). For cosmopolitanism, see Jacques Derrida, *Adieu à Emmanuel Lévinas* (Paris: Galilée, 1997), translated by Pascale-Anne Brault and Michael Naas as *Adieu: To Emmanuel Levinas* (Stanford: Stanford University Press, 1999); *Cosmopolites de tous les pays, encore un effort!* (Paris: Galilée, 1997), translated by Mark Dooley as "On Cosmopolitanism," in *On Cosmopolitanism and Forgiveness* (New York: Routledge, 2016); *Le droit à la philosophie du point de vue cosmopolitique* (Paris: Galilée, 1997). Derrida's late writings shift emphasis from the universalizing, ontological, cosmological import of "the world" to a thinking of "world" in relation to death and singularity—to the death of the other. Also see Jacques Derrida, *Surtout, pas des journalistes!* (Paris: Galilée, 2016), originally published in English as "Above All, No Journalists!," in *Religion and Media*, edited by Hent de Vries and Samuel Weber (New York: Fordham University Press, 2001), 24/62, 37–38/68–69, 49–50/74–75, 74/90.

2. For Derrida's remarks on death, see Jacques Derrida, "The Three Ages of Jacques Derrida," interview with Kristine McKenna, *LA Weekly* (November 8–14, 2002), and Jacques Derrida [with Maurizio Ferraris], "Il Gusto del Segreto," edited by Giacomo Donis and David Webb (Rome-Bari: Gius. Laterza & Figli Spa, 1997); *A Taste for the Secret*, translated by Giacomo Donis (Malden, MA: Polity Press, 2001), 88.

3. In *Aporias*, we note perhaps the first appearance of the phrase "nothing less than the end of the world, with each death" (A 131/75). Michael Naas and Pascale-Anne Brault's introduction to *The Work of Mourning*, "To Reckon with the Dead: Jacques Derrida's Politics of Mourning," should be credited for anticipating and bringing to our attention this "end of the world." (No doubt, Derrida picked up on this connection in the French edition, insofar as he chose it for the title of the book.) The death of the friend, they write in the introduction, hits us each time "like the end of the world" (15). Quoting Derrida, the editors remark that Althusser's death "takes away the world itself" (15). "In 'each death' there is an end of the world," thus, they further note, "the world is lost" (15). "With *each first death*, the whole world is lost" (15).

4. Derrida refers to *salut* as a "strange word" also in "TA" 39/xl.

5. As Derrida writes in "Faith and Knowledge," the history of the word "religion" would in principle forbid every non-Christian from using it (FK 47/36). For a superlative, detailed examination of "Faith and Knowledge," see Michael Naas, *Miracle and Machine: Jacques Derrida and the Two Sources of Religion, Science, and the Media* (New York: Fordham University Press, 2012).

6. Jacques Derrida, ". . . . . . ," *Les Cahiers du Grif* 3, no. 1 (1997): 131–166, translated by Pascale-Anne Brault and Michael Naas as ". . . . . . . ," in *The Work of Mourning* (Chicago: University of Chicago Press, 2001), 165–188. This text later appeared in abbreviated form in CFU.

7. In *H. C. for Life, That Is to Say* . . . Derrida refers to the two *salut*s as "the *salut* that salutes and the *salut* that saves [*le salut qui salue et le salut qui sauve*]" (H. C. 67/69). In "How to Name" he describes the relation as "the two *salut*s salute each other from near or afar, the one *as* well *as* the other one operating and co-operating within the other that remains nevertheless apart [*le deux saluts se saluent de près ou de loin, l'un comme l'autre, l'un opérant et co-opérant dans l'autre qui reste pourtant à part*]" (CN 185/194).

8. I carried out an initial investigation into the relationship between Derrida and Nancy concerning terms related to *salut* in "Salut-ations" in my *Apparitions—Of Derrida's Other* (New York: Fordham University Press, 2010).

9. Jacques Derrida, "Comment nommer," in *Le poète que je cherche à être*, edited by Yves Charnet (Paris: La Table Ronde/Belin, 1996), 184, translated by Wilson Baldridge as "How to Name," in Michel Deguy, *Recumbents: Poems* (Middletown, CT: Wesleyan University Press, 2005), 194.

10. In "Le temps des adieux," Derrida refers to *salut* as a synonym of "the ambiguous word *adieu*" ("TA" 38/xi).

11. On at least three occasions—in "How to Name" (1996), "A Time for Farewells" (1998), and *Rogues* (2003)—Derrida expressed his wish to separate and keep dissociated the two senses of *salut*.

12. Peggy Kamuf, *To Follow: The Wake of Jacques Derrida* (Edinburgh: Edinburgh University Press, 2010), 105.

13. This modifies slightly Michael Naas's translation of this passage in Michael Naas, *Derrida from Now On* (New York: Fordham University Press, 2008), 272 (trans. mod., for my emphasis).

14. In "Les temps des adieux," in which Derrida calls "this ambiguous word 'adieu' (synonym of another equivocal word "*salut*") ("TA" 38/xl, trans. mod.), he nicely describes the relation between *adieu* (farewell) and *au-revoir* (until we meet again) thus: "Always and forever, 'farewell' and 'goodbye, until we meet again [*l'adieu et au-revoir*]' will continue to haunt each other [*hanter l'un l'autre*]. One will always remain the specter of the other, spectrality itself" (45/xlvi, trans. mod.).

15. Using the same language in "Les temps des adieux," Derrida calls for "an other *salut* [*un autre salut*]" ("TA" 27/xxviii, trans. mod.) and "an other form of adieu [*une autre forme d'adieu*]" (37/xxxviii).

16. A thorough discussion of the phantasm would require another project.

17. I am here using the translation of "How to Name?" provided by Garry Sherbert and Christopher Elson in their admirable *In the Name of Friendship: Deguy, Derrida, and Salut* (Leiden: Brill/Rodopi, 2017). Regrettably this remarkable volume, whose editors I salute and whose book I heartily recommend, came to my attention very late in the process of the preparation of my manuscript. "How to Name?" demonstrates the indispensable role of the poetry of Michel Deguy for Derrida's emphasis on the other *salut*. Deguy's poetics is engaged in the reassessment and reconfiguration of the role of the poet. Deguy's poetics of *salut*, not satisfied with merely naming and saving but also calling, is assigned to a new task, a new poetic act.

18. For selected examples of this formulation, see "vive-et-morte, survivante [alive-dead, living on]" (Par 200/189) and "mort-vivant-survivant [dead-alive-surviving]" (CN 201/ 215). In *Demeure—Maurice Blanchot* the survivor is described as "living-dead [*mort-vivant*]," while in *H. C. for Life, That Is to Say*, we encounter "la survie du mort vivant [translated as the afterlife of the living dead]" (H. C. 136/154).

19. This book will not be the book that at one time I had hoped to write. Circumstances changed it into another entity. Its dedicatee deserved the most elegant prose, yet this writer's anguish forced him to settle for what he could manage.

Chapter 1. The World after the End of the World

1. Portions of this chapter were first presented at the fourth Derrida Today conference held at Fordham University, New York on May 30, 2014.

2. Derrida specifically leaves the last line of Celan's poem, "*Die Welt ist fort, ich muss dich tragen*," in German. A discussion of this line also appears in

the following works of Derrida: *Voyous: Deux essais sur la raison* (Paris: Galilée, 2003); *Rogues: Two Essays on Reason*, translated by Pascale-Anne Brault and Michael Naas (Stanford: Stanford University Press, 2005); *Chaque fois unique, la fin du monde* (Paris: Galilée, 2003); *Béliers. Le dialogue ininterrompu: entre deux infinis, le poème* (Paris: Galilée, 2003); "Rams," translated by Thomas Dutoit and Philippe Romanski in *Sovereignties in Question: The Poetics of Paul Celan*, edited by Thomas Dutoit and Outi Pasanen (New York: Fordham University Press, 2005); *Séminaire La bête et le souverain. Volume II (2002–2003)*, edited by Michel Lisse, Marie-Louise Mallet, and Ginette Michaud (Paris: Galilée, 2010); *The Beast and the Sovereign*, volume 2, translated by Geoffrey Bennington (Chicago: University of Chicago Press, 2011); "A Self-Unsealing Poetic Text: Poetics and Politics of Witnessing," translated by Rachel Bowlby, in *Revenge of the Aesthetic: The Place of Literature in Theory Today* (Berkeley: University of California Press, 2000), 180–207; revised English translation as "Poetics and Politics of Witnessing," in *Sovereignties in Question* (New York: Fordham University Press, 2005); expanded French version "Poétique et politique du témoignage," in *Derrida*, edited by Marie-Louise Mallet and Ginette Michaud (Paris: Editions de l'Herne, 2004), 521–539; and "Comment ne pas trembler," *Annali della Fondazione Europea del Disegno (Fondation Adami)*, vol. 2 (Milan: B. Mondadori, 2006).

3. See Ginette Michaud, "Juste le poème, peut-être (Derrida, Celan)," *Les Lettres Romanes* 64, no. 1–2 (2010): 3–47; 40. This article was collected in *Derrida, Celan. Just le poème, peut-être* (Paris: Hermann, 2017).

4. See Michael Naas, "Lifelines," *Epoché* 10, no. 2 (Spring 2006): 221–236, and *Derrida from Now On* (New York: Fordham University Press, 2008); Rodolphe Gasché, "De-closing the Horizon," in *Europe, or the Infinite Task: A Study of a Philosophical Concept* (Stanford: Stanford University Press, 2009); Ginette Michaud, "Singbarer Rest: Friendship, Impossible Mourning (Celan, Blanchot, Derrida)," *Oxford Literary Review* 31 (July 2009): 79–114, and "Juste le poème, peut-être (Derrida, Celan)," *Les Lettres Romanes* 64, nos. 1–2 (2010): 3–47, both collected in *Derrida, Celan. Just le poème, peut-être* (Paris: Hermann, 2017); J. Hillis Miller, "Derrida's Remains," in *For Derrida* (New York: Fordham University Press, 2009); Geoffrey Bennington, *Not Half No End: Militantly Melancholic Essays in Memory of Jacques Derrida* (Edinburgh: Edinburgh University Press, 2010); and Peggy Kamuf, "From Now On," in *To Follow: The Wake of Jacques Derrida* (Edinburgh: Edinburgh University Press, 2010), and "Teleiopoetic World," *SubStance* 43, no. 2 (2014): 10–19.

5. These must be considered merely as markers, in order not to fall into the trap of a developmental, historical narrative of the world.

6. My "account" is indebted to Rémi Brague, *La sagesse du monde. Histoire de l'expérience humaine de l'univers* (Paris: Fayard, 1999), translated by Teresa Lavender Fagan as *The Wisdom of the World: The Human Experience of the Universe in Western Thought* (Chicago: University of Chicago Press, 2003).

7. Hesiod *Theog.* 738.
8. Heraclitus DK 22 B1, 7, 53, 64, 66, 80, 90.
9. Empedocles DK 31 B13, 14.
10. Jeremiah 10: 16.
11. Pliny HN 2.3.4.
12. The first Platonic appearance of the word *kosmos* is in *Gorgias* 508a3.

13. Before the *Timaeus*, the term *kosmos* remained ambiguous and was far from the only one used by Plato to name the world. We find the terms *holon* ("all") and *ouranos* ("heavens") that are occasionally affirmed as synonyms and employed for one another. For *holon*, all (*Lysis* 214b6), *ouranos* and *kosmos* are used interchangeably in *Statesman* 269d, *Timaeus* 18b3. In the *Timaeus* itself, all these words are used, with all their ambiguity. *To holon* appears in 63a5. But does it only mean "the world" or the collection/entirety (ensemble) of things that make up the heavens (63a8)? *Kosmos* can mean "order" (29e4) or play on the sense of finery, jewelry (40a7). *Ouranos* can mean the celestial vault in which is contained all that there is. *To pan* is the most frequent term. It is not clear whether it is a matter of this world, this sky, or still the whole: *tode to pan, to pan tode, pan tode,* or simply *tode* (*Philebus* 28c4. Cf. Aeschylus, *Agamemnon* v. 160). The latter occurs in *Philebus*, in which Socrates speaks of *peri toude on kosmon legomen,* "this thing that we here call cosmos."

14. For further details, the reader is referred to Rémi Brague's *Aristote et la question du monde. Essai sur le contexte cosmologique et anthropologique de l'ontologie* (Paris: Presses Universitaires de France, 1988), an extremely rich and detailed account and analysis of the notion of the world, from which I have benefited.

15. See Juan Manuel Garrido's fine article, "Without World," *CR: The Centennial Review* 8, 3 (Winter 2008): 119–137; 121, where he wants to consider world "in itself," preceding all horizon, finitude, selfhood. That is, a "world *other* with respect to the lived world" (120). Cited further parenthetically in the text.

16. If there has been a contract or an agreement over millennia for there to be a "world," if there has been a ruse to make *as if* there is a "world," perhaps one justification to go along with this ruse—but not *in the name* of "the world"—would be for the sake of facilitating communication, exchange, economic and social progress for those who would not have access to them, for the sake of supporting institutions resisting a homo-hegemony, for the sake of political interventions beyond the nation-state, or for the sake of juridical reasons such as countering and prosecuting the so-called "crimes against humanity."

17. Cf. "Before being, I follow you [*avant d'être, je te suis*]" in Jacques Derrida, *L'animal que donc je suis*, edited by Marie-Louise Mallet (Paris: Galilée, 2006); *The Animal That Therefore I Am*, translated by David Wills (New York: Fordham University Press, 2008).

18. I will discuss portions of this preface in some detail as it still remains officially untranslated and requires in-depth commentary.

19. Rodolphe Gasché, "De-closing the Horizon," in *Europe, or the Infinite Task: A Study of a Philosophical Concept* (Stanford: Stanford University Press, 2009), 318.

20. Cf. Gasché, 318.

21. In "Teleiopoetic World" Peggy Kamuf argues that Derrida enlists *teleiopoesis* "in the deconstruction of the idea of a totalizable, unified world" (15) and eloquently demonstrates that each engagement with Celan's line "deconstructs the very idea of a unified, totalized, reconciled world" (16). The world, then, is always a "deconstructible world" (14). Kamuf's rich and perceptive piece concentrates more on a reading of Celan's line "*Die Welt is fort, ich muss dich tragen*," whereas this chapter focuses on "world" and its future.

22. From *Of Grammatology* (1967) to *The Truth in Painting* (1978), from *Signéponge* (1988) to *Khôra* (1993), from *Mal d'Archive* (1995) to *Artaud le Moma* (2002) and his last seminars, Derrida has always been very interested in the thought of the abyss and the *mise-en-abîme*, placement in the abyss. See, for example, *Of Grammatology* and *The Truth in Painting*. A treatment of the notion of abyss (*l'abîme*) throughout Derrida's work would require detailed elaboration.

23. The question of ground (*Grund*) is raised throughout German philosophy from Kant's reaction to Wolff in the first *Critique*, to the German Idealism of Fichte and Schelling and to Schopenhauer's 1813 thesis, *On the Fourfold Root of the Principle of Sufficient Reason*. Early on in *Being and Time*, as Heidegger explicates the components of the term "phenomenology," he remarks about the second part that "*logos* as *legomenon* can also mean ground, *ratio*" (SZ 34/32). In §58 of *Being and Time* he writes that Dasein *is* as thrown ground by projecting itself onto possibilities into which it has been thrown. It has been *released* (entlassen) from the ground so as to be *as the ground* (SZ 284). It should be noted that Heidegger displays reservations about viewing being as the ground of beings. The meaning of being, he writes, is not the "supporting ground of beings ['*Grund*' des Seienden]." Ground becomes accessible only as meaning, even if it is the abyss (*Abgrund*) of meaninglessness (SZ §32 152). This view can be supported by referring to Heidegger's *Nietzsche* (written in 1939), where he states that Being is the rejection of the role of grounding. Renouncing all grounding, "it is abyssal [*ab-gründing*]" (NII G 252/niv E 193).

In *The Metaphysical Foundations of Logic* (1928) Heidegger traces the appeal to ground back to Aristotle. In Aristotle's *Posterior Analytics*, Heidegger explains, to "understand" something is to know the grounds for something: "this reason is the *aitian*, the ground, the cause [*Ur-sache*] of the thing" (Book I, II, 71, b9ff.). Heidegger further comments that in Aristotle's *Metaphysics* (VII, I, 1028a, 36ff.) explanatory knowledge relies on *archē*, beginning, or departure (GA 26 136/110).

In the thirteenth session of the lecture course entitled *The Principle of Reason*, Heidegger explains that since *Grund* is the translation of *ratio*, this means that ratio has passed over into *Grund*. In the "Address" appended to this lecture course, Heidegger adds: "being is experienced as ground/reason [*Grund*]," which is interpreted as *ratio*, an account (GA 10 210/129). Derrida quotes extensively from this lecture course in the second volume of *The Death Penalty* seminars. Commenting on *Der Satz vom Grund*, Derrida writes that *Grund* can also be translated as "foundation or principle or axiom (*Grundsatz*)" (DP2 207/152). Derrida notes "the serious play" with *Satz*, which has several meanings, such as "the proposition that is put forth," and "the being that is ventured (*gesetzt*), the being that is posited, wagered, etc." and "the leap (*Satz*, also *Sprung*), discontinuity, the leap from the abyss or into the abyss (*Abgrund*)" (DP1 207/152). Heidegger, Derrida writes, believes that being should be understood as "ground [*fond*] and not as *ratio* or cause (*Ursache*) or rational grounding (*Vernunftgrund*) or reason (*Vernunft*), but as an assembling that lets the things before us be" (207/153). It is "on the basis of a thinking of *logos*, of *legein* as gathering" that this is embarked upon (207/153). Heidegger views Western history as that which thinks being as ground, a ground that is not a "causal and objective grounding" but "a ground of the ground, thus a ground without ground, a *Grund* that is also an *Ab-Grund*" (208/153). This ground is a ground underlying the ground; it is not a firmament, but rather abyssal. If Being is Reason, Being (*Sein*) and reason (*Grund*) are "the Same (*das Selbe*). Thus, "Being = *Ab-Grund*, abyss, both reason and without reason" (208/153). Therefore, reason is without reason. "It rests on itself, that is to say, on nothing [. . .]. In so far as it grounds, being has no grounding, it is without ground [*sans-fond*] (*Abgrund*)" (208/153). "What grounds [*fonde*], the grounding [*le fondement*], is necessarily ungrounded [*infondé*]" (208/153). Derrida interpolates his own endorsement of this view of foundations when he adds that "the positing (*Setzung*) of something [a State, of a law, or a constitution] is a leap since it is a matter of positing what was not there" (208/153). Hence there is a "relation of affinity" between *Satz* as proposition and *Satz* as leap (208/153). "Being reposes without repose since it rests on nothing that is" (209/154). "It is supported by no foundation, since it is a ground without ground [*fondement sans fondement*] (both *Grund* and *Abgrund*, *Abgrund Ab-grund*). The foundation founds only by remaining, for its part, unfounded (209/154).

Contributions to Philosophy (written during 1936–1938 but not published until 1989) offers a further glimpse. In *Beiträge* Heidegger refers to "Beyng [*Seyn*] as the ground in which all beings first come to their truth" and the ground in which beings are submerged (abyss) (GA 65 77/61). In fact, *beyng* essentially occurs in the manner of grounding. For Heidegger, the abyssal ground [*Ab-grund*] is the originary essential occurrence of the ground [*Grund*] (379/299). Moreover, time-space is grasped as abyssal ground [*Ab-grund*] (379/299).

24. On ground and the abyss, see my "Dying Alive," *Mosaic* 48, no. 3 (September 2015): 15–26, and "Calculus" in *Deconstructing the Death Penalty*,

edited by Kelly Oliver and Stephanie Marie Straub (New York: Fordham University Press): 139–155. What concerns me here is the rethinking of *the ground* in terms of the abyss.

25. See, for example, Martin Heidegger, *Contributions to Philosophy (Of the Event)*, where he writes that the abyssal ground is the originary or the first essential occurrence of the ground (GA 65 382/302). In his second major work, Heidegger further notes that the abyss is the originary unity of time and space. Time-space is grasped as abyssal ground (*Ab-grund*) (379/299). Also, see the discussion of the "abyssal character of Being as appropriating event [*die Einzigkeit de Abgründlichkeit des Seyns als Ereignis*]," in *Besinnung (1938/39)* (GA 66 88).

26. "The abyss is not the bottom [*le fond*], the originary ground (*Urgrund*), nor the bottomless depth (*Ungrund*) of some hidden base" (BSI 443/334). "The abyss, if there is an abyss, is that there is *more than one* ground [*plus d'un*]" (BSI 443/334). "More than a single single; no more single single [*Plus d'un seul seul*]" (BSI 443/334).

Chapter 2. Safe, Intact: Derrida, Nancy, and the "Deconstruction of Christianity"

1. See recent publications by Jean-Luc Nancy, *Tombe de sommeil* (Paris: Galilée, 2007), translated by Charlotte Mandell as *The Fall of Sleep* (New York: Fordham University Press, 2009), *Identité* (Paris: Galilée, 2010); *Partir. Le départ* (Paris: Bayard, 2011), and most recently *Exclu le juif en nous* (Paris: Galilée, 2018).

2. Hent de Vries finely distinguishes the differences between Derrida and Nancy, noting "nuances in vocabulary, tonality, and so on" but also "a difference in philosophical and theologico-political temperament" that reveals "a more substantial disagreement" between them about the deconstructibility of concepts and "the possibility of a deconstruction of Christianity." See Hent de Vries, *Religion and Violence: Philosophical Perspectives from Kant to Derrida* (Baltimore: Johns Hopkins University Press, 2005), 205.

3. References to the two aspects of *salut* in Derrida date back at least to Jacques Derrida, "Avances," in Serge Margel, *Le Tombeau du dieu artisan. Sur Platon* (Paris: Minuit, 1995), 11–43, further developed in several texts since 1996. "Circonfession," in *Jacques Derrida* [with Geoffrey Bennington] (Paris: Seuil, 1991, 2008), translated by Geoffrey Bennington as "Circumfession," in *Jacques Derrida* (Chicago: University of Chicago Press, 1993); "Foi et savoir: Les deux sources de la 'religion' aux limites de la simple raison," in *La Religion*, edited by Jacques Derrida and Gianni Vattimo (Paris: Seuil, 1996), translated by Samuel Weber as "Faith and Knowledge: The Two Sources of 'Religion' within the Limits of Mere Reason," in *Religion*, edited by Jacques Derrida and Gianni Vattimo (Stanford: Stanford University Press, 1998); *Adieu à Emmanuel Lévinas* (Paris:

Galilée, 1997), translated by Pascale-Anne Brault and Michael Naas as *Adieu: To Emmanuel Levinas* (Stanford: Stanford University Press, 1999); *Demeure—Maurice Blanchot* (Paris: Galilée, 1998), translated by Elizabeth Rottenberg as *Demeure: Fiction and Testimony* (Stanford: Stanford University Press, 2000), published with a translation of Maurice Blanchot's *The Instant of My Death*; "Prière d'insérer," in *Voyous. Deux essais sur la raison* (Paris: Galilée, 2003), translated by Pascale-Anne Brault and Michael Naas as *Rogues: Two Essays on Reason* (Stanford: Stanford University Press, 2005), *Le toucher, Jean-Luc Nancy* (Paris: Galilée, 2000), translated by Christine Irizarry as *On Touching—Jean-Luc Nancy* (Stanford: Stanford University Press, 2005).

4. On auto-immunity, see Jacques Derrida and Micaela Henich, *"Lignées"* (Paris: William Blake & Co., 1996), written in 1991, published in 1996; "Avances," in Serge Margel, *Le Tombeau du dieu artisan. Sur Platon* (Paris: Minuit, 1995), 11–43; "Faith and Knowledge"; *Spectres de Marx*; *Politiques de l'amitié* (Paris: Galilée, 1994), translated by George Collins as *Politics of Friendship* (New York: Verso, 1997); *Voyous. Deux essais sur la raison* (Paris: Galilée, 2003), translated by Pascale-Anne Brault and Michael Naas as *Rogues: Two Essays on Reason* (Stanford: Stanford University Press, 2005); Jacques Derrida and Jürgen Habermas, *Le «concept» du 11 septembre. Dialogues à New York (octobre–decembre 2001) avec Giovanna Borradori* (Paris: Galilée, 2004), 144–152, translated by Giovanna Borradori as *Philosophy in a Time of Terror: Dialogues with Jürgen Habermas and Jacques Derrida* (Chicago: University of Chicago Press, 2003), 94–99.

5. The clause "safe, intact" appears twice in Derrida's "Fors. Les mots anglées de Nicolas Abraham et Maria Torok," in *Le verbier de l'Homme aux loups* (Paris: Flammarion, 1976), translated by Richard Rand as "Fors: The Anglish Words of Nicolas Abraham and Maria Torok," in *The Wolf Man's Magic Word: A Cryptonymy* (Minneapolis: University of Minnesota Press, 1986): (1) when he writes that the process of incorporation preserves a certain topography "safe, intact [*sauve, intact*] untouched by the very relationship with the other" (26/xxii) and (2) where Derrida recalls that an English word—"mortgage"—has not stopped haunting him throughout his reading, "coming back safe, intact [*revenant sauf, intact*]" (53n/xxxvifn2). The translation reverses the order of the words.

6. See Michael Naas's exemplary *Miracle and Machine: Jacques Derrida and the Two Sources of Religion, Science, and the Media* (New York: Fordham University Press, 2012).

7. Émile Benveniste, "Le sacré," in *Le vocabulaire des institutions indo-européennes*, tome 2 (Paris: Minuit, 1969), 179–207; 183–184, translated as "The Sacred," by Elizabeth Palmer, in *Indo-European Language and Society* (Coral Gables: University of Miami Press, 1973), 445–469; 448–449.

8. The word "intact" appeared in Derrida's work from very early on, from *Of Grammatology* to later texts such as *Le toucher*. See OG 308/215; WD 298/200; Diss 137/111, 317/259, 360/297; Psy 74/60; PM 107–108, WA

130; LT 92. It has consistently signified what is "whole, complete, unimpaired, without damage."

9. In *Papier machine* Derrida describes "this strange word" immune as "synonymous to a certain degree with 'safe [*sauf*]' and 'unharmed [*indemne*],' even with sacred and saintly (*helig, holy*), to put this argument in an important relation [. . .] with the logic of immunology and auto-immunology [*auto-immunitaire*]." See Jacques Derrida, *Papier machine* (Paris: Galilée, 2001), 183n; *Negotiations: Interventions and Interviews, 1971–2001*, edited and translated by Elizabeth Rottenberg (Stanford: Stanford University Press, 2002), 269fn9.

10. For informative treatments of *Le toucher*, see J. Hillis Miller, *For Derrida* (New York: Fordham University Press, 2009), 245–305; Geoffrey Bennington, "Handshake," in *Not Half No End: Militantly Melancholic Essays in Memory of Jacques Derrida* (Edinburgh: Edinburgh University Press), 65–85; Martin McQuillan, "Toucher I: (The Problem with Self-Touching)," *Derrida Today* 1, no. 2 (2008): 201–211, and "Toucher II: Keep Your Hands to Yourself Jean-Luc Nancy," *Derrida Today* 2, no. 1 (2009): 84–108.

11. See note 14 in this chapter for Nancy's comments on "the untouchable."

12. For other discussions of resurrection by Nancy not discussed here, see "Résurrection de Blanchot," in Déc 135–146/89–97.

13. Nancy refers to Freud's *Totem and Taboo* (New York: Norton, 1950), 2: 2, where the principal prohibition is against touching.

14. The Untouchables (*Dalit*): "ground," "suppressed," "crushed," "broken to pieces" (Sanskrit). First used by Jyotirao Phule in the nineteenth century, historically associated with Hindus, the term Dalit refers to those who pursued activities and held occupations considered as "polluting" and ritually impure among the Hindus, such as those involving butchering and leatherwork, and removal of refuse, animal carcasses, and waste. They were segregated and banned from full participation in Hindu social life and consigned to work as manual laborers cleaning streets, latrines, and sewers. Note Derrida's disagreement in *Le toucher* on page 53 (LT 93n).

15. On *partance*, see Jean-Luc Nancy, *Partir—Le départ* (Paris: Bayard, 2011).

16. "He is the same without being the same, altered within himself [*en lui-même*]" (48/28). I discuss Nancy's reading of Blanchot in my "Thomas the Marvelous: Resurrection and Living-Death in Blanchot and Nancy," *Mosaic: A Journal for the Interdisciplinary Study of Literature* 45, no. 3 (September 2012): 1–16.

17. Jacques Derrida, "Avant-propos," in CFU 9–11.

18. On the whole, the appearance of the word "intact" in Nancy's writing seems to confirm the signification "firm, whole, untouchable." For example, in "Sur le seuil" in *Les muses* (1994), discussing Caravaggio's model for Mary, a woman drowned in the river Tiber, in the painting *The Death of the Virgin*,

Nancy writes: "*ce corps est ferme, entier, intact dans son abandon*/this body is firm, whole, intact in its abandon" (105/59). In the "Peinture" chapter of *Le sens du monde* (1993), Nancy associates the untouchable with the intact. He writes that painting separates the space between intactness and touching: "*Que la vue touche à la limite, qu'elle touche à sa limite, qu'elle se touche intacte. La peinture est toujours sur le seuil, elle fait seuil de l'intact et du toucher—de l'intact et du toucher de la lumière et de l'ombre . . . Le clair et l'obscur [. . .] demeurant pourtant infiniment intacts*" (131). // "So that the view should touch the limit, that it should touch its limit, that it should touch itself intact. Painting is always on the threshold. It makes up the threshold between intactness and touching—between the intactness and touching *of* light and shadow. . . . The clear and the obscure [. . .] nonetheless remain infinitely intact" (131/82). He writes, further, "*Dans le toucher, dans toutes les touches du toucher qui ne se touchent pas entre elles [. . .] les deux côtés du sens unique ne cessent de venir l'un à l'autre [. . .] touchant à l'intouchable, intact*" // "In touching, in all the touches of touching [. . .] the two sides of the one sense do not cease to come each toward the other [. . .] touching on the untouchable, intact, spacing of sense" (132/83). In *Corpus* (2000), "intact" is used alongside "untouchable." Nancy writes that all bodies are caught up in a network of signification and "no 'free body' floats beyond sense" but "sense itself will float," however not "as some unknown, intact, untouchable 'matter' [*quelle "matière" intacte, intouchable*]" (C 24/23). For, as he writes further on, "There is no intact matter [*matière intacte*]—or else there'd be nothing" (102/117).

The only exception to this way of treating the term "intact" may be in an essay, "Tenue, retenue," written for the catalogue of Lucile Bernard entitled *Lucile Bertrand: Sculptures*. There Nancy writes: "Calculation of the measure and the stance [are needed] if what does not need to be saved is to be safeguarded. Save that 'safe' here does not mean 'intact, unharmed, or unscathed.'" In other words, the word "safe" in "safeguarded" does not have the signification of "intact, unharmed, or unscathed." In fact, it seems to have the opposite meaning: "nascent, touched, breached once and for all." See Jean-Luc Nancy, "Tenue, retenue," in *Lucile Bertrand: Sculptures* (Paris: L'Arbre à Lettres, 1995), unpaginated, translated by Simon Sparks as "Held, Held Back," in *Multiple Arts*, edited by Simon Sparks (Stanford: Stanford University Press, 2006), 180.

19. Jean-Luc Nancy's "Consolation, désolation" first appeared in *Magazine littéraire* (April 2004): 58–60, and was subsequently collected in *La Déclosion*. All references are to the first cited article. All translations mine.

20. For "seul" in Derrida, see "R" 23/140, CFU, and BSI.

21. My translation of Sa (unpaginated download).

22. What is immortal is not susceptible to death and is as a result eternal. The English word "immortal" (late Middle English) is derived from L. *in* (no;

opposite of) + *mortalis* (from *mors*, death), L. *immortalis*, deathless, undying (referring to gods), imperishable, not susceptible to death. For "immortality (of the soul)," see Cicero, *Tusculan Disputations*.

23. "Car il y a déconstruction et déconstruction" (LT 74). Martin McQuillan in his analysis of the relation between Derrida and Nancy in "Toucher I: (The Problem with Self-Touching)," *Derrida Today* 1, no. 2 (November 2008): 201–211, refers to this phrase.

24. Jean-Luc Nancy, "The Deconstruction of Christianity," translated by Simon Sparks in *Religion and Media*, edited by Hent de Vries and Samuel Weber (Stanford: Stanford University Press, 2001), 113; 503–519, in the 1998 edition. This essay subsequently appeared in *La Déclosion*.

25. In a footnote in *Le toucher* (LT 273–4n/362fn) on the subject of "deconstruction" and "Christianity," Derrida refers to the following texts: "Comment ne pas parler," in *Psyché*, t. 1 (Paris: Galilée, 1987); *Donner la mort* (Paris: Galilée, 1999), translated by David Wills as *The Gift of Death*, second edition (Chicago: University of Chicago Press, 2008); "Passions," in *Passions* (Paris: Galilée, 1993), translated by David Wood as "Passions: 'An Oblique Offering,' " in *On the Name*, edited by Thomas Dutoit (Stanford: Stanford University Press, 1995); *Sauf le nom* (Paris: Galilée, 1993), translated by John P. Leavey Jr. as "Sauf le nom," in *On the Name*, and "Faith and Knowledge" in FK.

26. In Theses 19 and 20 of *Heidelberg Disputation* (1518), discussing the difference between Aristotelian Scholasticism's *theologia gloriae* and Paul's *theologia crucis*, Luther translates the Pauline term "destroy [*apolo*]" from I Corinthians 1 into Latin as *destruere*, "to pull down, to dismantle, to de-stroy." Heidegger first used the term *Destruktion* in his winter semester 1919–1920 lecture course, when referring to Luther's "*destruction*" of Aristotle. Also see John van Buren, "Martin Heidegger, Martin Luther," in *Reading Heidegger from the Start: Essays in His Earliest Thought*, edited by Theodore Kisiel and John van Buren (Albany: State University of New York Press, 1994), 159–174.

27. As a rejoinder, Nancy in *Dis-Enclosure* calls for a "closer examination" of the uses of *destructio* in Luther before an eventual revisiting of the employment of the terms *Destruktion/Zerstörung/Abbau* in Heidegger and of *Abbau* in Husserl" (Déc 216/189).

Chapter 3. Derrida Is the Death of Death

1. Françoise Dastur, *La mort: Essai sur la finitude* (Paris: Hatier, 1994), 5; *Death: An Essay on Finitude*, translated by John Llewelyn (London: Athlone, 1996), 4. The title of this chapter is a sentence borrowed from Geoffrey Bennington's "R.I.P.," in *Interrupting Derrida* (London: Routledge, 2000), 64.

2. Latin texts of the fifteenth century offer advice on the protocol and procedures of a good death, *ars moriendi*, the art of dying.

3. As Geoffrey Bennington writes in "R.I.P.," in *Interrupting Derrida*, philosophers "philosophise to overcome death" (61).

4. Plato, *Phaedrus* (233c), translated by Harold North Fowler, Loeb Classical Library (Cambridge, MA: Harvard University Press, 1914). Socrates says about himself that he is not "a being overcome by passion" when lovers praise him beyond due measure, but is "in full control" of himself. Rather than being a victim of love, he is the master of himself. For mastery over himself of the autarkic man, "a man sufficient unto himself," see Jacques Derrida, *Politiques de l'amitié* (Paris: Galilée, 1994), 238, translated by George Collins as *Politics of Friendship* (New York: Verso, 1997), 210. Also, see the relation to itself of the drive to dominate in "Spéculer—sur Freud," in *La carte postale: de Socrate à Freud et au-delà* (Paris: Aubier-Flammarion, 1980), 430, translated by Alan Bass as "To Speculate—on Freud," in *The Post Card: From Socrates to Freud and Beyond* (Chicago: University of Chicago Press, 1987), 403; and for the relation between sovereignty and ipseity, see *Voyous. Deux essais sur la raison* (Paris: Galilée, 2003), translated by Pascale-Anne Brault and Michael Naas as *Rogues: Two Essays on Reason* (Stanford: Stanford University Press, 2002).

5. In a discussion of *The Epic of Gilgamesh* Françoise Dastur notes Gilgamesh's obsession, after the death of his friend, Enkidu, to search for a remedy for and an escape from death. The relation to death is that of the relation to the death of the other. See *The Epic of Gilgamesh*, translated by Andrew George (London: Penguin, 2000), 54–62.

6. See Michel de Montaigne, "Que philosopher, c'est apprendre à mourir," in *Essais*, edited by Emmanuel Naya, Delphine Reguig-Naya, and Alexandre Tarrête (Paris: Gallimard, 2009), translated by Donald M. Frame as "That to philosophize is to learn to die," in *The Complete Essays of Montaigne* (Stanford: Stanford University Press, 1958), Book I, 56–68. In addition to Plato's *Phaedo*, Cicero's *Tusculanae Disputatio* (45 BC) also served as inspiration for Montaigne. See Cicero, *Tusculan Disputations*, translated by J. E. King, Loeb Classical Library (Cambridge, MA: Harvard University Press, 1927), I, 75.

7. Emmanuel Levinas, *Dieu, la mort et le temps* (Paris: Grasset, 1993), my translation.

8. See entry on "Eros," in Jean Laplanche and Jean-Bertrand Pontalis, *Vocabulaire de la psychanalyse* (Paris: Presses Universitaires de France, 1967), 143–144.

9. Decease from MF *décès*, from Latin *decessus*, departure, death, pp. of *decedere*, to depart, die, fr. *de-+cedere* to go, departure (depart, ME *departen* to divide, to go away, fr. OF *departir*, fr. *de-+partir* to divide, fr. L *partire*, fr. decease), *trépas* [from *trespasser*].

10. See Geoffrey Bennington, "Jacques Derrida: . . . A Life," in *Not Half No End: Militantly Melancholic Essays in Memory of Jacques Derrida* (Edinburgh: Edinburgh University Press, 2010).

11. Cicero, *De Finibus Bonurum*, translated by H. Rackham, Loeb Classical Library (Cambridge, MA: Harvard University Press, 1927).

12. See the discussion of "dead—immortal" in chapter 5 of the present volume.

13. "In my heart of heart" is often incorrectly rendered. Contrary to popular belief, Hamlet does not say "in my heart of hearts," but "in my heart of heart"— that is, at the "heart" (center) of his heart. See Shakespeare, *Hamlet*, edited by Harold Jenkins The Arden Shakespeare, second series (Walton-on-Thames, Surrey: Thomas Nelson & Sons, 1982; rpt. 1997), act 3, scene 2: 71–74. Addressing Horatio, Hamlet says that he reserves this region of his affection, his heart's core, for men who aren't slaves to their passion, who are governed by reason:

> Give me that man
> That is not passion's slave, and I will wear him
> In my heart's core, ay, in my heart of heart,
> As I do thee. (Act 3, scene 2, 71–74)

Chapter 4. Nancy's Resurrection

1. The eternal has a relation to time. To be eternal is to be everlasting and have infinite duration. Eternal (Late Middle English) from L. *aevum*, of an age, lasting, enduring, permanent, enduring, *aeternus*, Late L. *aeternalis*, Old French, late fourteenth-century *eternel*. For eternity, see Augustine, *Confessions*, Book XI, and Boethius, *The Consolation of Philosophy*, Book V. For Kant raising the issue of eternity (*Ewig[keit]*, "for ever") leads to a discussion of the immortality of the soul. See Immanuel Kant, "The Immortality of the Soul, as a Postulate of Pure Practical Reason," in *Critique of Practical Reason*, trans. Werner S. Pluhar (Indianapolis: Hackett, 2002), Ak. 122–124. By existence "continuing *ad infinitum* [forever]," Kant means "the immortality [*Unsterblichkeit*] of the soul" (122). The immortality of the soul is propounded as a postulate [an *imperative* for action] of *pure practical reason*. It springs from the teleology of moral behavior. In his essay "The End of All Things" (1794), Kant examines the common expression describing a dying person as "*going out of time into eternity.*" Eternity ought not be conceived as a time proceeding to infinity, Kant writes, for the person would not get outside time, but would progress from one time into another. This expression must mean, Kant suggests, "an *end of all time* along with the person's uninterrupted duration" (8: 327). Kant understands this duration as "a

magnitude wholly incomparable with time" (8: 327). See Immanuel Kant, "The End of All Things," trans. Allen W. Wood in *Religion and Rational Theology*, translated and edited by Allen W. Wood and George Di Giovanni (Cambridge: Cambridge University Press, 1996), Ak. 221–231.

2. Interestingly, the description of a dead person that Nancy provides uncannily fits Derrida's description of a specter. At first, Mary Magdalene does not recognize Christ, for, as Nancy explains, a dead person (*un mort*) "no longer properly appears [*proprement n'apparaît plus*]" (NMT 48/28). It is, Nancy writes, "the appearing of *an appeared and disappeared* [l'apparaître d'un *apparu et disparu*]" (48/28). "He is the same without being the same, altered within himself [*en lui-même*]" (48/28). In *Specters of Marx* Derrida describes the specter in a similar fashion: "There is something disappeared, departed [*Il y a du disparu*] in the apparition itself as reapparition of the departed [*disparu*]" (SM 25/6). What for Derrida is the definition of the (dis) appearing of the specter becomes for Nancy the definition of Christ's resurrection. See also, Derrida's reference to Christ as "the most spectral of specters [*le plus spectral que le spectral*]" (SM 229/144) and "that absolute specter [*ce spectre absolu*]" (231/145).

3. Liddell-Scott's *Greek-English Lexicon* provides the following translation of *anastasis*, *a raising up* of the dead, Aeschylus; *a setting up*, restoration; *a rising again, the Resurrection*, NT. *The Oxford English Dictionary*, resurrection—rising again from the dead; (1320) the rising again of Christ after His death and burial. Etymology OF. *resurreccium*, -ection, fr. *résurrection*, fr. *resurğere*, to resurge; usage in English, general resurrection dates back to at least 1300. *Webster's*: *anastasis*, resurrection, L. to rise again, fr. re- + *surgere*, to rise; the act of rising from the dead; the rising again to life of all the humankind before the final judgment.

4. See my "Thomas the Marvelous: Resurrection and Living-Death in Blanchot and Nancy," *Mosaic* 45, no. 3 (September 2012): 1–16.

5. The original version of *Thomas the Obscure*, published in 1941, which bore the designation of "novel" on its cover, was until recently only available in a much more truncated form, known as the "new version," authorized by Blanchot and published in 1950. *Thomas l'obscur* (Paris: Gallimard, 1941). Maurice Blanchot, *Thomas l'obscur, nouvelle version* (Paris: Gallimard, 1950). In 2005 the first version was republished as *Thomas l'obscur. Première version, 1941* (Paris: Gallimard, 2005).

6. It is curious that Nancy does make a reference to eternity here.

7. Jean-Luc Nancy's "Consolation, désolation" first appeared in *Magazine littéraire*, April 2004, 58–60, and was subsequently collected in *La Déclosion* (Déc 59/101).

8. Blanchot's quote is taken from the famous *Letter to Hulewicz* dated November 13, 1925. See *Rainer Maria Rilke, Briefe aus Muzot: 1921 bis 1926* (Leipzig: Insel-Verlag, 1937), 335–338; also in *Briefe: Zweiter Band 1914 bis*

1926 (Leipzig: Insel-Verlag, 1950); *Letters of Rainer Maria Rilke 1910–1926*, translated by Jane Bannard Greene and M. D. Herter Norton (New York: Norton, 1947–1948), 372–376.

9. "La déconstruction du christianisme" was a talk given in 1995, published in *Etudes philosophiques* 4 (1998): 503–519, and reprinted in *La Déclosion*.

10. Jean-Luc Nancy, *Partir—le départ* (Montrouge: Bayard, 2011).

11. "Le long échange que Jacques et moi avions autour de la 'résurrection'[. . .] ne s'agissait ni pour lui ni pour moi de croyance fantasmatique dans un retour des morts. Il s'agissait de beaucoup plus: de comprendre ce que nous veut cette éternité dont Spinoza dit que nous la sentons et que nous l'expérimentons comme nôtre. L'éternité, c'est-à-dire le dehors du temps. Non pas ce qui dure toujours, mais justement ce qui ne dure pas du tout. L'instant évanoui dans son évanouissement même—la trace inscrite dans son effacement, comme effacement [. . .] Les grandes pensées de la résurrection ne sont jamais des imaginations de corps revenus à la vie. Ce sont précisément des pensées sans image. Ce qui ressuscite, ce qui se redresse du corps allongé sous la terre et bientôt mêlé à elle, c'est l'absence d'image" (2). Nancy adds that two terms he used in his exchange with Derrida, "consolation" and "désolation," share the Latin *solor*, to soothe (*apaiser*), to comfort (*adoucir*), to relieve (*soulager*).

12. Giorgio Agamben notes on the first page of his *Homo Sacer* that Aristotle refers to God as having "a more noble and eternal life, *zōē aristē kai aidios*" (*Metaphysics*, Book Λ, 7, 1072b280). *Aidios* has also been translated as "everlasting." The Loeb edition provides the following translation: the essential actuality of God is life, and "God is life most good and eternal." Aristotle, *Metaphysics*, translated by Hugh Tredennic, Loeb Classical Library (Cambridge, MA: Harvard University Press, 1989. See Giorgio Agamben, *Homo Sacer: Sovereign Power and Bare Life*, translated by Daniel Heller-Roazen (Stanford: Stanford University Press, 1998). In his discussion of Agamben and Foucault in *The Beast and the Sovereign, 2*, Derrida refers to Heidegger's *Introduction to Metaphysics*: "Christ is the *logos* of redemption (*der Logos der Erlösung*), the *logos* of eternal life [*la vie éternelle*], the *logos* of zoē (*logos des ewigen Leben, logos zōēs*)" (BSII 426–427/ 321).

13. The first traceable idea of the eternal life is often attributed to Persian Zoroastrian influence. The importance of resurrection is what distinguishes biblical teaching from Zoroastrian and other religions' teaching, which have no place for resurrection. In the New Testament, the resurrection is variously understood as a) a vindication of Jesus's faithfulness (Mark 14: 62), echoing Daniel; b) a fulfillment of Old Testament prophesy (Luke 24: 44–46); c) a new creation through a new Adam (Roman 5: 12–21); and d) a heavenly exaltation (Philippians 2: 9, Ephesians 4: 6–8). See *Eerdmans Dictionary of the Bible*, edited by David Noel Freedman (Grand Rapids, MI: William B. Eerdmans, 2000), 429–430.

In the *Catechism of the Catholic Church* (London: Chapman, 1994), 226, Catholics are told of "belief in the resurrection of the dead" as "an essential element of Christian faith from its beginnings" (because of Cor. 15: 12–14). Article 12 of the third chapter of the *Catechism* is entitled "I believe in life everlasting." In part 1, The Profession of Faith, chapter 2, article 1, The Revelation of God ¶55, we find: "For he wishes to give eternal life to those who seek salvation by patience in well-doing." See *Catechism of the Catholic Church*, second edition (Vatican City: Liberia Editrice Vaticana, 1994). Topic 16 of *The Apostle's Creed* of the Catholic Church states: "I believe in the resurrection of the body and life everlasting." Also see Wittgenstein's cryptic description of eternal life as the time of the present: "If we take eternity to mean not infinite temporal duration but timelessness, then eternal life belongs to those who live in the present." See Ludwig Wittgenstein, *Tractatus Logico-Philosophicus*, translated by D. F. Pears and B. F. McGuiness (London: Routledge, 1961), 6.4311.

14. See "I give them eternal life, and they shall never perish" (John 10: 28–30 NIV); "For God so loved the world that he gave his one and only Son, that whoever believes in him shall not perish but have eternal life" (John 3: 16 NIV); "And this is eternal life, that they know you the only true God" (John 17: 3 NIV); "Christ Jesus might display his immense patience as an example for those who believe in him and receive eternal life" (1 Timothy 1: 16 NIV); "I write these things to you who believe in the name of the Son of God so that you may know that you have eternal life" (1 John 5: 13 NIV).

15. Jean-Luc Nancy, *La Déclosion (Déconstruction du christianisme, 1)* (Paris: Galilée, 2005); "Fin du colloque" in *Maurice Blanchot: Récits critiques* (Tours: Editions Farrago/Léo Scheer, 2003), 628. The quotation is from Maurice Blanchot, *L'entretien infini* (Paris: Gallimard, 1969), 458.

16. Jean-Luc Nancy, "Lettre à Jean-Pierre Rehm," *Journal FIDMarseille-04.07.05*, Festival International du Documentaire, Marseille, 2005, page 2. (This is item 477 in Nancy's bibliography.)

17. No reference to "la vie éternelle" is to be found in Pierre-François Moreau's six-hundred-page tome, *Spinoza: L'expérience et l'éternité*. Moreau claims that Spinoza clearly distinguishes between immortality and eternity, never using the former. See Pierre-François Moreau, *Spinoza: L'expérience et l'éternité* (Paris: Presses Universitaires de France, 1994).

18. We would have to leave to one side the vexing question of how to adequately translate Spinoza's *mens*. The French translations of Spinoza vary, opting for rendering *mens* as *âme* (mind in English, emphasizing the intellectual, one of the faculties or activities designated as mental) or *esprit* (mind or spirit). Martial Gueroult in *Spinoza II. L'âme (Ethique, II)* (Hildesheim: Georg Olms Verlag, 1974), 9, argues that *mens* must be translated as *âme* since Spinoza very rarely uses the word *spiritus*. In contrast, the most modern French translation

of the *Ethics* by Bernard Pautrat uses *esprit*. Pautrat, in his "Translator's Note," writes that the translation of *mens* as *âme* designates a long-standing prejudice, "bathing" the *Ethics* in a climate of "sacristy" (8). Pautrat's choice of *esprit*, he claims, avoids any risk of foundering in (*sombrer*) "a nebulous atmosphere." Bernard Pautrat, "Note de traducteur," in Spinoza, *Ethique*, new translation by Bernard Pautrat (Paris: Seuil, 1988), 8.

19. See, for example, Bernard Rousset, *La perspective finale de "L'Ethique" et le problème de la Cohérence du Spinozisme. L'autonomie comme salut* (Paris: Vrin, 1968), whose second part is entitled "La vie éternelle." He writes that "Spinozism is a philosophy of salvation [*salut*]" (14).

20. Victor Delbos, *La problème morale dans la philosophie de Spinoza et dans l'histoire du spinozisme* (Paris: Alcan, 1893; rpt. Hildesheim: Georg Olms Verlag, 1988).

21. Ferdinand Alquié, *Le rationalisme de Spinoza* (Paris: Presses Universitaires de France, 1981), 10–11. Alquié devotes chapter 19 of his book to "L'éternité de l'homme." For a discussion of beatitude, see Jean-Luc Nancy, "Fin du Colloque," in *Maurice Blanchot: Récits critiques*, edited by Christophe Bident and Pierre Vilar (Tours: Farrago/Léo Scheer, 2003) and *L'adoration (Déconstruction du Christianisme, 2)* (Paris: Galilée, 2010).

22. Ferdinand Alquié, "Note sur la vie éternelle selon Spinoza," *Archivio di Filosofia* 1 (1959): 183–186.

23. There is "a difference of nature between duration and eternity," Deleuze explains in *Expressionism in Philosophy*. See Gilles Deleuze, *Spinoza et le problème de l'espression* (Paris: Minuit, 1968), 292, translated by Martin Joughin as *Expressionism in Philosophy: Spinoza* (New York: Zone Books, 1992), 313. According to Deleuze, Spinoza avoids using the concept of immortality in the *Ethics* because it seems to him to involve "the most tiresome confusions" (292/313). Deleuze's entry for eternity in *Spinoza: Practical Philosophy* reads: "Eternity is the character of existence insofar as it is enveloped/incorporated [*enveloppé*] by essence (*Ethics* I, def. 8, trans. mod.)." See Gilles Deleuze, *Spinoza. Philosophie pratique* (Paris: Minuit, 1981), 100, translated by Robert Hurley (San Francisco: City Lights, 1988), 65. As Deleuze remarks in *Expressionism in Philosophy: Spinoza*: If we form the idea of ourselves (as it is in God), "to the extent that we form it, to the extent that we have it, we *experience* that we are eternal (*Ethics*, v. 23)" (293/315).

24. Pierre Macherey, *Introduction à L'Ethique: La cinquième partie* (Paris: Presses Universitaires de France, 1994), 118–119, 181. Subsequent quotations are parenthetically cited in the text.

25. This is also echoed in the demonstration of Proposition 29: "Eternity cannot be explained by duration [*aeternitas per durationem explicari nequit*]."

26. See Nancy's comments on the phrase "nous sentons et savons d'expérience que nous sommes éternels" (Ad 135).

27. See Martial Gueroult, "Appendix 17," in *Spinoza II, L'âme (Ethique II)* (Hildesheim: Georg Olms Verlag, 1974). However, in contrast, Edwin Curley

renders this phrase as "under a species." See Benedict de Spinoza, *Ethics*, in *A Spinoza Reader: The Ethics and Other Works*, edited and translated by Edwin Curley (Princeton, NJ: Princeton University Press, 1994). Also, see Baruch Spinoza, *Ethics*, in *Complete Works*, edited by Michael L. Morgan (Indianapolis: Hackett, 2002), where Samuel Shirley translates it as (the preferable) "under a form" of eternity.

28. Alexandre Matheron, "La vie éternelle et le corps selon Spinoza," *Revue philosophique de la france et de l'Etranger* 184, no. 1 (January–March 1994): 27–40. Subsequent quotations are parenthetically cited in the text.

29. This Proposition is rendered by Bernard Pautrat as: "Qui a un Corps apte [*aptum*] a un très grand nombre de choses, a un Esprit [*Mentem*] dont la plus grande part est éternelle [*cujus maxima pars est aeterna*]" and by Macherey as "qui a un corps apte au plus grand nombre de choses, celui-là a une âme dont la plus grande partie est éternelle" (182).

30. *Lexicon Spinozanum*, 2 vols., edited by Emilia Giancotti Boscherini (The Hague: Martinus Nijhoff, 1970). See Spinoza, *Theological-Political Treatise*, edited by Jonathan Israel, translated by Michael Silverthorne and Jonathan Israel (Cambridge: Cambridge University Press, 2007).

31. Steven Nadler, *Spinoza's Heresy: Immortality and the Jewish Mind* (Oxford: Clarendon Press, 2001), 48. Subsequent quotations are parenthetically cited in the text.

32. Maimonides, who codified Torah law and Jewish philosophy, compiled what he refers to as the *Shloshah Asar Ikkarim*, the "Thirteen Fundamental Principles" of the Jewish faith, as derived from the Torah. One of Maimonides's thirteen principles of the Jewish faith cited a belief in the resurrection of the body after death.

33. Nancy refers to Spinoza several times in *Adoration*, in one place saying, "The question is finding a new Spinozism" (Ad 132/91). He equates God, that is, "the totality of beings [*totalité de l'étant*]," with that which consists of "conceiving things under the aspect of eternity" (using the Pautrat translation) (135/94).

34. Ian James, in his book *The Fragmentary Demand*, notes that, unlike Derrida, "Nancy is happy to be a philosopher of existence, of the material and the concrete." See Ian James, *The Fragmentary Demand: An Introduction to the Philosophy of Jean-Luc Nancy* (Stanford: Stanford University Press, 2006), 148.

35. Juan Manuel Garrido, *Chances de la pensée: A partir de Jean-Luc Nancy* (Paris: Galilée, 2011), all translations are my own and quotations from this source are cited parenthetically in the text.

36. These references by Nancy appear in the following texts: to Psyche in *Corpus* (Paris: Metailié, 1992), to the dead body of the virgin in Caravaggio's *The Death of the Virgin* (1605–1606, Louvre Museum) in "Sur le seuil," in *Les Muses* (Paris: Galilée, 1994), and to resurrection in *Noli me tangere* (Paris: Bayard, 2003).

37. Spinoza, *Ethics*, Part II, Proposition 49, Scholium. Samuel Shirley translates *Dei nutu* as "God's command" (151) or "God's will" (276).

38. Alfonso Cariolato, *"Le Geste de Dieu" Sur un lieu de* l'Ethique *de Spinoza*, Marginalia of Jean-Luc Nancy (Chatou: Editions de la Transparence, 2011), 62. Subsequent quotations from this source are cited parenthetically in the text.

Chapter 5. The Desire for Survival?

1. Martin Hägglund, *Radical Atheism: Derrida and the Time of Life* (Stanford: Stanford University Press, 2008). All subsequent page numbers are given within the text. I have benefited from the astute analysis of Hägglund's work by the following commentators: Michael Naas, "An Atheism That (*Dieu merci!*) Still Leaves Something to Be Desired," *New Centennial Review* 9, no. 1 (2009): 45–68; Jacques de Ville, *Jacques Derrida: Law as Absolute Hospitality* (New York: Routledge, 2011); and Danielle Sands, Review Article in *Parrhesia* 6 (2009): 73–78.

2. The notion of desire appears throughout Derrida's writings. For a random sampling, see *La Dissémination* (Paris: Seuil, 1972), translated by Barbara Johnson as *Dissemination* (Chicago: University of Chicago Press, 1981), especially on the hymen 258–259/xx; *Eperons: Les styles de Nietzsche* (Paris: Flammarion, 1976), translated by Barbara Harlow as *Spurs: Nietzsche's Styles* (Chicago: Chicago University Press, 1979); *La vérité en peinture* (Paris: Aubier-Flammarion, 1978), translated by Geoffrey Bennington and Ian McLeod as *The Truth in Painting* (Chicago: University of Chicago Press, 1987); *Khôra* (Paris: Galilée, 1993), translated by Ian McLeod as "Khora," in *On the Name*, edited by Thomas Dutoit (Stanford: Stanford University Press, 1995).

3. Among those commending Hägglund's reading of Derrida, Ernesto Laclau, in "Is Radical Atheism a Good Name for Deconstruction?," *Diacritics* 38, nos. 1–2 (Spring–Summer 2008): 180–189, calls *Radical Atheism* a "substantial contribution" (188), describing Hägglund's "intellectual project" as "very much valuable" (181). However, he quibbles with Hägglund's dualistic opposition between mortality and immortality, which in his opinion views mortality as the reversal of immortality, and also questions whether there is "an elaborated theory of desire" in Derrida (182).

4. Plato, *Symposium and Phaedrus*, translated by Tom Griffith (New York: Everyman's Library/Knopf, 2000), and Plato, *Lysis, Symposium, Gorgias*, translated by W. R. M. Lamb, Loeb Classical Library (Cambridge, MA: Harvard University Press, 1996). Lamb renders the latter passage as: "I wish these things now present to be present also in the future."

5. In two potent criticisms, John D. Caputo in "The Return of Anti-Religion: From Radical Atheism to Radical Theology," *Journal for Cultural and Religious Theory* 11, no. 2 (Spring 2011): 32–125, calls Hägglund's work "deconstruction as logic not *écriture*" and "an abridged edition of Derrida cut to fit the new

materialism" (33). Caputo also, echoing other critics, disagrees with Hägglund about whether Derrida's primary interest is in "time" (53). Hägglund, according to Caputo, "flattens the movement of temporality in Derrida by silencing the call which always calls from 'beyond' the horizon of expectation" (58). In addition, he diverges from Hägglund about the precedence of the trace in relation to the constitution of time (62) and takes issue with his understanding of "infinite finitude" (60). Caputo's wide-ranging engagement with Hägglund raises a number of issues, however, it soon becomes clear after making one's way through his novella-length article (ninety-three pages) that the terms of the debate with Hägglund (atheism/theism) and its entire predeconstructive vocabulary are framed by the metaphysical tradition that both interlocutors are hoping to escape.

It would be hard here not to conceive of Hägglund Enterprises as a oneman marketing cottage industry, a calculated ploy to secure attention through polemical saber-rattling, amassing established figures to have "debates" with, tallying the number of debates on his personal website and using these as means for self-promotion and self-aggrandizement. Resembling tired parlor games replete with the jargon of academic business, these "debates" do not succeed in advancing any meaningful understanding of the issues under consideration. But that would be churlish of me to say so.

6. Nass, "An Atheism," 49. Michael Naas's article contains the most detailed, minute—surgical even—dissection of Hägglund's logic, done in the nicest way possible, at times appearing so subtle that his remarks would elude the harried reader. In his review, Naas uses the terms of the very discourse that he is dealing with, in other words, Hägglund's discourse, such as "the best," and "the worst" (terms enamored by Hägglund), and, of course, "desire." For example, Naas argues that "the very *worst* way to react" to Hägglund's book "would be simply to praise and affirm it without really engaging it" (46). He calls *Radical Atheism* "a work that claims to say it all about Derrida, a work that comprehends and explains Derrida's work from beginning to end without remainder," but adds a caveat, "insofar as it would leave no future for Derrida scholarship," it would be "the very worst, the most inaccurate and most unfaithful" (46). The book, then, Naas observes, "leaves something to be desired, indeed . . . it leaves everything to be desired" (46). Naas who calls his response to Hägglund not a critique but a "friendly supplement," adds that even if we desire only what is mortal, impure, open to difference, and so on, as Hägglund claims, we still need to give an account of all those things metaphysics claims to desire and their enduring history (46). In assessing Hägglund's discourse, Naas shows that deconstruction does not operate simply on the level of being, truth, or knowledge, but also as a deconstruction of the discourses of being, truth, and knowledge (49). He notices that in his arguments Hägglund shifts from "the more active notions of refutation and deconstruction" to "more passive notions of self-refutation and self-deconstruction" (50). In analyzing Hägglund's strategy, Naas explains that

the former's strategy bears a resemblance to "the strategy of metaphysics" itself (50). Even though Hägglund dismisses the normative and prescriptive dimensions of deconstruction, Naas demonstrates the ineluctable necessity of these aspects of deconstruction and "other modalities of thought" (52). Insisting on the logic of the phantasm that "requires other forms of analysis, from linguistics to psychoanalysis," his argument points to the necessity of using these forms of analysis to question the enduring vestiges of metaphysical thought (54). Naas shows an equivocation on the part of Hägglund regarding desire and what can be desirable. In Naas's view, Hägglund seems to be saying that metaphysics did not actually or could not possibly have desired the things that it purportedly desired. It is "this more radical version," Naas perceptively argues, that "allows Hägglund to undercut or undermine the very basis for prescriptive or normative appropriation of deconstruction" (61–62). If Hägglund "wishes to exclude from the deconstructive enterprise any kind of prescription," then "he must restrict himself to ontological claims" (62). Throughout his article Naas puts forward the notion of the phantasm as a hinge term in order to address what he deems to be lacking in Hägglund's approach, an approach that simply addresses the being or truth of things. Even though I cannot be in agreement with all the things Naas says about the phantasm—I may agree with the first clause of his last sentence but certainly not the second for reasons I have tried to show in other chapters of this book: "For every absolute is a phantasm and every phantasm a phantasm of the absolute—to be deconstructed"—his argument effectively shows the shortcomings of Hägglund's approach (63).

7. Hägglund does not pay adequate attention to spacing, even though he mentions its importance on page 72.

8. For two appreciative accounts of Hägglund, see Jean-Michel Rabaté, "Dying from Immortality: Notes for a Discussion with Martin Hägglund," *Derrida Today* 6, no. 2 (2013): 169–181, and Henry Staten, "Writing: Empirical, Transcendental, Ultratranscendental," *CR: The New Centennial Review* 9, no. 1 (Spring 2009): 69–85. Rabaté's article, which also takes into consideration Hägglund's second book, *Dying for Time* (2012), generally praises Hägglund for his interpretation of Derrida, in particular for his renewal of a notion of survival to counterbalance the all-too-religious readings of Derrida. For Rabaté, however, Hägglund holds several unorthodox views about Freud: he categorically denies such a thing as the death-drive (calling it "a pure contradiction"), which Rabaté argues there is a need for, and appealing to the lack of clinical evidence, Hägglund also denies that the unconscious is unaware of time (171). In contrast, Hägglund's argument for survival maintains that to live on is to be subjected to temporal finitude. Rabaté complains exasperatedly that Hägglund "constantly reiterates that the wish for immortality boils down to a fantasy of a life lived in an endless time" (178), even though Freud, in "On Transcience," had already rejected the wish for eternity, arguing that the value of life would be enhanced

by its fleeting nature. Henry Staten, at the beginning of "Writing: Empirical, Transcendental, Ultratranscendental," speaks admiringly of *Radical Atheism*, calling it "the most accurate, insightful, and complete account anyone has produced so far of Derrida's thought" (69). While he compliments Hägglund's "flair" and "clarity" (69), his article contends that Hägglund's book blurs the crucial distinction between *arche*-writing and empirical writing. Staten is emphatic that this distinction needs to be maintained before going on to explore the ramifications of Derrida's discussion of the relation of spacing (which he takes to be the "key concept in [Hägglund's] exposition" (78) to time and what Derrida calls the "outside" with the inside before trailing off into speculative reverie.

9. Derrida mentions "radical atheism" in *Sauf le nom* (103/80).

10. Jacques Derrida, "Penser ce qui vient," in *Derrida pour les temps à venir*, edited by René Major (Paris: Stock, 2007).

11. Raoul Mortley, *French Philosophers in Conversation: Levinas, Schneider, Serres, Irigaray, Le Doeuff, Derrida* (London: Routledge, 1991), 101.

12. Jacques Derrida, "Dialangues," in *Points de suspension. Entretiens*, selected and presented by Elisabeth Weber (Paris: Galilée, 1992), 143, translated by Peggy Kamuf et al. as "Dialanguages," in *Points . . . Interviews, 1974–1994* (Stanford: Stanford University Press, 1995), 137.

13. Rodolphe Gasché, *The Tain of the Mirror: Derrida and the Philosophy of Reflection* (Cambridge, MA: Harvard University Press, 1988), 317.

14. Geoffrey Bennington, "Derridabase," in *Jacques Derrida* (Paris: Seuil, 1991), translated by Geoffrey Bennington as "Derridabase," in *Jacques Derrida* [With Geoffrey Bennington] (Chicago: University of Chicago Press, 1993), 117 and 115.

15. Geoffrey Bennington, *Not Half No End: Militantly Melancholic Essays in Memory of Jacques Derrida* (Edinburgh: Edinburgh University Press, 2010), 85.

16. Rodolphe Gasché, "Structural Infinity," in *Inventions of Difference* (Cambridge, MA: Harvard University Press, 1994).

17. G. W. F. Hegel, *Science of Logic*, translated by A. V. Miller (Atlantic Highlands, NJ: Humanities Press, 1989), 144.

18. Martin Heidegger, *Sein und Zeit* (Tübingen: Max Niemeyer Verlag, 1953), 329; *Being and Time*, translated by John Macquarrie and Edward Robinson (New York: Harper & Row, 1962), 378.

19. In a footnote in "Violence and Metaphysics," Derrida writes that Henri Birault's study "Heidegger et la pensée de la finitude" shows that the theme of *Endlichkeit* is progressively abandoned by Heidegger (WD 20 n2/141fn70). Birault claims that Heidegger no longer mentions finitude after *Kant and the Problem of Metaphysics*.

20. One could interpret Heidegger's rethinking of finitude partly as a response to the strong tendency in the philosophical tradition to privilege the finite. For example, Malebranche, Leibniz, and Spinoza all viewed the infinite as ontologically secondary in relation to infinity.

21. Héraclite, *Fragments*, text established, translated, and commented on by Marcel Conche (Paris: Presses Universitaires de France, 1986), 369–371. DK frag 162; Frag 106 of the Conche edition.

22. This is pointed out by Ginette Michaud's incisive analysis in *Tenir au secret (Derrida, Blanchot)* (Paris: Galilée, 2006), 56. Michaud's text demonstrates the destabilization between fiction and autobiographical truth in Blanchot's *récit* (56–57). Also see René Major, "Faire la verité," *TTR: traduction, témoignage, rédaction* 11, no. 2 (1998): 234, and *Au commencement. La vie la mort* (Paris: Galilée, 1999).

23. Derrida defines eternity, the best treatment of which is found in "Ousia and Grammē: Note on a Note from *Being and Time*," as another name for the presence of the present (M 34/32). In *Being and Time* Heidegger announces "the determination of the meaning of being as *parousia* or as *ousia*, which in the ontologico-temporal order means 'presence' (*Anwesenheit*)" (M 33–34). The ontological *project* can be understood in relation to time. "The entity is grasped in its being as 'presence' (*Anwesenheit*), that is, it is understood by a reference to a determined mode of time, the present (*Gegenwart*)" (M 34). In a note, Derrida continues quoting Heidegger from *Kant and the Problem of Metaphysics*, who states that metaphysics has understood the Being of the entity as *permanence* and *persistence* (*Beständigkeit*). The project relative to time lies at the basis of the comprehension of Being. Even eternity, taken as *nunc stans*, the eternal now, is conceivable as "now" and "persistent" only on the basis of time. Being is synonymous with "permanence in presence"(M 33–34/32). In the essay Derrida explains that, for Hegel, everything that receives the predicate of eternity (the Idea, Spirit, the True, etc.) must not be thought outside (or necessarily inside) time (M 50/45). "Eternity as presence is neither temporal nor intemporal. Presence is intemporality in time or time in intemporality" (M 51/45–46). Eternity, then, is another name for the presence of the present. Though, as Derrida notes, Hegel distinguishes this presence from the present as now (M 50–51/45–46).

24. The quote is from "Literature and the Right to Death," translated by Lydia Davis, which appears in Maurice Blanchot, *La part du feu* (Paris: Gallimard, 1949), 325; *The Work of Fire*, translated by Charlotte Mandell (Stanford: Stanford University Press, 1995), 337, trans. mod. throughout.

Chapter 6. For a Time: The Time of Survival

1. Cicero, *Laelius de Amicitia* vii 23; *Old Age, Friendship, Divination*, translated by W. A. Falconer, Loeb Classical Library (Cambridge, MA: Harvard University Press, 1923), 133. This is translated as friends, "though dead, are yet alive."

2. In *Aporias* Derrida writes that he recently came upon Paul Valéry's remarks in his preface to James G. Frazer's *La crainte des morts*, who writes of "the Ancient belief that *the dead are not dead, are not quite dead* [les morts ne sont pas morts, ou ne sont pas tout à fait morts]" (A 112/62, JD's italics).

3. Portions of this chapter were originally presented at a SPEP session on Michael Naas's *Miracle and Machine* in Eugene, Oregon, on October 24, 2013, and later published in *Journal of French and Francophone Philosophy* 23, no. 2 (2015): 122–130.

4. Michael Naas, *Miracle and Machine: Jacques Derrida and the Two Sources of Religion, Science, and the Media* (New York: Fordham University Press, 2012), 21. Further citations shall be given parenthetically in the body of the text.

5. Rodolphe Gasché in "In Love of Life: Michael Naas' *Miracle and Machine*," *Research in Phenomenology* 43 (2013): 73–91, hails Naas's "extremely rich and highly illuminating reading of Derrida's complex work that permits us to gauge the stakes of this absolutely unique text in Derrida's corpus" (73). Gasché describes *Miracle and Machine* as "an attempt at *reading*" in the strong sense of the word (75), and extols the book's "impressive stylistic achievements" (74) and Naas's attentiveness to the intimate intertwinement of "the text's argumentative and thetic nature *and* its formal structure and resources" (75). For Gasché, Naas's book demonstrates that the biased belief regarding Derrida's purported nihilistic thinking about death is, in fact, indicative of "a love without reserve for life" (74).

While Agata Bielik-Robson chooses Michael Naas's *Miracle and Machine*, "among the symphony of Derrida's commentators," to navigate the complicated terrain of Derrida's text, "Faith and Knowledge," Bielik-Robson's "The Marrano God: Abstraction, Messianicity, and Retreat in Derrida's 'Faith and Knowledge,'" *Religions* 10(1), no. 22 (29 December, 2018): 1–23, an exceptionally detailed and sophisticated examination of Derrida's "Faith and Knowledge," claims that Derrida "experiments with a new concept of non-Marrano religiosity" (2). In her view "Derrida's critical treatment of the Hegelian-Kantian model of God's demise complicates the dualistic picture painted by Hägglund, based on the simple opposition of the God who by definition cannot die, on the one hand, and the radical atheism which accepts the premise that whatever is alive must be mortal, on the other" (10). Bielik-Robson argues that "religious traditions [engage in an error] by staking their survival on averting all dangers of impurity and contamination, which eventually takes over the whole of their actual life, for the sake of an idealized, abstracted, more-than-life, hyper-pure essence of their identity" (13).

Penelope Deutscher's "Auto-immunity, Sexual Violence, and Reproduction: Response to Michael Naas, *Miracle and Machine*," *Research in Phenomenology* 43 (2013): 108–117, focuses on the question of sexual violence discussed in two chapters of *Miracle and Machine* pertaining to the singling out of women as victims and in particular the reproductive life of women. Deutscher is particularly concerned with the violence perpetrated against women's reproductive life, overtly strategic violence "aimed at achieving a dissolution of, or a manipulation of, reproductive futures" (112). She looks at these sexual assaults in the context of ethno-religious conflicts that take on a specific form that she calls genocidal (111). The question she wants to pose regarding "the role of reproductive life in the indemnification of community" is how to think the specific forms of auto-immunity in the contexts where the life of the community is deemed more important than women's lives (117).

6. The *Robert Dictionnaire de la langue française* dates the appearance of the feminine noun "survivance" to 1606. The term is said to have belonged to legal terminology since 1521.

7. Georges Didi-Huberman, "La Survivance nous divise-t-elle?," in *Aperçues* (Paris: Minuit, 2018), 207–209. Further citations are given parenthetically in the body of the text.

8. Didi-Huberman extensively develops the notion of survivance in *L'image survivante: Histoire de l'art et temps des fantômes selon Aby Warburg* (Paris: Minuit, 2002).

9. I owe an investigation of the work of Georges Didi-Huberman and his reference to survivance to a recommendation by Ginette Michaud.

10. Jacques Derrida, "Des tours de Babel" (1985) in *Psyché, Invention de l'autre, t. 1 (nouvelle édition augmentée)* (Paris: Galilée, 1998). Further citations are given parenthetically in the body of the text.

11. Jacques Derrida, "Deconstruction in America: An Interview with Jacques Derrida," *Critical Exchange* 17 (Winter 1985): 1–33.

12. This rehearses the argument in "Des tours de Babel" (Psy 214/xx).

13. Interestingly, Derrida makes mention of a "survival movement [*mouvement de survie*]," in conjunction with the death sentence or stay of death in "+R" in *The Truth in Painting* (TP 182/160).

14. On survival, see Michael Naas, especially the chapter entitled "The Passion of Literature," in *Miracle and Machine*, and Geoffrey Bennington in *Not Half No End* throughout.

15. Jacques Derrida, *L'oreille de l'autre. Otobiographies, transferts, traductions. Texte et debats aved Jacques Derrida*, edited by Claude Levesque and Christie V. McDonald (Montreal: VLB Editions, 1982) (EO 161/121–122). Further citations are given parenthetically in the body of the text.

16. "Dialogue entre Jacques Derrida, Philippe Lacoue-Labarthe et Jean-Luc Nancy," *Rue Descartes* 52 (2004): 86–99, 93. Cited further parenthetically in the text.

17. Jacques Derrida, "Je suis en guerre contre moi-même," *Le Monde*, October 12, 2004, vi–vii.

18. Jacques Derrida, *Apprendre à vivre: Entretien avec Jean Birnbaum* (Paris: Galilée, 2005), 26; *Learning to Live Finally: The Last Interview*, translated by Pascale-Anne Brault and Michael Naas (Hoboken, NJ: Melville House, 2007), 26.

19. It will be recalled that in *A Taste for the Secret*, a book-length interview with Maurizio Ferraris, Derrida noted: "I do not believe that one lives on post mortem," in Jacques Derrida [with Maurizio Ferraris], *A Taste for the Secret*, translated by Giacomo Donis (Malden, MA: Polity Press, 2001), 88, originally published as "Il Gusto del Segreto," edited by Giacomo Donis and David Webb (Rome-Bari: Gius. Laterza & Figli Spa, 1997). This book has subsequently appeared in French *as Le Goût du secret* (Paris: Harmattan, 2018).

20. Among the terms used by Derrida with the intransitive *-ance* suffix we could name: *mouvance* (M 9/9), *aimance* (PFr 23/7, 88/69; 144/123 [translated as "lovence"]); *demeurance* (D 89/69, 101/77, 108/81); *demourance* (D 108/81); *désistance* ("Désistance" in Psy2); *destinérrance* (Psy 360/351, 369/360); *fiance* (PFr 31/14, 33/16, 220/194 [translated as "fidence"]); *mourance* (H. C. 114/127 [translated as "dying"], CN 203/218 [translated as "passing-on"]); *pré-férance* (A 103/56); *revenance* (Par 151/140 [translated as "'phantom-like' revenance"]; PFr 20/3, H. C. 95/103; BSII 46–50), *arrestance* (Par 200/188); *survivance* (H. C. 101/111; BSII [rendered as "*survivance*" and italicized in English] 176/117, 193/130, 194/131; D 80/63, 135/100), and *vivance* (H. C. 102/112 [translated as lovingness]; DP1 279/376).

21. Raoul Mortley, *French Philosophers in Conversation: Levinas, Schneider, Serres, Irigaray, Le Doeuff, Derrida* (London: Routledge, 1991), 99.

22. Jacques Derrida, "Sémiologie et grammatologie," in *Positions* (Paris: Minuit, 1972), 39, translated by Alan Bass as "Semiology and Grammatology," in *Positions* (Chicago: University of Chicago Press, 1981), 27.

23. A mood expresses how the speaker feels about the action, a wish, a suggestion, a command, a condition that is contrary to fact.

24. See "absolute mortality" in *Apprendre à vivre*, 24.

25. Jean-Pierre Vernant, "La belle mort et le cadavre outragé," in *L'individu, la mort, l'amour: Soi-même et l'autre en Grèce ancienne* (Paris: Gallimard, 1989), 41; "A 'Beautiful Death' and the Disfigured Corpse in Homeric Epic," in *Mortals and Immortals: Collected Essays*, edited by Froma I. Zeitlin (Princeton, NJ: Princeton University Press, 1991), 50. The translation from Homer, *Iliad* (22.304–305), provided here does not match the cited source. Homer, *Iliad*, translated by Richmond Lattimore (Chicago: University of Chicago Press, 1951).

26. Michael Naas, "The Tragedy of Renown: Aeschylus, Nietzsche and the Might Have Been," *Philosophy Today* 35, no. 3 (Fall 1991): 277–290.

27. Jean-Pierre Vernant, "La belle mort et le cadavre outragé," in *L'individu, la mort, l'amour: Soi-même et l'autre en Grèce ancienne* (Paris: Gallimard, 1989), 50; "A 'Beautiful Death' and the Disfigured Corpse in Homeric Epic," in *Mortals and Immortals: Collected Essays*, edited by Froma I. Zeitlin (Princeton, NJ: Princeton University Press, 1991), 55.

28. Jacques Derrida, *Apprendre à vivre enfin: Entretien avec Jean Birnbaum* (Paris: Editions Galilée/*Le Monde*, 2005), 25; *Learning to Live Finally: The Last*

Interview, translated by Pascale-Anne Brault and Michael Naas (Hoboken, NJ: Melville House, 2007), 24.

Chapter 7. Dying Alive: The Phantasmatics of Living-Death

1. Phenomenologically, the noematic content differs from the real content of our experiences. The noema is that through which the object is grasped. The object can be destroyed, like Husserl's famous example of the apple tree, but the noematic content cannot.

2. Derrida takes Robinson's greatest fear, a fear that is Robinson's, the fear of dying alive, and makes it into a general structural component of survivance.

3. Michael Naas, "*Comme si, comme ça*: Following Derrida on the Phantasms of the Self, the State, and a Sovereign God," first presented as a keynote speech at the Mosaic conference in 2006, subsequently published in *Mosaic* and then collected in *From Derrida Now On* (New York: Fordham University Press, 2008), 192. Cited further parenthetically.

4. While the set of words or quasi-concepts such as specter, ghost, phantom, spectrality, fantomaticity, and haunting have a similar structure and function, Michael Naas in "*Comme si, comme ça*" wonders whether these terms are "quasi-synonyms or nonsubstitutable synonyms for the same phenomenon?" (189). He adroitly and persuasively argues for the phantasm as a special case and provides definitions for it. But would it not be possible, perhaps for different reasons, to reserve for other terms, for example, the *revenant* (*revenant*) a special status too? Derrida distinguishes "the revenant" from the specter, phantom, or ghost in *For What Tomorrow*. The *revenant* would be the ghost or spirit that *returns* (perhaps from the other world, as entries in French dictionaries suggest). To think the event and haunting together, Derrida remarks in *For What Tomorrow*, would be to think the *revenant* rather than the specter or the ghost (FWT 256–257/159). Furthermore, in *Echographies* Derrida isolates *revenance* from the series of more or less equivalent words because it does not necessarily have a reference to visibility (E 129/115). There are also frequent places in Derrida's work where he recites or reels off, as it were, a list of several terms such as images, phantasms, simulacra, and specters using them almost synonymously, as in *Archive Fever* ("a phantasm or a specter" [xx/95]), *Le toucher* ("phantasmes, spectres" [66/xx]), and *The Beast and the Sovereign, 2* ("the phantasm, the *phantasmata*, the phantoms and the revenants" [BSII 263/185]), to cite just three examples. In addition, to be able to present a fuller picture of the phantasm we would have to examine its particular function in *Glas*. All of these instances would, it would seem, trouble or disturb the description or definition of the phantasm provided by Naas.

5. In another context, Jean-François Lyotard speaks of an "affection that owes nothing to the sensible." See Jean-François Lyotard, *Heidegger et «les juifs»* (Paris: Galilée, 1988), 78; *Heidegger and "the Jews*,*"* translated by Andreas Michel and Mark Roberts (Minneapolis: University of Minnesota Press, 1990), 44. Also see especially 34–35/15–17 where Lyotard refers to an "unconscious affect" and its temporality. Daniel Giovannangeli finds this idea problematic for phenomenology, because the latter cannot give an account of it. See his *La passion de l'origine. Recherches sur l'esthétique transcendantale et la phénoménologie* (Paris: Galilée, 1995).

6. Jacques Derrida, *Apories* (Paris: Galilée, 1996), translated by Thomas Dutoit as *Aporias* (Stanford: Stanford University Press, 1993). The English version is a translation of an article "Apories: Mourir—s'attendre aux limites de la vérité" published in *Le passage des frontières. Autour du travail de Jacques Derrida*, edited by Marie-Louise Mallet (Paris: Galilée, 1993).

7. Martin Heidegger, "Das Ding," in *Vorträge und Aufsätze* (1954), 171; translated as "The Thing" by Albert Hofstadter in *Poetry, Language, Thought* (New York: Harper & Row, 1971), 176.

8. "Editor's Introduction," in Sigmund Freud, *The Ego and the Id and Other Works* in *The Standard Edition of the Complete Psychological Works of Sigmund Freud* (London: The Hogarth Press, 1961), SE XIX (1923–1925): 3–11.

9. Sigmund Freud, "Zur Psychopathologie des Altagslebens," in *Gesammelte Werke* vol. 4 (Frankfurt am Main: S. Fischer Verlag, 1941, 1990), 305fn, translated as *The Psychopathology of Everyday Life*, SE VI (1901), 275n.

10. Herman Nunberg and Ernst Federn, eds., *Minutes of the Vienna Psychoanalytic Society, Volume III: 1910–1911*, translated by M. Nunberg with the assistance of H. Collins (New York: International Universities Press, 1974), 307, cited further parenthetically. I owe this reference to Kelly Noel-Smith's *Freud on Time and Timelessness* (London: Palgrave Macmillan, 2016), 146.

11. Sigmund Freud, "Das Unbewusste," in *Studienausgabe* Bd III "Psychologie des Unbewussten" (Frankfurt am Main: Fischer Verlag, 1969–1975): [*Die Vorgänge des Systems* Ubw sind zeitlos*, d.h., sie sind nicht zeitlich geordnet, warden durch die verlaufende Zeit nicht abgeändert, haben überhaupt keine Beziehung zur Zeit, Auch die Zeitbeziehung ist an die Arbeit des Bw-Systems geknüpft*]," SA III, 145–146; "The Unconscious," SE XIV, 187.

12. Sigmund Freud, *Die Traumdeutung*, SA II: 580; *The Interpretation of Dreams*, SE V, 613.

13. Sigmund Freud, "Zeitgemässes uber Krieg und Tod," SA IX: 56; "Thoughts for The Times on War and Death," SE XIV, 296.

14. Sigmund Freud, *Jenseits des Lustprinzips* in *Studienausgabe* Bd III "Psychologie des Unbewussten," 238; *Beyond the Pleasure Principle*, SE XVIII: 28.

15. Sigmund Freud, *Das Ich und das Es* in *Studienausgabe* Bd III Psychologie des Unbewussten SA 284/14; G.W., 13; *The Ego and the Id*, SE XIX: 14.

16. Sigmund Freud, *Neue Folge der Vorlesungen zur Einführung in die Psychoanalyse in Studienausgabe* vol. 1. (SA 511); *New Introductory Lectures on Psychoanalysis and Other Works*, SE XXII, 73. Further quotations are cited parenthetically in the text.

17. See Jean-François Lyotard's interesting comments regarding the timelessness of "the system of UCS" in *Lectures d'enfance*, where he writes that the processes of the Ucs are timeless in the sense that time is a chain, that time links. But, he adds, time is also stasis (*stase*) when it occurs, and at that point there is not yet any time that links. See Jean-Francois Lyotard, *Lectures d'enfance* (Paris: Galilée, 1991), 51, translated by Christopher Fynsk as "Prescription," in *Toward the Postmodern*, edited by Robert Harvey and Mark S. Roberts (Atlantic Highlands, NJ: Humanities Press, 1993), 187.

18. In a footnote, the translator of "Freud and the Scene of Writing," Alan Bass, writes that in *Being and Time* and *Kant and the Problem of Metaphysics*, Heidegger "deconstructs" Kant's posited timelessness of the cogito, a position taken over from Descartes, in order to develop an "authentic" temporality. See Jacques Derrida, *Writing and Difference*, trans. Alan Bass (Chicago: University of Chicago Press, 1978), 215.

19. Derrida's remarks on the unconscious guard against simplifying it as a mere dimension, a system, or a process.

20. See chapter 4, "The Desire for Survival?," in this book.

21. Krzysztof Ziarek, examining Heidegger's use of the noun *Geflecht* (weave or plait) in the essay "On the Way to Language," observes that Heidegger later found his choice of this term a poor one and preferred the use of *falten* (folding). See Krzysztof Ziarek, *Language after Heidegger* (Bloomington: Indiana University Press, 2013), 26.

22. Accentuation translates *Tonart*, emphasis, intensification, "accentuation" in French, which is rendered as "tonality" in Martin Heidegger, *The Principle of Reason* (Bloomington: Indiana University Press, 1991).

23. The first accentuation understands Leibniz's maxim as a statement about *beings*: "every being has a reason," while the second accentuation reveals the principle of reason as a principle of being.

24. "Being *qua* being grounds," writes Heidegger. In other words, Being comes to be as grounding. It is ground-like. Martin Heidegger, *The Principle of Reason*, translated by Reginald Lilly (Bloomington: Indiana University Press, 1991), 51.

25. On ground, also see my "Calculus," in *Deconstructing the Death Penalty: Derrida's Death Penalty Seminars*, edited by Kelly Oliver and Stephanie Marie Straub (New York: Fordham University Press, 2018).

26. Jacques Derrida, *Demeure—Maurice Blanchot* (Paris: Galilée, 1998); *Demeure: Fiction and Testimony*, translated by Elizabeth Rottenberg (Stanford: Stanford University Press, 2000), published with Maurice Blanchot's *The Instant*

of My Death. Jacques Derrida, "Avances," in Serge Margel, *Le Tombeau du dieu artisan. Sur Platon* (Paris: Minuit, 1995), 11–43; *Advances*, translated by Philippe Lynes (Minnesota: University of Minnesota Press, 2017).

27. Jacques Derrida, *Apprendre à vivre enfin: Entretien avec Jean Birnbaum* (Paris: Galilee/*Le Monde*, 2005), translated by Pascale-Anne Brault and Michael Naas as *Learning to Live Finally: The Last Interview* (Hoboken, NJ: Melville House, 2007), 32.

28. For a discussion of some of these torsions and the relation between experience and trauma, see Geoffrey Bennington, *Not Half No End: Militantly Melancholic Essays in Memory of Jacques Derrida* (Edinburgh: Edinburgh University Press, 2010), 6fnn. 5 and 6.

29. The OED dates the adjective "intemporal," *not* temporal, to 1656, while the word "timeless" dates back to 1628.

30. One should exercise caution about seeking a location for the unconscious. Resisting a reliance on the predominance of the conscious, the unconscious would be the contamination or haunting of consciousness, its becoming-enigmatic.

Bibliography

Agamben, Giorgio. *Homo Sacer: Sovereign Power and Bare Life*. Translated by Daniel Heller-Roazen. Stanford: Stanford University Press, 1998.

Alquié, Ferdinand. *Le rationalisme de Spinoza*. Paris: Presses Universitaires de France, 1981.

Alquié, Ferdinand. "Note sur la vie éternelle selon Spinoza." *Archivio di Filosofia* 1 (1959): 183–186.

Bennington, Geoffrey. *Not Half No End: Militantly Melancholic Essays in Memory of Jacques Derrida*. Edinburgh: Edinburgh University Press, 2010.

Bennington, Geoffrey. *Interrupting Derrida*. London: Routledge, 2000.

Bennington, Geoffrey. "R.I.P." In *Interrupting Derrida*. London: Routledge, 2000.

Bennington, Geoffrey. "Derridabase." In *Jacques Derrida*, translated by Geoffrey Bennington. Chicago: University of Chicago Press, 1993.

Benveniste, Émile. *Le vocabulaire des institutions indo-européennes*, tome 2. Paris: Minuit, 1969. Translated by Elizabeth Palmer as *Indo-European Language and Society*. Coral Gables: University of Miami Press, 1973.

Boscherini, Emilia Giancotti, ed. *Lexicon Spinozanum*, 2 vols. The Hague: Martinus Nijhoff, 1970.

Brague, Rémi. *La sagesse du monde: Histoire de l'expérience humaine de l'univers*. Paris: Fayard, 1999. Translated by Teresa Lavender Fagan as *The Wisdom of the World: The Human Experience of the Universe in Western Thought*. Chicago: University of Chicago Press, 2003.

Brague, Rémi. *Aristote et la question du monde: Essai sur le contexte cosmologique et anthropologique de l'ontologie*. Paris: Presses Universitaires de France, 1988.

Cariolato, Alfonso. *"Le Geste de Dieu" Sur un lieu de l'Ethique de Spinoza*, Marginalia of Jean-Luc Nancy. Chatou: Editions de la Transparence, 2011.

Dastur, Françoise. *La mort: Essai sur la finitude*. Paris: Hatier, 1994. Translated by John Llewelyn as *Death: An Essay on Finitude*. London: Athlone, 1996.

Delbos, Victor. *La problème morale dans la philosophie de Spinoza et dans l'histoire du spinozisme*. Paris: Alcan, 1893; rpt. Hildesheim: Georg Olms Verlag, 1988.

Deleuze, Gilles. *Spinoza et le problème de l'espression*. Paris: Minuit, 1968. Translated by Martin Joughin as *Expressionism in Philosophy: Spinoza*. New York: Zone Books, 1992.

Deleuze, Gilles. *Spinoza. Philosophie pratique*. Paris: Minuit, 1981. Translated by Robert Hurley as *Spinoza: Practical Philosophy*. San Francisco: City Lights, 1988.

Derrida, Jacques. "Biodegradables: Seven Diary Fragments." Translated by Peggy Kamuf. *Critical Inquiry* 15 (1989): 812–873.

de Vries, Hent. *Religion and Violence: Philosophical Perspectives from Kant to Derrida*. Baltimore: Johns Hopkins University Press, 2005.

de Vries, Hent, and Samuel Weber, eds. *Religion and Media*. Stanford: Stanford University Press, 2001.

Garrido, Juan Manuel. *Chances de la pensée: A partir de Jean-Luc Nancy*. Paris: Galilée, 2011.

Garrido, Juan Manuel. "Without World." *CR: The Centennial Review* 8, no. 3 (Winter 2008): 119–137.

Gasché, Rodolphe. *Europe, or the Infinite Task: A Study of a Philosophical Concept*. Stanford: Stanford University Press, 2009.

Gasché, Rodolphe. *Inventions of Difference*. Cambridge, MA: Harvard University Press, 1994.

Gasché, Rodolphe. *The Tain of the Mirror: Derrida and the Philosophy of Reflection* Cambridge, MA: Harvard University Press, 1988.

Giovannangeli, Daniel. *La passion de l'origine: Recherches sur l'esthétique transcendantale et la phénomenologie*. Paris: Galilée, 1995.

Gueroult, Martial. *Spinoza II. L'âme (Ethique, II)*. Hildesheim: Georg Olms Verlag, 1974.

Hägglund, Martin. *Radical Atheism: Derrida and the Time of Life*. Stanford: Stanford University Press, 2008.

Hegel, G. W. F. *Science of Logic*. Translated by A.V. Miller. Atlantic Highlands, NJ: Humanities Press, 1989.

James, Ian. *The Fragmentary Demand: An Introduction to the Philosophy of Jean-Luc Nancy*. Stanford: Stanford University Press, 2006.

Kamuf, Peggy. "Teleiopoetic World." *SubStance* 43, no. 2 (2014): 10–19.

Kamuf, Peggy. *To Follow: The Wake of Jacques Derrida*. Edinburgh: Edinburgh University Press, 2010.

Kamuf, Peggy. "From Now On." In *To Follow: The Wake of Jacques Derrida*, 89–107. Edinburgh: Edinburgh University Press, 2010.

Kant, Immanuel. "The Immortality of the Soul, as a Postulate of Pure Practical Reason." In *Critique of Practical Reason*, translated by Werner S. Pluhar, 155–157. Indianapolis: Hackett, 2002.

Kant, Immanuel. "The End of All Things." Translated by Allen W. Wood in *Religion and Rational Theology*, translated and edited by Allen W. Wood and George Di Giovanni, 217–231. Cambridge: Cambridge University Press, 1996.

Levinas, Emmanuel. *Dieu, la mort et le temps*. Paris: Grasset, 1993. Translated by Bettina Bergo as *God, Death, and Time*. Stanford: Stanford University Press, 2000.

Lyotard, Jean-François. *Lectures d'enfance*. Paris: Galilée, 1991. Translated by Christopher Fynsk as "Prescription." In *Toward the Postmodern*, edited by Robert Harvey and Mark S. Roberts, 176–191. Atlantic Highlands, NJ: Humanities Press, 1993.

Lyotard, Jean-François. *Heidegger et «les juifs»*. Paris: Galilée, 1988. Translated by Andreas Michel and Mark Roberts as *Heidegger and "the Jews."* Minneapolis: University of Minnesota Press, 1990.

Macherey, Pierre. *Introduction à L'Ethique. La cinquieme partie*. Paris: Presses Universitaires de France, 1994.

Major, René. *Au commencement. La vie la mort*. Paris: Galilée, 1999.

Major, René. "Faire la verité." *TTR: traduction, témoignage, rédaction* 11, no. 2 (1998): 234.

Matheron, Alexandre. "La vie éternelle et le corps selon Spinoza." *Revue philosophique de la france et de l'Etranger* 184, no. 1 (January–March 1994): 27–40.

McQuillan, Martin. "Toucher I: (The Problem with Self-Touching)." *Derrida Today* 1, no. 2 (2008): 201–211.

McQuillan, Martin. "Toucher II: Keep Your Hands to Yourself Jean-Luc Nancy." *Derrida Today* 2, no. 1 (2009): 84–108.

Michaud, Ginette. "Juste le poème, peut-être (Derrida, Celan)." *Les Lettres Romanes* 64, nos. 1–2 (2010): 3–47.

Michaud, Ginette. "Singbarer Rest: Friendship, Impossible Mourning (Celan, Blanchot, Derrida)." *Oxford Literary Review* 31 (July 2009): 79–114.

Michaud, Ginette. *Tenir au secret (Derrida, Blanchot)*. Paris: Galilée, 2006.

Miller, J. Hillis. *For Derrida*. New York: Fordham University Press, 2009.

Montaigne, Michel de. *Essais*. Edited by Emmanuel Naya, Delphine Reguig-Naya, and Alexandre Tarrête. Paris: Gallimard, 2009. Translated by Donald M. Frame as *The Complete Essays of Montaigne*. Stanford: Stanford University Press, 1958.

Moreau, Pierre-François. *Spinoza: L'expérience et l'éternité*. Paris: Presses Universitaires de France, 1994.

Mortley, Raoul. *French Philosophers in Conversation: Levinas, Schneider, Serres, Irigaray, Le Doeuff, Derrida*. London: Routledge, 1991.

Naas, Michael. "An Atheism That (*Dieu merci!*) Still Leaves Something to Be Desired." *New Centennial Review* 9, no. 1 (2009): 45–68.

Naas, Michael. *Derrida from Now On*. New York: Fordham University Press, 2008.

Naas, Michael. "Lifelines." *Epoché* 10, no. 2 (Spring 2006): 221–236.

Nadler, Steven. *Spinoza's Heresy: Immortality and the Jewish Mind.* Oxford: Clarendon Press, 2001.
Noel-Smith, Kelly. *Freud on Time and Timelessness.* London: Palgrave Macmillan, 2016.
Nunberg, Herman, and Ernst Federn, eds. *Minutes of the Vienna Psychoanalytic Society, Volume III: 1910–1911.* Translated by M. Nunberg with the assistance of H. Collins. New York: International Universities Press, 1974.
Rilke, Rainer Maria. *Briefe: Zweiter Band 1914 bis 1926.* Leipzig: Insel-Verlag, 1950.
Rilke, Rainer Maria. *Letters of Rainer Maria Rilke, 1910–1926.* Translated by Jane Bannard Greene and M. D. Herter Norton. New York: Norton, 1947–1948.
Rilke, Rainer Maria. *Briefe aus Muzot: 1921 bis 1926.* Leipzig: Insel-Verlag, 1937.
Rousset, Bernard. *La perspective finale de "L'Ethique" et le problème de la Cohérence du Spinozisme. L'autonomie comme salut.* Paris: Vrin, 1968.
Saghafi, Kas. "Calculus." In *Deconstructing the Death Penalty: Derrida's Death Penalty Seminars,* edited by Kelly Oliver and Stephanie Marie Straub, 139–155. New York: Fordham University Press, 2018.
Saghafi, Kas. "Dying Alive." *Mosaic* 48, no. 3 (September 2015): 15–26.
Saghafi, Kas. "Thomas the Marvelous: Resurrection and Living-Death in Blanchot and Nancy." *Mosaic* 45, no. 3 (September 2012): 1–16.
Saghafi, Kas. *Apparitions—Of Derrida's Other.* New York: Fordham University Press, 2010.
Shakespeare. *Hamlet.* Edited by Harold Jenkins, The Arden Shakespeare, second series. Walton-on-Thames, Surrey: Thomas Nelson & Sons, 1982; rpt. 1997.
Spinoza, Baruch. *Ethics.* In *Complete Works,* edited by Michael L. Morgan, 213–382. Indianapolis: Hackett, 2002.
Spinoza, Benedict de. *Ethics.* In *A Spinoza Reader: The* Ethics *and Other Works,* edited and translated by Edwin Curley, 85–276. Princeton, NJ: Princeton University Press, 1994.
Spinoza, Benedict de. *Ethique.* New translation by Bernard Pautrat. Paris: Seuil, 1988.
Spinoza. *Theological-Political Treatise.* Edited by Jonathan Israel, translated by Michael Silverthorne and Jonathan Israel. Cambridge: Cambridge University Press, 2007.
van Buren, John. "Martin Heidegger, Martin Luther." In *Reading Heidegger from the Start: Essays in His Earliest Thought,* edited by Theodore Kisiel and John van Buren, 159–174. Albany: State University of New York Press, 1994.
Vernant, Jean-Pierre. "La belle mort et le cadavre outragé." In *L'individu, la mort, l'amour: Soi-même et l'autre en Grèce anciennes,* 41–97. Paris: Gallimard, 1989. Translated as "A 'Beautiful Death' and the Disfigured Corpse in Homeric Epic." In *Mortals and Immortals: Collected Essays,* edited by Froma I. Zeitlin, 50–74. Princeton, NJ: Princeton University Press, 1991.

Wittgenstein, Ludwig. *Tractatus Logico-Philosophicus*. Translated by D. F. Pears and B.F. McGuiness. London: Routledge, 1961.
Ziarek, Krzysztof. *Language after Heidegger*. Bloomington: Indiana University Press, 2013.

Classical Sources

The Epic of Gilgamesh. Translated by Andrew George. London Penguin, 2000.
Cicero. *Tusculan Disputations*. Translated by J. E. King. Loeb Classical Library. Cambridge, MA: Harvard University Press, 1927.
Cicero. *De Finibus Bonorum*. Translated by H. Rackham. Loeb Classical Library. Cambridge, MA: Harvard University Press, 1927.
Cicero. *Laelius de Amicitia* vii 23. Translated by W. A. Falconer as *Old Age, Friendship, Divination*. Loeb Classical Library. Cambridge, MA: Harvard University Press, 1923.
Héraclite. *Fragments*. Text established, translated, and commented on by Marcel Conche. Paris: Presses Universitaires de France, 1986.
Plato. *Symposium and Phaedrus*. Translated by Tom Griffith. New York: Everyman's Library/Knopf, 2000.
Plato. *Lysis, Symposium, Gorgias*. Translated by W. R. M. Lamb. Cambridge, MA: Harvard University Press, 1996. Loeb Classical Library.

Biblical Sources

Catechism of the Catholic Church, second edition. Vatican City: Liberia Editrice Vaticana, 1994; London: Chapman, 1994.
Freedman, David Noel, ed. *Eerdmans Dictionary of the Bible*. Grand Rapids, MI: William B. Eerdmans, 2000.

Index

abyss, xxvii, 11, 15–16, 32, 59–62, 87, 126, 128, 140fn22–23, 141fn24, 142fn25–26; *Ur*-abyss, 15
address, xxviii, xxx–xxxi, 21, 31–32, 133
adieu, xxvii, 39, 136fn10, 137fn14–15
afterlife, 40, 69–70, 98–100, 104–107, 137
afterworld, 40, 98, 104
Agamben, Giorgio, 150n13
alone, xxiii, xxviii, 3, 5, 10–13, 16, 31–32, 118
Alquié, Ferdinand, 66–67, 152n21–22
anastasis, 14, 29–31, 57, 59, 71, 149fn3
another world, 64, 90, 98–99, 107
Aristotle, 7, 66, 81, 140n23, 146fn26, 150n13
auto-immunity, 21–23, 143fn4, 159fn5
l'autre côté, 60, 98

Bass, Alan, 164fn18
to bear; bearing, xxiii, 3–5, 11–13, 16, 89, 91, 99–100, 102–105, 122, 130; bearing witness, xxiv

belief, 23, 29–30, 62, 65, 69–70, 80, 86, 98, 105, 150fn14, 153fn32, 159fn2, 159fn5; belief in God, 36; Christian belief, 65
Bennington, Geoffrey, 5, 41, 79, 83, 147fn3, 160fn14, 165fn28
Benveniste, Emile, xxv, 23–24
Bergson, Henri, 41, 96
Bible, 28, 65, 150fn14
Bielik-Robson, Agata, 159fn5
Blanchot, Maurice, xxv–xxvi, 9, 59–66, 70, 87–92, 101, 125, 142fn3, 144fn16, 149fn5, 149fn8, 158fn22, 158fn24
Brague, Rémi, 6–8, 138fn6, 139fn14

calling, xxvii, xxix–xxx, 77, 100, 137fn17
Caputo, John D., 154fn5
Cariolato, Alfonso, 73
to carry; carrying, xxiii, xxviii, xxx, 4–5, 10–13, 16, 31, 51, 103
Celan, Paul, 4–5, 10–13, 100, 137fn2, 140fn21
Christianity, 8–9, 20, 26–30, 33–36, 40, 61–62, 70–74, 97, 142fn2, 146fn25
Cixous, Hélène, 49–50, 123–124
consolation, 31, 106, 150fn12

contamination, xxx, 23, 48, 116, 159fn5, 165fn30
côté, 49–50, 59–60, 98–99, 145fn18
courage, 3, 122

Darwin, Charles, 100
Dastur, Françoise, 39, 147fn5
the dead, 12, 21, 31–33, 39, 48, 55–61, 62–65, 69–74, 85–86, 90, 92, 104, 106, 112, 116–117, 125, 131–133, 149fn3, 150fn14, 159fn2; the dead and the living 92, 104, 125
DeArmitt, Pleshette, xxviii
death, xxiii, xxiv, xxix–xxx, 3–5, 13–16, 21, 26, 29–33, 35–36, 39–50, 55–67, 70–74, 86–93, 97–110, 116–117–120, 123–124, 125–127, 128–130, 132–133, 135fn1, 136fn3, 146fn22, 147fn2–3, 147fn5, 153fn32; being-toward-death, 61, 86–87, 125; death-drive, 42, 156fn8; death of God, 35; death of the other, xxiv, xxvii, xxx, 4, 10, 11, 13–15, 40, 48, 99, 107, 109–110, 135fn1, 147fn5; death penalty, 35–36, 63; my death, 40, 48, 102, 105–106, 109, 130. *See also* living death
deconstruction, xxvi, 10, 19–21, 33–36, 56, 61–63, 72, 79, 115, 142fn2, 146fn25, 154fn5, 155fn6
Defoe, Daniel, xxx
Delbos, Pierre, 66
Deleuze, Gilles, 152fn23
DeLillo, Don, 96
departure, xxvii, 140fn23, 147fn9
Derrida, Jacques, works, *Apories*, 40–41, 45–48, 61, 86–87, 136fn3, 159fn2; *Mal d'Archive. Une impression freudienne*, 82, 99, 101, 129; *L'animal que donc je suis,* 139fn17; "Avances," xxv; "Circonfession," 100; *Chaque fois unique, la fin du monde,* xxvi, 13–14, 16, 31, 110, 133; "Comment nommer," xxvii–xxx, 136fn7, 137fn18; *Demeure,* xxv, 87–90, 161fn20; *La Dissemination*, 127; *Echographies—de la television,* 82, 110, 130, 162fn4; "De l'écrit à la parole: table ronde animée par Jacques Munier," 82; "Foi et savoir," xxv, 22–24, 82, 136fn5; "Fors: Les mots anglées de Nicolas Abraham et Maria Torok," 143fn5, 162n4; *De quoi demain . . . Dialogue,* 162fn4; *Donner le temps: 1. La fausse monnaie,* 81–82; "H. C. pour la vie, c'est a dire . . .," 49–51; *Idiomes, nationalités, déconstructions: Rencontre de Rabat avec Jacques Derrida,* 110; *Le toucher, Jean-Luc Nancy,* xxv, xxviii, 25–27, 33–34, 56, 83, 144fn14, 146fn23, 146fn25; *Marges—de la philosophie,* 81, 104, 122, 158fn23, 161fn20; *Mémoires d'aveugle: L'autoportrait et autres ruines,* 6; *Le Monolinguisme de l'autre ou la prothèse d'origine,* xxiv; *Mémoires—pour Paul de Man,* 100; *De la grammatologie,* 41–42, 48, 81–83; *Sauf le nom,* 82; *Introduction à "L'Origine de la géométrie" de Husserl,* 83, 122; *Parages,* 101–102, 107–108, 137fn18, 161fn20; *La carte postale: de Socrate à Freud et au-delà,* 42–45; "Penser ce qui vient," 80; *Politiques de l'amitié,* 102–103, 161fn20; *Le problème de la genèse dans la philosophie de Husserl,* 83; *Papier machine. Le*

ruban de machine à écrire et autres réponses 114; *Points de suspension. Entretiens.* 113–114; *Psyché. Invention de l'autre,* t. 1 82–83, 161fn20; *Béliers. Le dialogue ininterrompu: entre deux infinis, le poème* xxiii, 4–5, 10–12, 16; *Voyous. Deux essais sur la raison* xxvii–xxviii, 34; *Schibboleth—Pour Paul Celan* 100; *Spectres de Marx. L'Etat de la dette, le travail du deuil et la nouvelle Internationale,* 82, 104–105, 149fn2; "Le temps des adieux: Heidegger (lu par) Hegel (lu par) Malabou," xxv–xxvi, 136fn10, 147fn14–15; *La vérité en peinture,* xxv, 49, 82, 160fn13; *La voix et le phénomène,* 81–83; *L'Ecriture et la différance,* 82–83, 100, 122, 157fn19; *The Work of Mourning,* xxiv, 31, 109, 136fn3; seminars; *Séminaire La bête et le souverain, Volume I (2001–2002),* 51, 131, 142fn26; *Séminaire La bête et le souverain, Volume II (2002–2003),* 9, 12, 16, 74, 92–93, 100, 104, 106, 111–114, 116–119, 122, 125–133, 150fn13; *La peine de mort, Volume I (1999–2000),* 35–36, 62–63, 82, 90, 133, 140fn23; *La peine de mort, Volume II (2000–2001),* 131, 140fn23
desire, xxv, xxvii–xxviii, 21–22, 30, 36, 42, 63, 77–80, 80–83, 85–87, 92–93, 103, 108, 112–114, 117, 154fn2, 154fn3, 155fn6
Destruktion, 34, 146fn26–27
Deutscher, Penelope, 159fn5
Diderot, Denis, 45–46
Didi-Huberman, Georges, 99–100, 160fn8
différance, 43, 83–84, 104, 125

de Duve, Thierry, xxvi
dying alive, xxx, 6, 29, 45, 57, 61–64, 74, 112–118, 125, 127–130, 162fn2

the end, xxviii–xxix, 13–14, 34, 36, 39, 43, 45–46, 48, 51, 55, 98, 104, 106
the end of the world, xxiii–xxiv, xxvii, xxx, 4–5, 10–11, 13–15, 30–31, 106–107, 109–110, 136fn3
eternal, 66–70, 89, 108, 146fn22, 148fn1, 152fn23, 158fn23
eternal life, 30, 36, 55, 64–74, 106, 150fn13–14
eternity, 58, 65–68, 74, 85, 89, 95, 148fn1, 149fn6, 150fn14, 151fn17, 152fn23, 152fn25, 153fn33, 156fn8, 158fn23
the event, xxix, xxx, 46–48, 80, 88, 110, 114–115, 123–124, 162fn4

faith, 3, 7, 26, 29–30, 36, 55, 62, 70, 97, 110, 150fn14
finitude, 10, 36, 50, 61, 63, 77, 79–80, 83–85, 87, 92, 98, 106–110, 125, 139fn15, 154fn5, 156fn8, 157fn19–20
Fortleben, 101–102, 125
Freud, Sigmund, 25, 42–45, 71–72, 83, 119–122, 124, 127, 129, 131–132, 144fn13, 156fn8

Gadamer, Hans-Georg, xxviii, 11, 13
de Gandillac, Maurice, 101
Garrido, Juan-Manuel, 72–74, 139fn15
Gasché, Rodolphe, 5, 14, 79, 83–84, 127–128, 159fn5
Genet, Jean, 97–98
Gide, André, 97–98
globalization, xxiv, 33, 135fn1

God, xxv, 6, 8–9, 14, 28, 31, 35, 66–68, 73, 77–78, 80, 82, 115, 150fn13–14, 151fn15, 152n23, 153fn33, 153fn37, 159fn5
greeting, xxiv, xxvi–xxviii, 21
ground, 3, 9, 11–12, 15–16, 126, 128–129, 140fn23, 141fn24, 142fn25–26, 164fn24–25; groundless ground, 126, 128
Guéroult, Martial, 68, 151fn18

Hägglund, Martin, 77–80, 84–87, 154fn3, 154fn5, 155fn6, 156fn7–8, 159fn5
haptics, 26
haptology, 27
haunting, 103, 105, 115, 124, 129, 162fn4, 165fn30
to heal; healing, xxv, 21, 24, 26, 32
health, xxiv–xxv, xxvii, xxix, 20, 24, 32
Hegel, G.W.F., 29, 34, 40, 57–58, 82, 84, 91, 96, 102, 113, 132, 158fn23, 159fn5
Heidegger, Martin, xxx, 4, 7–9, 12, 15, 22, 24, 34, 40–41, 48, 61, 63, 83–85, 96, 109, 118–119, 122, 127–128, 140fn23, 142fn25–27, 157fn19–20, 158fn23, 164fn18, 164fn21–22, 164fn24
holy, xxv, 19, 22–24, 36, 144fn9
Homer, 5, 86, 108
horizon, xxix–xxx, 4, 9–10, 24, 42, 48, 106, 139fn15, 154fn5

Immortality, 40, 66, 68–70, 78–80, 85–92, 103–107, 130, 146fn22, 148fn1, 151fn17, 152fn23, 154fn3
Immunity, xxiv, xxv, 22–27, 42. See also auto-immunity
indemnification, xxv, 22, 24, 159fn5
indemnity, xxv, xxviii, 22, 35

Kamuf, Peggy, xxviii, 5, 140fn21
Kant, Immanuel, 9, 24, 34, 82, 85, 96, 122, 133, 140fn23, 148fn1, 159fn5, 164fn18
khōra, 97, 108

Laclau, Ernesto, 154fn3
Levinas, Emmanuel, 39–41, 48, 82, 83, 92, 109, 133
living death, xxx, 111–114, 118–119, 128–129, 131, 133
living on, 97, 99, 101–108, 112, 137fn18
Lyotard, Jean-François, 163fn5, 164fn17

Macherey, Pierre, 67–68, 153fn29
machine, 23, 41–42, 97, 110, 112, 126
Maimonides, 70, 153fn23
Major, René, 158fn22
Marrano, 48–49, 159fn5
Matheron, Alexandre, 68
melancholy, 4–5, 15
metonymy, xxvii
Michaud, Ginette, 5, 11, 158fn22
Miller, J. Hillis, 5, 144fn9
miracle, 30, 58, 97, 110
mondialisation, 33, 97, 135fn1
mourning, xxiii, xxvii–xxviii, xxx, 3–5, 12, 15, 39, 48, 103–105, 107

Naas, Michael, 5, 11, 79, 95–99, 102, 105–110, 115, 136fn3, 136fn5, 154fn1, 155fn6, 159fn5, 160fn14, 162fn3–4
Nachleben, 99–100
Nadler, Steven, 69–70
name, xxviii–xxix, 6, 32, 42, 48, 71–74, 77, 86, 100, 103, 122, 126, 131, 139fn16

naming, xxvii, xxix, 96, 112, 137fn17
Nancy, works, *L'adoration,* 55,
70–74, 152fn26, 153fn33;
Corpus, 145fn18; "Consolation,
desolation," 31–32; *La Déclosion
(Deconstruction du christianisme 1),*
32, 57–59, 146fn27, 149fn7; "Fin
du colloque," 65–66; *L'intrus,* xxvi;
Les muses, xxvi; *Noli me tangere.
Essai sur la levée du corps,* 28–30,
56–57, 144fn16, 149fn2; *Partir—
Le depart,* 63–64; "Reste, viens,"
55; "Salut à toi, salut aux aveugles
que nous devenons," 33

obligate; obligation, 3, 11, 22

Pautrat, Bernard, 151fn18, 153fn29, 153fn33
Persian, 150fn14
phantasm, xxx, 22–23, 36, 65, 72, 74, 97, 111–119, 122–125, 128, 130–133, 155fn6, 162fn4
Plato, xxv, xxx, 6–7, 39, 40, 78, 83, 84, 86, 89, 113, 127–128, 139, 147fn4, 154fn4
poetics, xxviii, xxx, 73, 123–124, 137fn17
porter, 3–4, 11–13, 102–103
prayer, xxx, 25, 112
the proper, 42–45, 48, 68–69, 82
psychoanalysis, 81, 83, 117, 126, 155fn6

Rabaté, Jean-Michel, 156fn8
reappropriation, 44
redemption, xxiv–xxvi, xxviii–xix, 24, 35–36, 107, 133, 150fn13
Rehm, Jean-Pierre, 64–65, 70
religion, xxiv, xxvi–xxviii, 21–26, 28, 30, 31, 33, 35–36, 48–49, 55, 64, 90–91, 95–98, 136fn5, 150fn14

remains, xxiii, xxvi–xxvii, xxx, 10, 21–22, 24–27, 31, 47, 50, 64, 67–68, 72, 82, 86, 104, 114–115, 128–129, 136fn7
resurrection, xxvi, xxix, 14–15, 27–31, 35–36, 55–61, 64–65, 69, 71–72, 74, 86, 88, 99–100, 107, 133, 144fn12, 149fn2–3, 150fn12, 150fn14, 153fn32, 153fn36
revenance, 86–87, 90, 102–105, 107–108, 114, 125, 129, 161fn20, 162fn4
Rilke, Rainer Maria, 59–60
Robinson Crusoe, 111–113, 125
Rousset, Bernard, 152fn19

sacred, xxv, 22–25, 28, 144fn9; sacredness, 23
salut, xxiii–xxi, 21, 22–24, 26, 31–33, 55, 59, 97, 136fn4, 136fn7–8, 136fn10–11, 137fn14–15, 137fn17, 142fn3, 152fn19
salutation, xxvii–xxx, 21, 31–33
salvation, xxiv–xxix, 21, 22–24, 26, 31–32, 35, 55, 63, 66, 74, 97, 108, 133, 150fn14, 152fn19
Santiago, Hugo, 70
saving, xxv–xxvii, 24, 32, 137fn17
secret, 24, 42, 48–49, 97
shibboleth, 42, 48
Sophocles, 46
Spinoza, Baruch, 40, 65–69, 70, 73, 84, 151fn17–18, 152fn23, 152fn27, 153fn33, 153fn37, 157fn20
Staten, Henry, 156fn8
Survival, xxiii, xxx, 4, 10, 14, 36, 66–68, 74, 77–80, 85–88, 90–93, 97, 99–108, 112, 125–130, 133, 156fn8, 159fn5, 160fn13–14; survivals, 99–100
survivance, xxix–xxx, 4, 77, 88, 90–92, 99–110, 112, 124–130,

survivance *(continued)*
  133, 160fn6, 160fn8, 161fn20, 162fn2
survie, 74, 86, 99–104, 112, 126–127, 133, 137fn18, 160fn13
sur-viving, 90, 99, 102
survivor, xxiii, 5, 10–15, 91, 102–103, 107–109, 126, 129–130, 137
survivre, 97, 99–105
syntagma, xxiii–xxiv, xxx, 7, 48

to-come, xxviii–xxix, 108
touch, 19, 21, 25–32, 117, 145fn18
touching, 25–30, 71, 83, 144fn13, 145fn18
tragen, 4, 11–12, 137fn2, 140fn21
Tylor, Edward B., 99–100

Uberleben, 101–102, 125
undecidable, 50, 116; undecidability, xxvii, 114

unscathed, xxiv–xxv, xxviii, 19, 21, 22–25, 26–27, 31, 33, 35–36, 63 145fn18
untouchable, 21, 23, 25–30, 32, 144fn14, 145fn18
untouched, 19, 21–22, 143fn5

Vernant, Jean-Pierre, 109, 161fn25
Vries, Hent de, 142fn2

Warburg, Aby, 99
Wittgenstein, Ludwig, 150fn14
world, xxiii–xxiv, 3–16, 31, 33–34, 40–41, 55, 62, 64, 70–74, 90, 98–99, 106–107, 109–110, 120, 123, 130, 135fn1, 136fn3, 138fn5, 139fn13–16, 140fn21, 162fn4. *See also* the end of the world

Ziarek, Krzysztof, 164fn21
Zoroastrian, 7, 150fn14

www.ingramcontent.com/pod-product-compliance
Ingram Content Group UK Ltd.
Pitfield, Milton Keynes, MK11 3LW, UK
UKHW041919140426
5217IPUK00013B/220